VICTORIAN RELIGION

VICTORIAN RELIGION

Faith and Life in Britain

Julie Melnyk

VICTORIAN LIFE AND TIMES
Sally Mitchell, Series Editor

Westport, Connecticut
London

Library of Congress Cataloging-in-Publication Data

Melnyk, Julie.
Victorian religion : faith and life in Britain / Julie Melnyk.
     p. cm. — (Victorian life and times, ISSN 1932–944X)
   Includes bibliographical references (p.   ) and index.
   ISBN-13: 978–0–275–99124–1 (alk. paper)
  1. Great Britain—Religion—19th century.   2. Great Britain—Religious life and customs.
   I. Title.
  BR759.M39   2008
  274.1′081—dc22   2007044366

British Library Cataloguing in Publication Data is available.

Library of Congress Catalog Card Number: 2007044366
ISBN-13: 978–0–275–99124–1
ISSN: 1932-944X

First published in 2008

Praeger Publishers, 88 Post Road West, Westport, CT 06881
An imprint of Greenwood Publishing Group, Inc.
www.praeger.com

Printed in the United States of America

The paper used in this book complies with the
Permanent Paper Standard issued by the National
Information Standards Organization (Z39.48–1984).

10 9 8 7 6 5 4 3 2 1

CONTENTS

LIST OF ILLUSTRATIONS
AND TABLES

ILLUSTRATIONS

TABLES

SERIES FOREWORD

Although the nineteenth century has almost faded from living memory—most people who heard first-hand stories from grandparents who grew up before 1900 have adult grandchildren by now—impressions of the Victorian world continue to influence both popular culture and public debates. These impressions may well be vivid yet contradictory. Many people, for example, believe that Victorian society was safe, family-centered, and stable because women could not work outside the home, although every census taken during the period records hundreds of thousands of female laborers in fields, factories, shops, and schools as well as more than a million domestic servants—often girls of fourteen or fifteen—whose long and unregulated workdays created the comfortable leisured world we see in Merchant and Ivory films. Yet it is also true that there were women who had no household duties and desperately wished for some purpose in life but found that social expectations and family pressure absolutely prohibited their presence in the workplace.

The goal of books in the Victorian Life and Times series is to explain and enrich the simple pictures that show only a partial truth. Although the Victorian period in Great Britain is often portrayed as peaceful, comfortable, and traditional, it was actually a time of truly breathtaking change. In 1837, when eighteen-year-old Victoria became queen, relatively few of England's people had ever traveled more than ten miles from the place where they were born. Little more than half the population could read and write, children as young as five worked in factories and mines, and political power was entirely in the hands of a small minority of men who held property. By the time Queen Victoria died in 1901, railways provided fast and cheap transportation for both goods and people, telegraph messages sped to the far corners of the British Empire in minutes, education was compulsory, a man's religion (or lack of it) no longer barred him from sitting in Parliament, and women were not only wives and domestic servants but also physicians, dentists, elected school-board members, telephone operators, and university lecturers. Virtually every aspect of life had been transformed either by technology or by the massive political and legal reforms that reshaped Parliament, elections, universities, the army, education, sanitation, public health, marriage, working conditions, trade unions, and civil and criminal law.

The continuing popularity of Victoriana among decorators and collectors, the strong market for historical novels and for mysteries set in the age of Jack the Ripper and Sherlock Holmes, the new interest in books by George Eliot and Charles Dickens and Wilkie Collins whenever one is presented on television, and the desire of amateur genealogists to discover the lives, as well as the names, of nineteenth-century British ancestors all reveal the need for accurate information about the period's social history and material culture. In the years since my book *Daily Life in Victorian England* was published in 1996 I have been contacted by many people who want more detailed information about some area covered in that overview. Each book in the Victorian Life and Times series will focus on a single topic, describe changes during the period, and consider the differences between country and city, between industrial life and rural life, and above all, the differences made by class, social position, religion, tradition, gender, and economics. Each book is an original work, illustrated with drawings and pictures taken from Victorian sources, enriched by quotations from Victorian publications, based on current research and written by a qualified scholar. All of the authors have doctoral degrees and many years' experience in teaching; they have been chosen not only for their academic qualifications but also for their ability to write clearly and to explain complex ideas to people without extensive background in the subject. Thus the books are authoritative and dependable but written in straightforward language; explanations are supplied whenever specialized terminology is used, and a bibliography lists resources for further information.

The Internet has made it possible for people who cannot visit archives and reference libraries to conduct serious family and historical research. Careful hobbyists and scholars have scanned large numbers of primary sources—nineteenth-century cookbooks, advice manuals, maps, city directories, magazines, sermons, church records, illustrated newspapers, guidebooks, political cartoons, photographs, paintings, published investigations of slum conditions and poor people's budgets, political essays, inventories of scientists' correspondence, and many other materials formerly accessible only to academic historians. Yet the World Wide Web also contains misleading documents and false information, even on educational sites created by students and enthusiasts who don't have the experience to put material in useful contexts. So far as possible, therefore, the bibliographies for books in the Victorian Life and Times series will also offer guidance on using publicly available electronic resources.

Both private belief and public worship were central to Victorian life in ways that are now often puzzling. Even people who have read a large number of the period's novels may be baffled by the difference between a vicar, a rector, a canon, a curate, a deacon, and a dean, though that difference is clearly important to a novel's characters, whether they're women choosing a husband or men seeking to advance their career. People interested in genealogy and family history may realize that the Church of England was the established church without knowing what that meant in social and legal terms. What's an Anglo-Catholic, a Tractarian, a Puseyite? Are Nonconformists and Dissenters the same thing? What might the distinction between "chapel" and "church" suggest about someone's class standing or political affiliation? And even with a grasp of concepts and terminology, the doctrinal disputes within and between nineteenth-century religious denominations and the effect of discoveries in science or textual criticism are hard to appreciate. Using our own understanding of issues that are still with us only makes the confusion worse, since both terms and concepts have changed. "Evangelical," for example, meant something quite different to Victorians than it does to us; and the disputes about science and religion are in some ways more divisive in the early twenty-first century than they were in the nineteenth.

Julie Melnyk's *Victorian Religion: Faith and Life in Britain, 1829–1901* provides authoritative and easy-to-understand explanations. Chapters cover the changing relationship of church and state, the history of various denominations, a typical clergyman's career, religious practice in ordinary people's lives, movements for philanthropy and reform, religion's impact on literature, women's role in religious life, and the causes and consequences of various challenges to religious faith. The book's clarity and its plentiful examples make it enormously useful to novel-readers, to teachers, and to anyone interested in the political and social as well as the theological meanings attached to religion.

Sally Mitchell, Series Editor

ACKNOWLEDGMENTS

I would to thank Sally Mitchell, the general editor of the *Victorian Life and Times* Series, first for asking me to write this book and then for guiding me and sharing with me her wisdom, her prodigious knowledge, and her enthusiasm for Victorian lives in all their fascinating detail. Her comments and encouragement have been invaluable.

I would also like to thank Suzanne Staszak-Silva, our editor at Praeger, for her patience and support, particularly in the latter stages of the project.

The staff of the Division of Special Collections, Archives, and Rare Books at Ellis Library, and Matthew Bailey at the National Portrait Gallery, London, also deserve thanks for all the help they gave me in acquiring many of the illustrations I have used in this volume.

I am also grateful to my boss, Stuart Palonsky, the Director of the Honors College at the University of Missouri, Columbia, for his understanding, flexibility, and deep commitment to learning and teaching. Without him, I would not have the opportunity to be both an administrator and a scholar.

I would like to thank my parents, Russell and Faye Peavyhouse, who taught me how important religion is to how a life is lived, and my professors at Haverford College, Steve Finley and Joanne Hutchinson, who introduced me to the complexities and beauties of Victorian culture and literature.

Finally, though no thanks could be sufficient, I would like to thank my husband, Andrew, for his unfailing love and support. This book is dedicated to him.

CHRONOLOGY

1826   University College, London, is founded to provide higher education for Dissenters barred from Oxford and Cambridge, but it is not able to grant degrees.

1827   Publication of John Keble's *The Christian Year*.

1828   Repeal of Test and Corporations Act officially allows Dissenters to hold office in municipal government.

1829   Catholic Emancipation Act allows Roman Catholics to serve in Parliament and hold most other state offices.

1833   Church rate abolished in Ireland.

John Keble preaches his Assize sermon on National Apostasy, generally seen as the start of the Tractarian movement. The first of the *Tracts for the Times* is published.

Having led the fight to abolish the slave trade in 1806, Evangelicals succeed in passing parliamentary legislation abolishing slavery in British territories from August 1834.

1835   Franchise granted to Jews who meet the usual property qualifications for voting.

1836   University of London founded to provide degree examinations for University College and King's College, London: For the first time, Dissenters were able to earn university degrees.

Publication of A.W.N. Pugin's *Contrasts* provides theoretical foundation for Gothic revival, which had a significant effect on Victorian church architecture.

1836   Marriage Act introduces civil marriages and allows marriages to be performed in dissenting houses of worship.

1837	Civil registration of births, marriages, and deaths begins on July 1.
1838	First of two Pluralities Acts limits the holdings of plural livings by clergymen and reduces the number of nonresident incumbents.
1841	John Henry Newman causes a storm of protest when he publishes Tract 90, in which he argues that the Thirty-Nine Articles, the fundamental statement of Anglican belief, could be interpreted in a Catholic sense. This marks the end of the *Tracts for the Times*.
	Evangelical novelist Charlotte Elizabeth Tonna publishes the first industrial novel, *Helen Fleetwood*, protesting working conditions and hours.
	Marian Hughes, the first Anglican nun, takes her religious vows.
1842	Judge Erskine's decision in *Shore v. Wilson* sets a new standard for blasphemy, which now requires "scoffing" at God or the Bible, and excludes works that question Christian doctrine "soberly and reverently."
1845	John Henry Newman, a central Tractarian leader, converts to Roman Catholicism.
	Jews permitted to hold municipal offices.
	First Anglican convent founded in Park Village West, London.
1846	First full English translation of D.F. Strauss's *Leben Jesu* (1835) published as *Life of Jesus*, translated by George Eliot (Marian Evans).
1847	Jewish financier Lionel de Rothschild is elected MP for the City of London but is unable to take the required Christian oath and cannot take his seat.
1848	Chartist revolts provide inspiration for the start of Christian Socialism.
1850	A second Pluralities Act further strengthens regulations about the holding of plural livings by clergymen.
1850	A papal bull restores the Roman Catholic hierarchy in England; Nicholas Wiseman is declared Roman Catholic Archbishop of Westminster and made a Cardinal.
1851	On Sunday, March 20, a religious census is taken, which reveals significant growth of dissenting denominations.
	First organized atheist group, the Central Secular Society, is founded by George Jacob Holyoake.
1854	Papal proclamation of the Immaculate Conception of the Virgin Mary declares that Mary was born without taint of original sin.
	Dissenters and Jews are admitted to university degrees at Oxford.
	English translation of Feuerbach's demythologizing *Das Wesen des Christentums* (1841) published as *The Essence of Christianity*, translated by George Eliot (Marian Evans).
1856	Dissenters and Jews admitted to university degrees at Cambridge.
1858	Lionel de Rothschild becomes first Jew admitted to Parliament.

1859   Publication of Charles Darwin's *Origin of Species*.

1860   Publication of *Essays and Reviews*.

T.H. Huxley and Samuel Wilberforce, Bishop of Oxford, debate Darwinian theory at the British Association for the Advancement of Science.

Revival of the Order of Deaconesses in the Church of England: Anglican "Mildmay Deaconesses" founded in London.

1861   First edition of *Hymns, Ancient and Modern*, the most widely used Anglican hymnal, is published.

1865   William and Catherine Booth found the East London Christian Mission, which will become the Salvation Army in 1878.

1868   Compulsory church rate abolished in England and Wales.

1869   T.H. Huxley coins the word "agnostic" to describe a person who suspends judgment about the existence or nonexistence of God.

1870   Proclamation of the doctrine of Papal Infallibility.

1871   The Church of Ireland, the Irish branch of the Anglican Church, is disestablished.

Dissenters and Jews permitted to hold fellowships at Oxford and Cambridge Universities.

1873   American revivalists, Dwight L. Moody and Ira D. Sankey, begin their first tour of Britain, preaching throughout the country until 1875.

1874   Public Worship Regulation Act makes many ritualist practices of the Anglican High Church illegal.

1880   Charles Bradlaugh, an avowed atheist and Liberal Party candidate, is elected MP for Northampton, but is prevented from taking his seat in Parliament.

Burial Act allows Dissenters the right to be buried in Anglican churchyards by their own ministers and according to their own rites.

1881   Pogroms in Russia cause Jewish population in Britain to skyrocket.

1886   Charles Bradlaugh, an avowed atheist, is finally allowed to take his seat in Parliament as MP for Northampton.

INTRODUCTION

To understand the Victorians and the Victorian period, we have to understand their religious beliefs and institutions. Religion permeated Victorian lives and culture in ways that modern readers may find hard to reimagine. It affected nineteenth-century men and women in their private lives—in their sense of personal identity and self-worth, their moral beliefs and behaviors, their family relationships and friendships, their spending habits, and their use of leisure time. But it also had a powerful influence on public life. It contributed significantly to making the Victorian era the Age of Reform, with thousands of societies and charitable organizations working toward some vision of social improvement. At the local level, the church or chapel was often the center of community life, particularly in villages and small towns. And religion had influence at the national level as well. Partly because the Anglican Church was the Established Church of England, a crucial institution explained in greater detail later in this Introduction and in Chapter 1, religious issues, ideas, and language played an important role in all political life, from local councils and school boards to parliamentary debate. Religion was entangled with most of the major issues of the period, including class relations, the pursuit of scientific knowledge, imperialism, and women's place in society.

Religion also influenced Victorian culture, especially Victorian literature. Every careful reader of Victorian novels or poetry recognizes the impact of religion on these works. Religious issues and characters crop up everywhere: the clergymen in the novels of Anthony Trollope and George Eliot, the ubiquitous scriptural allusions in Charlotte Brontë's writing, the struggles with religious doubt in Tennyson's masterpiece *In Memoriam*, the many voices of religious doubt and faith in Robert Browning's dramatic monologues (e.g., "Cleon," "An Epistle of Karshish," "Caliban upon Setebos"), even the hostile portraits of non-Anglican Christians in Charles Dickens's novels and the more sympathetic portrait in Elizabeth Gaskell's *Ruth* testify to the centrality of religion in the culture.

But twenty-first century people who want to understand this crucial element of Victorian life face significant obstacles. Some of these are a result of our own preconceptions. People raised within a Christian denomination may assume that Victorian Christianity shared the same beliefs and practices. Even within particular denominations—Anglican/Episcopal, Baptist, or Methodist—this is a dangerous assumption. We need to approach Victorian religious life, as we need to approach other aspects of Victorian culture, as anthropologists seeking to understand a wholly different culture. Some aspects of Victorian religious life will seem familiar, others unexpectedly alien, but we need to remain constantly aware of our own possibly misguided preconceptions.

Another barrier to understanding is the bewildering diversity of Victorian religious life and belief. The Victorian era was a religious age, but it was not an era of peaceful faith and doctrinal conformity—it was an era of religious controversy and, increasingly, of religious freedom. Throughout the period, the dominant Christian sect in England was the Church of England, which is often referred to as the Anglican Church; the Church of England was the established state church of England and Wales, and many Victorians saw membership in this church as a matter of national identity. Nevertheless, a significant number of Victorians were "Dissenters," members of a non-Anglican Christian denomination—Methodist, Baptist, Congregationalist, Unitarian, Plymouth Brethren, Quaker, or, more controversially, Roman Catholic. Even within denominations, however, there was a surprising diversity of belief and practice. The Anglican Church contained three major divisions—Low Church or Evangelical, High Church, and Broad Church—which held significantly different sets of beliefs. Baptists could be General Baptists, Particular Baptists, or Strict and Particular Baptists. Methodism spawned many splinter groups within the denomination, including Primitive Methodists, Kilhamites, and Bible Christians. In addition to these many Christian denominations, there was also a significant and growing Jewish population in Britain. To add further complexity, as the century progressed, many people, including J.S. Mill, Harriet Martineau, and T.H. Huxley, rejected belief in God altogether, becoming atheists or, less militantly, agnostics.

The Victorian era was also a time of rapid change, and religious life and belief altered significantly over the course of the nineteenth century. So in addition to diversity of individual and denominational systems of belief, we must add the differences in Victorian religion as it was practiced in 1837, in 1865, and in 1901.

In short, any sentence beginning, "The Victorians believed that . . . " is almost certainly false—at least for some Victorians at some point in the century.

A final barrier to understanding is the enormous one of historical context. Victorian attitudes toward religion and its place in society were formed in the context of a tumultuous religious history, which, if it is not entirely forgotten, looms much less large for people today. In the remainder of this Introduction, I will give an overview of the history of religious belief and conflict in Britain, from the Reformation through the early nineteenth century, filling in some of the background of Victorian religious life, and then provide a description of the state of religion in Britain at the start of the nineteenth century.

HISTORICAL BACKGROUND

Until the 1530s the state religion of England—and most of the rest of Europe—was Roman Catholicism. Lutheranism was beginning to make inroads in parts of Germany, but the doctrinal issues that motivated some European Christians to break with Catholicism had relatively little impact on the English Reformation. In Britain, issues of political power and royal succession rather than doctrine led to the founding of the Anglican Church. It is a common over-simplification to attribute the origin of the Church of England to the desire of Henry VIII for a divorce: In fact, by that point in his reign, the king had struggled with papal authority for years. But the struggle did come to a head when Henry, anxious because his wife, Catherine of Aragon, seemed unable to provide him with a male heir to the throne, asked Pope Clement VII to annul the marriage so that he could marry Anne Boleyn, already pregnant with his child. When the Pope refused to grant him an annulment, Henry broke with Rome altogether. In 1534, Parliament passed the Act of Supremacy, which made the English monarch the head of the Anglican Church. Henry seized the property of Roman Catholic institutions, including monasteries and convents, and required the clergy to swear an oath of allegiance to him as supreme head of the church. Some clergymen chose martyrdom rather than repudiate the authority of the Pope. However, Henry initiated few changes in religious practice, retaining much traditional Catholic ritual and doctrine.

There followed years of religious turmoil. Henry was succeeded by his son, Edward VI, and under his reign the Anglican Church, influenced by European reform movements, began to diverge further from its Roman Catholic origins. But when Edward died childless, Henry's daughter by Catherine of Aragon, Queen Mary, took the throne. She quickly had the Reformation legislation passed by Henry repealed and made England once again a Roman Catholic country. Her nickname, Bloody Mary, recalls her enthusiastic persecution of Protestants; during her five-year reign, 283 people were burned at the stake for heresy. When her half-sister Elizabeth, daughter of Henry VIII and Anne Boleyn, took the throne in 1558, she initiated a new Act of Supremacy (1559), which reinstated the Protestant reform legislation passed during her father's reign.

The reign of Queen Elizabeth I produced what came to be called the Elizabethan Settlement, in which Anglican doctrine was codified and Anglicanism legally entrenched as the established religion. Edward VI had instituted the use of a Book of Common Prayer in 1549, with a revised version in 1552, which exorcised many traditional Catholic practices. Elizabeth I again revised and published an Anglican Book of Common Prayer in 1559, and through the 1559 Act of Uniformity made it the sole legal form of worship in England. The Act also required weekly attendance at Anglican religious services. Anglican doctrine was further codified in 1563, when the Thirty-Nine Articles, which set out the fundamental teachings of the Anglican Church, were compiled, and in 1571, Parliament made adherence to the Thirty-Nine Articles a legal requirement.

The Elizabethan Settlement aimed to produce an Anglican Church that would prove acceptable to almost all of Elizabeth's subjects, including those with strong Roman Catholic sympathies and those who favored a Lutheran brand of Protestantism. As a result, the revised Prayer Book and the Thirty-Nine Articles used deliberately ambiguous language, language that made it possible for different Christian groups to interpret these documents as reflecting their own understanding of Christian doctrine. Elizabeth's compromises allowed the Anglican Church to develop and to flourish, though their ambiguities would pose significant problems for the Victorian church.

But this "settlement" did not wholly settle the religious controversy or end religious violence in England. Pope Pius V had excommunicated Queen Elizabeth in 1570, releasing her subjects from their oath of allegiance to her government. While previously Roman Catholic priests might have been charged with heresy, now they were also guilty of the capital crime of treason: all Roman Catholics in England came under suspicion. Although most English Catholics remained loyal citizens, a few actively plotted against the crown. Elizabeth's successor, James I, faced a series of assassination attempts by Roman Catholics who wanted to return England to Roman Catholicism. The most famous and most significant of these was the Gunpowder Plot of 1604, in which conspirators, including Guy Fawkes, planned to blow up the Houses of Parliament, while James I was there for the state opening. The foiling of this plot is still celebrated annually in England on Guy Fawkes Day, the fifth of November, and historically this celebration has kept alive the idea of Catholicism as a threat to public order. This turbulent history of the English Reformation had a long-term effect on the civil rights of Catholic citizens of England and set up the prejudice against Roman Catholics that would continue into the twentieth century.

But the most serious threat to the English monarchy in the seventeenth century came not from the Roman Catholics, but from the Puritans. The Puritans were a group of English Protestants strongly influenced by continental Calvinism who wanted to reform the Anglican Church by repudiating any remnants of Catholic doctrine and practice and remaking England according to their own religious ideals. In the 1630s, they had begun to fear that King Charles I, who had taken as his queen a devout Roman Catholic, was gradually undoing the Protestant Reformation, gradually reinstating Roman Catholic ritual and practice, and Puritan members of Parliament set themselves up in opposition to the king. These Puritan MPs led the revolt against royal power, which became the English Civil War in 1642 and culminated in the beheading of Charles I in 1649. From 1653 to 1658, England was governed by the Puritan leader, Oliver Cromwell, who was declared Lord Protector. Under the Protectorate or "Commonwealth," while Anglicans and Roman Catholics experienced some religious persecution, toleration was extended to Jews and to all non-Anglican Protestant sects, and Puritan legislation attempted to reform England ecclesiastically and morally. But the Protectorate depended upon Cromwell's powerful leadership, and when he died and was succeeded by his son, Richard Cromwell, Richard proved unable to sustain his father's position. In 1660, Charles II, the son of the dead king, who had been living in exile in France, returned to England to resume the throne—and headship of the Anglican Church.

After the restoration, Charles II published a new Book of Common Prayer (1662) and Parliament passed another Act of Uniformity. This Act extended some tolerance to non-Anglican Protestants, but many Puritans, as well as Baptists, Presbyterians, Congregationalists, and others, could not in good conscience submit to the new law. They became known as "dissenters" or "nonconformists," and they were regarded as potentially dangerous to the new, fragile peace. In fact, there was a reaction against all kinds of religious enthusiasm, which had shown its destructive power. The Established Church began to preach a more moderate form of Christianity, focusing on rational assent and moral behavior and eschewing strong religious emotions. The Enlightenment, with its Deism and its rationality, also tended to promote this religious moderation, and it looked as though the secularization that was gradually transforming Europe would proceed similarly in England. But it did not, as a result of two events: the religious awakening in the mid-eighteenth century and the French Revolution.

Many English men and women found the rational Christianity of the Established Church, which de-emphasized the emotional aspects of religious belief, unsatisfying, and simultaneously several eighteenth-century Anglican clergymen initiated a return to religious enthusiasm and emotional expression. The most important of these were George Whitefield (1714–1770) and John Wesley (1703–1791). These men led a revival in English Christianity that had a profound influence on Victorian religious life. Wesley's followers were called "Methodists," and for a long time they remained a group within the Anglican Church, but doctrinal and practical differences eventually led to a break with Anglicanism, and Methodism became the largest dissenting denomination in England, identified as "New Dissent." Despite considerable official opposition, the followers of Whitefield and other leaders largely remained within the Anglican Church and founded the Established Church's Evangelical wing. The traditional dissenting denominations, known as "Old Dissent," especially the Baptists and Congregationalists, were also influenced by this revival, and large portions of those dissenting denominations adopted evangelical beliefs and emphases. By the end of the eighteenth century, the Evangelical revival had turned English religion away from the "high and dry" practices of the post-Civil War period toward a much more emotional, enthusiastic form of worship and more active participation in national life.

The other event that temporarily reversed the secularizing trend in England was the French Revolution in 1789 and its aftermath. The revolutionaries in France wanted to get rid of the corrupt and autocratic French monarchy, but they also wanted to do away with other aspects of the establishment, so that they could remake society on rational, Enlightenment principles. One of their major targets was, of course, the church and religious belief in general. The revolutionary state was officially secular, and the revolutionary leaders were often avowed atheists, which horrified English onlookers found at least as shocking as their political ideology. The descent of the Revolution into the violence of the Terror (1793) and then the dictatorship of Napoleon Bonaparte, who took power in 1799 and had himself crowned emperor in 1804, confirmed English judgments that religion was the only sound basis for stable government and public morality. Antirevolutionary and pro-religious sentiment was further strengthened by the lengthy Napoleonic Wars (1803–1815), in which England fought to stop Napoleon from forcibly liberating Europeans from their monarchical governments. By the time that Napoleon was finally defeated, the reaction in Britain was firmly established. Politics had taken a conservative turn, and the Established Church was widely regarded as central to Britain's national life and, indeed, its very survival as a nation. Religion, with its inculcation of morality, was also seen as a guarantor against any working-class uprising, which might bring the horrors of the French Revolution to Britain.

RELIGION IN THE EARLY NINETEENTH CENTURY

Despite gains by Methodism in the late eighteenth century and the continued existence of other non-Anglican sects, in 1800 the Anglican Church still dominated religious life in England and Wales. Contemporary and later Victorian reformers tended to paint a grim picture of the state of the Anglican Church in the early nineteenth century: they portrayed it as an institution riddled with corruption, morally lax and spiritually barren, preaching mild morality and reason rather than the powerful transcendent truth of Christian doctrine. While these critics in their religious fervor may have exaggerated the extent of the problems, some problems certainly existed. Jane Austen, whose family included seven Anglican clergymen—her father, two brothers, and four cousins—and whose novels, all published in the first two decades of the nineteenth century, portray the role of the clergy in village life, provides us with illustrations of some of these problems.

Several of the main complaints against the church of this period concerned the clergy. A man of the early nineteenth century did not think of choosing a clerical career in terms of vocation, but of prudence and general aptitude. It was one of a handful of careers deemed appropriate for a member of the gentry without independent fortune. In Austen's *Mansfield Park* (1814), when Mary

Crawford discovers (to her dismay) that Edmund Bertram is planning to be ordained, she brings up the matter in conversation:

> "So you are to be a clergyman, Mr. Bertram. This is rather a surprise to me."
> "Why should it surprise you? You must suppose me designed for some profession, and might perceive that I am neither a lawyer, nor a soldier, nor a sailor."[1]

Edmund regards a clerical career as one more among several possible alternatives. His choice is partly determined by personal inclination—and Austen makes it clear that he will be an excellent clergyman—but also partly by the knowledge that his father will be able to appoint him to a parish that will provide him a comfortable living:

> "[T]he knowing that there was such a provision for me probably did bias me. Nor can I think it wrong that it should. There was no natural disinclination to be overcome, and I see no reason why a man should make a worse clergyman for knowing that he will have a competence early in life."[2]

Like the fictional Edmund, the Reverend Thomas Gisborne, a well-respected Evangelical author and clergyman of the period, sees nothing wrong with choosing a clerical career according to such prudential considerations, as he suggests in his high-minded book, *An Enquiry into the Duties of Men in the Higher and Middle Classes of Society* (1794):

> [T]o him who sees no reason to think that he shall not promote the glory of God and the good of mankind as much in the church as in any other profession . . . the prospect of obtaining, by the aid of his friends and relations, a competent provision in the church may lawfully be the motive which determines him to that line in preference to another.[3]

"Friends and relations" were often in a position to ensure such a "competent provision" because of the way clergymen were appointed to benefices, or permanent clerical posts. Out of 11,600 benefices in England and Wales, church authorities could appoint clergymen to only 2,500 of them. A further 600 appointments belonged to Oxford and Cambridge colleges and important public schools; these benefices generally went to ordained employees—fellows or schoolmasters—who wished to exchange the life of a celibate academic for that of a married minister. On behalf of the king or queen, the prime minister could appoint clergymen in 1,100 parishes, and these positions generally went to his political supporters. But fully 5,500 benefices, just under half of the total,

were in the gift of private citizens, who could appoint any ordained clergyman that they might choose. Such patrons regularly appointed sons, nephews,
friends, or friends' relations to the positions in their gift; on the theory that if
you want a job done right you have to do it yourself, a man could even appoint
himself to a living.

In *Sense & Sensibility* (1811), Colonel Brandon offers to appoint Edward
Ferrars to a living in his gift after only a brief acquaintance, partly because he
is a friend of Elinor Dashwood, as he explains to her:

> "I have seen Mr. Ferrars two or three times in Harley-street, and am
> much pleased with him. He is not a young man with whom one can be
> intimately acquainted in a short time, but I have seen enough of him to
> wish him well for his own sake, and as a friend of yours, I wish it still
> more . . . Will you be so good as to tell him that the living of Delaford, now
> just vacant, as I am informed by this day's post, is his, if he think it worth
> his acceptance . . . It is a rectory, but a small one; the late incumbent,
> I believe, did not make more than 200£ per annum, and though it is
> certainly capable of improvement, I fear, not to such an amount as to
> afford him a very comfortable income."[4]

In *Pride and Prejudice* (1813), Mr. Collins's excessive deference to the patron
who appointed him to his living, Lady Catherine de Bourgh (Mr. Darcy's aunt),
is partly a result of the system of private patronage in the church. When at
the end of the novel Mr. Bennet informs Mr. Collins about the engagement
of Elizabeth and Darcy, his cynical remark—"Console Lady Catherine as well
as you can. But, if I were you, I would stand by the nephew. He has more to
give"[5]—probably refers to the fact that Darcy will have even richer clerical
livings in his own gift.

The right to appoint a clergyman in a particular parish, known as an "ad-
vowson," could be sold; one could buy the right to just the next appointment
or to all appointments in the future. Advowsons were sometimes sold by auc-
tion and were regularly advertised in the newspapers, as Irene Collins reports:
"The value of the living was advertised . . . along with the life expectancy of the
existing incumbent,"[6] that is, the clergyman currently occupying that position.

The uncle of Jane Austen's father, George Austen, actually purchased the
next presentation of two livings, planning to appoint George to whichever one
came open first.[7] And in *Mansfield Park*, Sir Thomas Bertram finds himself
forced to sell the next presentation at Mansfield because of financial reverses.
But his tender conscience on the subject suggests that Austen was not happy
with this kind of commercialization.

While Victorian reformers and the modern reader may be disturbed by
the careerism, favoritism, and nepotism of the system, these were taken for
granted in the nineteenth-century church, as in other areas of public life,
including the civil service and the armed forces. Anglicans of the period were
also generally comfortable with pluralism, or the holding of multiple clerical

positions simultaneously. A pluralist clergyman would have the responsibility for—and the income from—more than one parish. About one-third of the clergymen in the early decades of the century were pluralists. Some accepted multiple benefices out of economic necessity: in 1802, about a third of benefices paid £150 or less, which was considered a minimally middle-class income. Others, like Jane Austen's brother James, who had three parishes, were looking to increase a more-than-adequate income. As a result, as many as 40 percent of parishes lacked a resident clergyman.

Though it fell short of the ideal, the system was not, perhaps, quite as bad as it sounds. Officially, if the parishes to be held simultaneously were more than thirty miles apart, a clergyman would have to get his bishop's permission; in practice, though, bishops were fairly lax about granting such permissions. If a clergyman could not adequately serve the parishes he was responsible for, he could hire an ordained minister to serve as curate, paying him some portion of the income from the benefice. In Austen's *Persuasion*, it is a curacy under the increasingly infirm Dr. Shirley that Charles Hayter hopes to obtain.

But, while some pluralist clergymen and a few bishops with rich livings might make a fortune in the church, clerical salaries, determined by ancient tradition, were notoriously inequitable and variable.

Originally, clergymen were supposed to derive their income from the "tithe," which was a levy on parishioners amounting to 10 percent of the agricultural output of the parish, and the "glebe," or church lands belonging to the parish. There were two kinds of tithes: the great tithes were levied on wheat, oats, and other cereal crops, and were the most lucrative, while the small tithes came from all other farm produce, including fruit, chickens, eggs, lamb, and so forth. The rector of the parish, who was in theory its clergyman, received both the great and small tithes. But a landowner sometimes wanted the great tithes for himself, and, if the living was in his gift, appointed himself (and his heirs) rector of the parish in which his estate was located. He would then appoint a "vicar" to serve as the parish clergyman. The word "vicar," in fact, is related to the prefix "vice," and similarly means "substitute"; the vicar is the substitute for the rector. So some parishes would have a rector as their incumbent, or permanent clergyman, and others would have a vicar, according to their historical circumstances. In general, rectors, receiving the full tithes, were better off, but the incomes of both rectors and vicars varied with farm incomes, which were notoriously volatile, so that the clergyman's income could vary considerably from year to year. Clergymen could also supplement their income through their use of the glebe. They could either farm the land themselves or rent it out to local farmers and increase their incomes in that way. An incumbent was usually provided with a house—the "rectory" or the "vicarage"—though the quality of the housing varied significantly, and the incumbent was responsible for the upkeep and improvement of his church-provided housing.

Because their income derived from the land rather than being received as a salary, rectors and vicars were considered gentlemen—and, often, if unmarried, quite eligible. Once a clergyman was appointed to a parish, he became a "freeholder" of his position and lands; he could not be fired by the patron of the living and the lands and income were his to use as he saw fit, although he could not sell the church property. This status as freeholder also entitled him to be one of the few voters in the parish, since voting was generally restricted to males with a freehold worth at least forty shillings.

While most incumbents were either rectors or vicars, a few were "perpetual curates." These clergymen were paid a salary by the diocese rather than relying on tithe and glebe for their income, but they enjoyed many of the privileges of other incumbents, and their situation was considerably better than that of the curates, considered below. Whether the incumbent was a rector, vicar, or perpetual curate depended upon the particular history of each parish.

Worse off than the incumbent clergymen were the curates. A curate could be hired by a clergyman to assist him with the overwhelming duties in a large parish or, more frequently in this period, to serve in his place as resident clergyman for the parish. Curates thus relied upon the salary paid them by the rector or vicar of the parish, which often amounted to only a small income. In 1803 William Jones wrote in his diary: "a journeyman in almost any trade or business, even a brick-layer's labourer or the turner of a razor grinder's wheel" was "generally better paid than a . . . curate."[8] At the end of the eighteenth century, an average curate might receive only £35, well below middle-class standards. A curate also had no job security. If the clergyman who had hired him became dissatisfied with his work, moved to another parish, died, or simply decided he could not afford a curate's salary any longer, the curate had to look for a new position. Needless to say, this poverty and insecurity made the curates less eligible as prospective husbands than their fellow clergymen. In *Sense and Sensibility* (1811) Mrs. Jennings anticipates the marriage of her niece, Lucy Steele, and the soon-to-be-ordained but as-yet-unemployed Edward Ferrars, with some trepidation:

> "Wait for his having a living!—Aye, we all know how *that* will end— they will wait a twelvemonth, and finding no good comes of it, will set down upon a curacy of fifty pound a-year, with the interest of his two thousand pounds, and what little matter Mr. Steele and Mr. Pratt can give her. Then they will have a child every year! And Lord help 'em! How poor they will be!—I must see what I can give them towards furnishing their house."[9]

Even though Edward will be able to supplement his curate's salary with investment income, Mrs. Jennings recognizes that he will still be unable comfortably to support a family. Jane Austen had a chance to see the curate's plight close up: her brother Henry Austen as curate of Chawton received only a little over £50 a year.

In addition, there was no pension for a superannuated clergyman, and most could not afford to retire. Upon retirement, clergymen lost not only their incomes but also their homes. Sometimes a clergyman too infirm to do his duties could hire a curate to take his place and retain enough income to survive, but that was not always possible. Clergy widows were also generally unprovided for. One of the poorest characters in Austen's fiction is Mrs. Bates in *Emma*, the widow of a clergyman, who has exchanged a middle-class life in the vicarage for a precarious existence in rented town lodgings, where she survives only through the generosity of her friends.

The Victorian church inherited all these problems and inequities, and, though they were not eliminated by the end of the nineteenth century, they were substantially ameliorated, as we will see in the next few chapters. But while problems with the system for selecting, appointing, monitoring, and compensating clergymen were serious, reformers were also disturbed by the doctrinal and religious teachings of the church in the late eighteenth and early nineteenth centuries.

Partly as a reaction against the violent emotion of the Civil War and its aftermath, the English Church had rejected an emotional form of worship in favor of a more rational style. Also, influenced by the Enlightenment, the church de-emphasized the supernatural and mystical content of Christianity, focusing instead on "natural religion," that is, a set of beliefs derivable from observation of the natural world and human nature. It took, in many respects, a more "scientific" approach to religion. Enlightenment Christians agreed with—and often quoted—the view of John Tillotson, Archbishop of Canterbury from 1691 to 1694, who claimed that "the great design of the Christian religion" was "to restore and reinforce the practice of the natural law or, which is all one, of moral duties."[10] This Enlightenment religion was concerned mainly with a rational Creator-God and, on the earthly plane, with ethical precepts of good behavior. In 1803 William Jones, clearly a critic of this rational religion, complained in his journal about the sermons at the local church: "the name of Christ is scarce ever heard, nor any of the characteristic doctrines of His holy religion. The watchword or *catchword*... is 'Morality.'"[11] Jane Austen's novels are all imbued with this calm, rational, Enlightenment Christianity.

But other currents were beginning to stir up British Christianity. In particular, Evangelicalism was gaining significant strength inside the Anglican Church, bringing with it a more emotional style of worship, generally associated with dissenters, and a greater emphasis on the revelation of God in the Bible, as well as an earnest and active attitude toward life. Though the Evangelicals constituted only a small minority of Anglicans, their enthusiasm and social activism made them more influential than their numbers would suggest. In the last years of the eighteenth and the first years of the nineteenth century, they founded dozens of charitable and reforming organizations dedicated to many different causes: the Society for the Relief of Persons Imprisoned for Small Debts; the Society for the Reformation of Prison Discipline; the Indigent Blind Institution; the Foundling Hospital; the British and Foreign Bible Society; and the Religious Tract Society. Famously, too, they led the public campaign against slavery, which brought about the abolition of the slave trade in 1807.

When Jane Austen's sister, Cassandra, encouraged her to read an Evangelical novel, Hannah More's *Coelebs in Search of a Wife* (1808), Austen objected strenuously—and ironically: "My disinclination for [the novel] before was affected, but now it is real; I do not like the Evangelicals. Of course, I shall be delighted when I read it, like other people, but till I do I dislike it."[12] Despite her claims here, many critics see Evangelical ideas beginning to have an influence in her novels, particularly *Mansfield Park*, where the heroine is the serious-minded and pious Fanny Price. In any case, the Evangelicals at the start of the nineteenth century were clearly having an effect on British religious and social life, and that effect would only increase through the early Victorian period.

So, in the first part of the nineteenth century, the reaction in the wake of the French Revolution consolidated the power of the Established Church and reestablished the importance of religion in private as well as in national life. Religion in Britain was still dominated by the tradition of Enlightenment Christianity, with its emphasis on natural religion and ethics. But the growing influence of Anglican Evangelicals and of Evangelical Dissenters such as Methodists was setting the stage for a century of enthusiastic religious activity, rapid change, and intense controversy in religious life and belief. In the chapters that follow I provide an overview of Victorian religious life, mapping its diversity, exploring its ramifications in public and private life, and recording important milestones and changes over the course of the century. I also try to recapture what religion meant to ordinary Victorian believers, how they experienced it, and how it shaped their lives and ideas.

Chapters 1 and 2 describe the major religious denominations in Victorian Britain, their theological differences as well as their social positions. Chapter 3 examines the life of the Victorian clergyman and distinguishes between the many kinds of Victorian clerics, while Chapter 4 looks at the way religion affected ordinary people in their daily lives. Chapters 5 and 6 discuss religion's influence on reform movements and on literature, respectively, while Chapter 7 analyzes Victorian women's experience of religion. The final chapter, Chapter 8, recounts the unsettlement of Victorian religion and the growth of various forms of unbelief, while the conclusion points out significant parallels between Victorian and contemporary religious issues.

1

Church and State: Politics and the Victorian Church of England

Throughout the nineteenth century the Anglican Church was the Established Church in England and Wales. Exactly what that meant—or should mean—was a subject of considerable controversy during the first half of the century; prominent writers and public figures including Samuel Taylor Coleridge, W.E. Gladstone, and Thomas Arnold, the famous headmaster of Rugby School, weighed in on the question. Despite the disputes, however, it is possible to summarize the general principles and salient facts about the relationship between church and state in Victorian England.

Church and state in nineteenth-century England were intimately connected. The church participated directly in the government of the state. Twenty-seven bishops sat with the peers of the realm in the upper house of Parliament, the House of Lords, and voted to pass or defeat new laws. Moreover, until its repeal in 1828, the Test and Corporations Act mandated that only Anglicans could hold any public office at any level of government, from local council to Parliament. In practice, exemptions were often granted, so that prominent Dissenters did in fact hold local office, but the law remained on the books well into the nineteenth century, and the vast majority of elected and appointed officials continued to be members of the Church of England. Church courts also wielded great power, exercising jurisdiction over wills and marriage law, as well as more narrowly religious issues, through much of the period.

Just as the church participated in the government of the state, so the state participated in the government of the church. The reigning monarch was both head of state and head of the church; the bishops and archbishops were selected by royal appointment. The state was also responsible for the financial support of the Established Church through a separate tax known as the "church rates." Parliament regularly debated and passed legislation regulating religious practices, from bills restricting activities legally permissible on the Sabbath to those setting minimum levels of remuneration for parochial clergy.

These legal and practical links between church and state both reflected and fostered a sense of mutual responsibility. The church was very much part of the ruling establishment, and it often adopted conservative political positions aimed at the maintenance of the political status quo. The state, in turn, looked to the church as a guarantor of public morality and hence of public order. Beyond that, many Anglican government officials felt responsible for the promotion of religious truth, as embodied in the beliefs of their own Anglican Communion. While they could practice a degree of religious tolerance, they could not treat truth and falsehood the same by granting equal rights to other religious denominations.

Two issues of great public concern illustrate some of the complications of this relationship between church and state: the observance of the Sabbath and the regulation of divorce.

The Victorian Sunday

Remember the sabbath day, to keep it holy. Six days shalt thou labour, and do all thy work: But the seventh day is the sabbath of the Lord thy God: in it thou shalt not do any work, thou, nor thy son, nor thy daughter, thy manservant, nor thy maidservant, nor thy cattle, nor thy stranger that is within thy gates: For in six days the Lord made heaven and earth, the sea, and all that in them is, and rested the seventh day: wherefore the Lord blessed the sabbath day, and hallowed it.
—Exodus 20: 8–11

British law and custom had long recognized Sunday as a day of rest and worship. Factory workers and farm laborers alike enjoyed their weekly day of leisure, and many Britons attended one or more religious services in a church or chapel. But toward the end of the eighteenth century, most Evangelicals, Anglicans and Dissenters, began to take a higher view of the Sabbath. In order to keep the Sabbath day holy, they restricted their activities to worship, prayer, and meditation. They eschewed all business concerns as well as all secular amusements such as sports, theatre, and novel reading, spending Sunday instead attending services, taking walks, and reading improving literature. People who were subjected to this regime as children seldom remembered it with affection; Mary Hughes describes her experience late in the century in *A London Child in the 1870s* (1934):

The afternoons hung heavy. It seemed to be always 3 o'clock. All amusements, as well as work, were forbidden. It was a real privation not to be allowed to draw and paint. However, an exception was made in favour of illuminated texts and we rivalled the old monks in our zeal for copying

Scripture, with the same kind of worldly decorations that they devised. Naturally our main stand-by was reading, but here again our field was limited by mother's notions of what was appropriate for Sunday. *Tom Brown, Robinson Crusoe, Hans Andersen's Tales,* and *Pilgrim's Progress* were permitted, but not the *Arabian Nights,* or Walter Scott, or indeed any novel. We had to fall back on bound volumes of *Good Words for the Young,* which were not so bad as the title suggests and contained plenty of stories.... The Bible proved often more entertaining than the "good" books. One day when my brother was desperate for a new story I recommended Esther as being as good as the *Arabian Nights.* He hung back, however, until I urged the point that God was not mentioned in it. "No, really?" he cried, seized the Bible, and soon became absorbed in the plot.[1]

Hughes's parents were not particularly pious, but, like many Christians, they voluntarily adopted Sabbath restrictions on the activities of their household. But was such private recognition of the Sabbath enough? All around them these religious people saw evidence of Sabbath-breaking, ranging from a comparatively innocent game of cricket, or an excursion to the country, to real drunkenness and dissipation. Would not God punish Britain as a nation (as He had so often punished Israel in the Old Testament) for taking no action to protect the sanctity of the Sabbath? In 1831 Sir Andrew Agnew and other like-minded Christians—known as "sabbatarians"—formed the Society for the Observance of the Lord's Day to push for parliamentary action on the keeping of the Sabbath. After all, because the church and state were so closely intertwined, the state had religious as well as secular responsibilities. As the Sabbath Observance Bill of 1833 put it, "[I]t is the bounden duty of Parliament to promote the observance of the Lord's day, by protecting every class of society against being required to sacrifice their comfort, health, religious privileges, and conscience, for the convenience, enjoyment, or supposed advantage of any other class on the Lord's day."[2] The bill prohibited most Sabbath trading, and seriously restricted travel on the Sabbath by forbidding the hiring of coaches and the opening of locks and turnpike gates, and it prohibited a large number of leisure activities, including public lectures, hunting, cockfighting, betting, and "any pastime of public indecorum, inconvenience or nuisance."[3]

In the attempt to legislate the observance of the Sabbath, however, the Evangelicals encountered considerable opposition—and largely failed to achieve their aims. One of the most vehement opponents of sabbatarian legislation was Charles Dickens, who created a memorable portrait of the tedium of a pious Sunday in *Little Dorrit.* His most effective intervention in the debate, however, was a pamphlet entitled "Sunday Under Three Heads" (1836), in which he argued that sabbatarian legislation disproportionately affected the poor, whose activities on their only day of leisure were severely restricted, while the lives of the rich were barely affected. Because a special provision of the bill allowed for personal servants to labor on the Sabbath (despite scriptural injunctions about "thy manservant nor thy maidservant"), rich families with their own cooks and kitchens, their own carriages and coachmen, and their own housekeepers and butlers could either travel or spend a tranquil and even luxurious Sabbath in their comfortable homes. But the poor, who depended on bakeshops to roast their meat, on public transportation to get them away from the city, and on public spaces as refuges from cramped and overcrowded tenements, would be deprived of nearly every comfort, and, in Dickens's words, the "law [will] convert the day intended for rest and cheerfulness, into one of universal gloom, bigotry, and persecution."[4]

The 1833 bill failed. In 1855 a much less ambitious bill regulating trade in London on Sundays actually sparked large public protests. The sabbatarian legislation had to be passed piecemeal: Sunday postal delivery was first abolished altogether, then one Sunday delivery was restored; licensing hours for pubs were restricted; in Scotland, railways did not run on Sundays, though no such restriction was ever imposed in England; efforts to open public attractions in London on Sunday—the Crystal Palace, the British Museum, the National Gallery—were soundly defeated. Still, the results were disappointing for the sabbatarians, though the laws managed to put a damper on city life, giving birth to the famous saying: "Ennui was born in London on a Sunday." Queen Victoria herself privately expressed her opposition to sabbatarianism: "I am not at all an admirer or approver of our very dull Sunday."

These attempts to restore observance of the Lord's day earned Evangelicals the (often exaggerated) reputation of being dour, prudish killjoys and won them widespread resentment. And the continuing controversy over legal restrictions of behavior on the Sabbath illustrated the problems of the intertwining of Established Church and increasingly diverse state.

Divorce

The Pharisees also came unto him, tempting him, and saying unto him, Is it lawful for a man to put away his wife for every cause? And he answered and said unto them, Have ye not read, that he which made them at the beginning made them male and female, And said, For this cause shall a man leave father and mother, and shall cleave to his wife: and they twain shall be one flesh? Wherefore they are no more twain, but one flesh. What therefore God hath joined together, let not man put asunder. They say unto him, Why did Moses then command to give a writing of divorcement, and to put her away? He saith unto them, Moses because of the hardness of your hearts suffered you to put away your wives: but from the beginning it was not so. And I say unto you, Whosoever shall put away his wife, except it be for fornication, and shall marry another, committeth adultery: and whoso marrieth her which is put away doth commit adultery.

—Matthew 19: 3–9

Although marriage was not a sacrament for Anglicans as it was for Roman Catholics, the Anglican Church and English law generally regarded marriages as holy and indissoluble. The rich and influential had only one way to escape an intolerable marriage, by requesting a special act of Parliament, a process that middle-class Mr. Bounderby describes to the miserably married factory hand, Stephen Blackpool, in Dickens's *Hard Times*:

> "Why, you'd have to go to Doctors' Commons with a suit, and you'd have to go to a court of Common Law with a suit, and you'd have to get an Act of Parliament to enable you to marry again, and it would cost you (if it was a case of very plain-sailing), I suppose from a thousand to fifteen hundred pound," said Mr. Bounderby. "Perhaps twice the money."
>   "There's no other law?"
>   "Certainly not."[5]

Women could almost never get a divorce, whatever the circumstances. In the 1850s, however, inspired in part by the sufferings of Caroline Norton, whose abusive husband used his full legal advantages to deny her access to her children and confiscate her property, people began to agitate for a change in the law. The Matrimonial Causes Bill was proposed in 1857. Under the bill, a husband could sue for divorce on the grounds of adultery, a wife for adultery plus a further offence (cruelty, desertion, bigamy, sodomy, bestiality, incest). Divorced wives were also offered additional financial protection: a wife was able to protect her own earnings from her ex-husband, and a court could order the husband to pay alimony.

The bill provoked differing reactions from Victorian Christians. Many Evangelicals regarded this step as a weakening of the sacredness of marriage and opposed the bill. In this vein, Evangelical Emma Jane Worboise wrote a novel, *The Wife's Trials*, demonstrating how remaining in an abusive marriage could perfect the Christian character of the wife and even achieve the conversion of the wicked husband.

Other Christians, including bishops in the House of Lords, saw the legislation as acceptable largely because of its adherence to Christ's teachings. In support of this position, W.E. Gladstone, MP and soon-to-be prime minister, wrote a detailed analysis of the Biblical texts on divorce for the *Quarterly Review*. As Owen Chadwick put it, the question that confronted Parliament clearly in this matter was this: could "the law of England . . . contradict the law of Scripture"?[6] How should the Anglican state legislate not for Anglicans only, but for all its citizens?

In the end the bill passed, and matrimonial affairs, which had long been under the jurisdiction of ecclesiastical courts, were from this point to be decided by a newly constituted state court.

Conflict over divorce, like conflict over Sabbath-breaking, revealed tensions in the relationship of church and state, of Christian commitment and good government, and the passage of the Matrimonial Causes Act of 1857 represented perhaps the last time that the interpretation of Scripture would prove key to the determination of English law.

CHALLENGES TO THE CHURCH OF ENGLAND: CHANGE AND DIVERSITY

For many nineteenth-century English men and women, attending the local Anglican Church on Sunday was an expected and largely habitual form of participation in community life, an act that had a social significance that outweighed its religious meaning. For them, the Anglican Church was a fact of life, taken for granted both as their ancestral faith and as part of their national identity. But the Established Church faced significant challenges over the course of the century, challenges that threatened to change forever its role in English society and government.

Some of these challenges came from political radicals, who saw religion and particularly the Established Church as a powerful force opposing reform and claiming supernatural justification for the status quo; they wanted to free the state from what they saw as religious interference. But such radicals remained outside the Victorian political mainstream, and their campaigns for disestablishment never posed a very serious threat to the Church of England. In fact, the threat of radical political change often shored up support for the church, especially during periods when fear of revolution was most acute, for instance during the Chartist agitation in 1848.

A more serious challenge came from the fact that increasing numbers of British citizens were not Anglican at all. Some of these non-Anglicans lived in other parts of Britain. Scotland had its own national church, which was not Anglican but Presbyterian. So though both Scotland and England were governed by the same monarch and Parliament, their religious structures were entirely different. In Scotland, Presbyterians belonged to the national church, while those with ties to the Anglican Church (called, then as now, Episcopalians) were a protected dissenting minority, while over the border in England, Anglicans enjoyed significant political and social privileges denied to all other Christians, and the Presbyterians were the Dissenters. The situation was even more anomalous in Ireland. The majority of people in Ireland were Roman Catholic, but the Established Church of Ireland was Anglican. This contradiction caused significant unrest, eventually leading to the disestablishment of the Irish Church in 1871.

Even in England itself, however, the number and influence of non-Anglicans was increasing, and what their rights as citizens should be was becoming a more pressing issue. In 1833, over 300,000 non-Anglicans signed a petition addressed to Parliament, asking for relief from five "grievances" that weighed heavily on Dissenters. The first three all concerned the Anglican monopoly over important rites of passage. Births could be registered only in the local Anglican Church. Marriages could be performed only by an Anglican clergyman in an

Anglican Church (though special arrangements had already been made for Jews and Quakers). And Anglican churchyards were the only legal sites for burials. Dissenters were not allowed to use the burial rites of their own denomination: they had to be buried according to the Anglican rites or in total silence. The fourth grievance concerned the Anglican monopoly in higher education. All three English universities, at Oxford, Cambridge, and Durham, were Anglican institutions, and in order to receive a degree, a man had to subscribe to Anglican doctrine as expressed in the Thirty-Nine Articles. Dissenters were also barred from holding academic appointments at the universities: nearly all university fellowships could be held only by ordained Anglican clergymen, and even the few that allowed laymen required an acceptance of Anglican doctrinal statements. University College, London, had been established in 1826 to allow Dissenters the chance to pursue higher education, but it was not yet legally permitted to grant degrees. Fifth and finally, Dissenters objected to paying church rates, providing compulsory financial support to the Anglican Church.

But how far could the state go in extending tolerance to other forms of Christian practice and in granting equal rights to non-Anglicans without compromising the status of the Established Church? As relief for each of the disabilities was debated and, eventually, granted, the question kept recurring.

While the Established Church faced significant external challenges, the most serious threat to the establishment of the church came from the splintering of religious views within the Church of England. The Elizabethan settlement had deliberately couched Anglican doctrine in ambiguous language in order to allow Christians with different convictions—those still loyal to Roman Catholic doctrine, those influenced by Lutheranism—to remain within the Established Church. But in the nineteenth century, this ambiguity led to a significant division within the church as different groups insisted on the primacy of their own interpretation of the Prayer Book and the Thirty-Nine Articles. Three major parties developed within the nineteenth-century Anglican Church: the Evangelicals (sometimes called the Low Church); the Tractarians and their descendents, the Ritualists (sometimes called the High Church or the Anglo-Catholics); and the more liberal Broad Church party. Each of these had distinctive doctrines and ritual practices, and they struggled throughout the nineteenth century for dominance within the Anglican Church, even as the church struggled with issues of how to—and sometimes whether to—accommodate such varieties of religious belief within one state church.

Evangelicalism

Anglican Evangelicalism had its origins in the eighteenth-century religious revival that also produced Methodism. The term "evangelical" can be confusing because it can refer not only to a particular party within the Church of England, but, more broadly, to an interdenominational movement with some shared doctrinal emphases, a movement that included many Dissenters. Some writers attempt to distinguish these usages by using the term capitalized to refer to Anglican Evangelicals and lowercase to refer to dissenting evangelicals. Relations between Anglican and dissenting evangelicals were at times cordial, allowing cooperation in charitable and reform organizations, at other times markedly more distant. For, though they shared much doctrine, they differed in their view of the role of the church and its relationship to the state. In this chapter, the focus will be on Anglican Evangelicals; Dissenters who shared some of their doctrines will be discussed in the next chapter.

Evangelicals were characterized by certain fundamental doctrinal emphases:

Conversion. Evangelicals emphasized the individual need for conversion and salvation by faith, with a corresponding stress on the atoning work of Jesus. Their focus on the crucifixion contrasted with the increasing emphasis on Jesus's incarnation as the central doctrine of Christianity.

Biblical authority. They regarded the Bible as God's authoritative revelation, often as the only reliable source of authoritative teaching; they tended to reject church doctrine as it developed over the centuries as having any significant authority, though, as Anglicans, they maintained allegiance to the Thirty-Nine Articles. Generally, they regarded these articles as supported by biblical teaching, though on certain issues, such as baptismal regeneration, the two seemed in clear conflict. Unlike some dissenting sects, Anglican Evangelicals did not insist that the Bible was perfectly accurate (inerrant) on all subjects, only in its religious and moral teaching.

Priesthood of the believer. Though Evangelicals within the Church of England had a higher view of the role of the clergy than did many dissenting evangelicals, all evangelicals stressed the immediacy of the individual believer's relationship to God (through Jesus) and de-emphasized or denied the need for the mediation of the clergy. These emphases led to a highly individualistic brand of Christianity, even when tempered by membership in the Established Church.

Doctrine of assurance. Unlike the Puritans before them, Evangelicals held that a believer who underwent a conversion experience could be certain of his or her salvation. Those outside the movement could interpret this "blessed assurance" as self-satisfaction or even smugness. Within the movement, however, it was regarded as a great blessing that conferred freedom to look beyond the self; no longer obsessed by anxieties about their own salvation, believers could turn their attention to other people and to the problems of the society at large.

Social activism. Perhaps as a result of the doctrine of assurance, nineteenth-century Evangelicalism was characterized by almost frenetic levels of social activity, including attempts to spread the gospel of salvation to people at home and abroad as well as a concerted effort to remake British society according to divine standards. Some of this activity took the form of pushing for state action on central humanitarian and moral issues. It was Evangelicals, including the influential MP, William Wilberforce, who took the lead in the campaigns to abolish the slave trade (1803) and, eventually, slavery (1833) in British territories. As well as working to pass sabbatarian laws, they were also instrumental in the passage of factory legislation, including the Ten Hours Act (1847), which limited working hours for women and teenagers. The first industrial novel, *Helen Fleetwood* (1841), which highlighted the poor living and working conditions of factory workers, was written by an Evangelical novelist and editor, Charlotte Elizabeth Tonna.

Most of their efforts at reform, however, did not involve state action but private philanthropy. They founded dozens of societies from the Society for the Suppression of Vice, to the Ragged Schools Union, to the Royal Society for the Prevention of Cruelty to Animals. In fact, one estimate holds that in the later Victorian period, three-quarters of charitable organizations "were Evangelical in character and control."[7]

Evangelicals were also among the first to call for reform and revival in the Anglican clergy. They wanted clergymen to embody a higher standard of spirituality and seriousness about their pastoral duties, and they opposed practices in the church that prevented clergy from ministering to their people, including pluralism and absenteeism. But they also engaged the efforts of armies of lay workers, including many women, who found in Evangelical philanthropy and church work a rare outlet for their energies and talents.

The style of worship in churches led by Evangelical clergy tended to be relatively simple, without much ritual. Evangelical parishes were also the first to adopt the practice, already common in many dissenting sects, of congregational hymn singing, and Evangelical writers were major contributors to Victorian hymnody. Evangelicals were also strongly protestant and thus frequently anti-Catholic and anti-Tractarian, as we will see.

While Evangelical Dissenters were often politically liberal and strongly individualistic, the Church of England Evangelicals were usually conservatives—Tories—committed to preserving the status and national character of the Established Church. There was also a class distinction between evangelicals and Evangelicals: Dissent tended to be identified with the lower-middle class, while higher classes (and those who aspired to those classes) were much more likely to be Anglicans. George Eliot used an Evangelical character in *Middlemarch* (1871) to record this distinction: "[W]hile true religion was everywhere saving, honest Mrs. Bulstrode was convinced that to be saved in the Church was more respectable."[8]

Evangelicals exerted tremendous influence on the nature of Victorian society. Many people attribute Victorian earnestness, enthusiasm, and energy to their influence. But the Evangelicals' high seriousness and energetic pursuit of personal holiness and social reform also left them open to criticism, much of it carried on in literature. This was no accident. The relationship of Evangelicals to imaginative literature was conflicted. Most opposed the theatre on the ground of "profaneness on stage, the low moral reputation of actresses and the specious appeal to the senses."[9] And while many loved poetry, novels were treated with much greater suspicion. Despite the overgeneralizations of popular discussions, few Evangelicals actually forbade novel reading. While they regarded most novels as a (possibly sinful) waste of time and potentially corrupting, most Evangelicals saw in the genre a further potential for doctrinal and moral edification, and Evangelical novelists from Charlotte Elizabeth Tonna to Emma Jane Worboise found a ready readership.

But many mainstream novelists participated in the critique of Evangelicalism. Because Evangelicals preached high standards of moral conduct, they were left open to charges of hypocrisy when they failed to live up to their own standards. In *Jane Eyre*, for instance, Charlotte Brontë lambasts the hypocritical master of Lowood School who forces the girls at the school to renounce luxuries and fine clothes, while his plump wife and daughters parade themselves in expensive dresses. Dickens indicts the hypocrisy of the drunken Evangelical minister, Mr. Stiggins, in the *Pickwick Papers*. Evangelicals were also often represented as killjoys, insisting on devoting Sundays to religion and most leisure time to serious pursuits. Dickens opposed Evangelical sabbatarian legislation, and Eliot's *Middlemarch* represented the early Victorian Evangelicals as transforming provincial England into a markedly less merry place: "Evangelicalism had cast a certain suspicion as of plague-infection over the few amusements which survived in the provinces."[10]

But even when they criticized it, no Victorian escaped the influence of Evangelicalism, and many eminent Victorians had their characters formed by pious Evangelical upbringing—including John Ruskin, George Eliot, and even the leading light of the Tractarians, John Henry Newman. In the 1830s it was Tractarians such as Newman who would inherit the Evangelical traditions of personal spirituality and earnest devotion to duty and transform them through a return to the Catholic origins of Anglicanism.

Tractarianism and Ritualism

The Tractarians were the High Church party in the Church of England in the 1830s and 1840s. "High Church" refers to the elevated view they took of the authority of the church over all spiritual matters. They argued strongly against Parliament granting equal civil rights to those outside the church, Dissenters and Roman Catholics, seeing such laws as failures to distinguish between true believers and heretics. Salvation was available through the church, and anything that discouraged membership in the church was to be resisted. They also fought against any state interference in church government, and some went so far to as oppose the establishment of the church on the grounds that it compromised the church's authority by granting the state some jurisdiction over church matters. Most, however, wanted the Anglican Church to remain the Established Church, with all its rights and privileges. The Evangelicals, in contrast, were dubbed the

"Low Church" and tended to represent salvation as a matter of personal faith rather than church membership or ritual; they were much more tolerant of Dissenters and often joined forces with them for charitable purposes.

The name "Tractarian" derives from a series of ninety pamphlets, called *Tracts for the Times*, which leading Anglican High Churchmen published between 1833 and 1841, each one arguing for a particular point of doctrine or practice that they regarded as important to the Church of England. The group was also called the Oxford Movement, because so many of the leading figures, including John Keble, Edward Pusey, John Henry Newman, and Hurrell Froude, were academics at Oxford. Their detractors tended to call them "Puseyites," after Edward Pusey, because, as Owen Chadwick noted, "the sound was smooth and comic and disrepectful."[11]

The origin of the movement is usually traced to a sermon entitled "National Apostasy" preached by John Keble in July of 1833 in strong opposition to a recent government decision about the Irish Church. Although a large majority of the Irish people were Roman Catholics, the Established Church of Ireland was Protestant, in essence the Irish branch of the Anglican Church, and the Irish people were required to pay tithes for its upkeep. The Whig government of the day saw a need for reform, and put forward a bill that would abolish the positions of ten Irish Anglican bishops and also allow for the transfer of church funds to be used for the benefit of the people—to found secular or Roman Catholic schools, perhaps even to support Roman Catholic clergy. In the end, a compromise bill eliminated the transfer of funds, but the interference of Parliament with the authority of the Irish Church alarmed and inflamed a group of Oxford dons, and Keble addressed the issue in his famous sermon.

The influence of Keble's sermon may well have been exaggerated, but it certainly affected John Henry Newman powerfully, and later that year, he wrote and published the first of the *Tracts for the Times*.

Like the Evangelicals, the Tractarians believed that England was in need of spiritual revival and the church in need of reform, particularly with regard to the clergy. They also tended to share the Evangelicals' deep piety and seriousness about religion. But in other respects, the parties were profoundly different. Some of the differences derived from the gap in class and education that separated members of the two groups. As its name implies, the Oxford Movement was largely associated with well-educated men and with men and women of the upper middle classes. Evangelicals, on the other hand, often de-emphasized the importance of education, focusing instead on depth and sincerity of faith, and they tended to come from a slightly lower social stratum. Other differences between the groups, however, had more to do with religious practice and doctrine.

Evangelicals embraced an emotional style of worship, and they were eager to share their faith, imparting the gospel to others. Because they believed that religion should permeate their social and intellectual lives, they talked openly about religious matters, often quoting Scripture in ordinary conversation. For the same reason, Evangelical novels are full of Biblical references and sermonic passages. To outsiders, however, such biblical discourse, whether in daily discussions or in fiction, often appeared sanctimonious or hypocritical.

Tractarians rejected the emotionalism of the Evangelicals and their religious conversation. They defended the "doctrine of reserve," best described in Tract 80, which held that some spiritual truths should not be communicated promiscuously to the uninitiated. Tractarians tended not to discuss sacred matters in secular contexts, and Tractarian novels tended to convey religious teaching less directly, striking the modern reader as less religious and more literary than their Evangelical counterparts. Evangelicals, however, regarded such reserve with suspicion, as reflecting at best a genteel shame about the gospel of Jesus Christ and at worst insincerity and secrecy about Tractarian beliefs.

While this difference might be considered as much about style as substance, other differences derived from opposing interpretations of Anglican doctrine. As we saw in the Introduction, the formulations of doctrine in the Thirty-Nine Articles and the Prayer Book had been carefully written to accommodate a wide variety of interpretations in order to placate those with Protestant and with Roman Catholic sympathies. In the nineteenth century, the Evangelicals generally stressed the Protestant elements of the Anglican Church, while the Tractarians tended to stress the church's Roman Catholic traditions. Thus, the Evangelicals, like the Lutherans, believed that the Bible was the sole reliable authority for the Christian. The Tractarians, however, saw the development of church doctrine through time as a source of authority independent of the Bible, and they assiduously studied not only the Bible but also the early church fathers, Christian writers of the first through fifth centuries, who had been largely neglected in English tradition since the Reformation. They also placed increased emphasis on the postbiblical Catholic saints, celebrating saints' days and publishing new lives of the saints.

Similarly, Evangelicals defined the role of the clergy in a way closer to the tradition of European Protestantism, while the Tractarians saw the clergy as fulfilling priestly roles. Evangelicals tended to regard their clergy more as fellow Christians called to particular duties of care and teaching, and they encouraged widespread lay participation in the church and its mission. Tractarians, however, regarded the clergy as set apart by their ordination, invested with spiritual power and moral authority over their congregations; many spiritual functions could only be properly performed by ordained clergy, and lay participation was more limited. This high concept of clerical authority was defined and supported by a strong Tractarian emphasis on the doctrine of Apostolic Succession. According to this doctrine, which is held by Roman Catholics as well as by Tractarians, Jesus Christ himself ordained his Apostles to lead the young church, and this authority was passed down by them through ordination to a new generation of bishops, who in turn ordained their successors, and so on, in unbroken succession, down to the present day. Priestly authority comes, through this unbroken line of ordination, from the Savior himself. For this reason, Tractarians regarded dissenting ministers as illegitimate, since they were not ordained within this succession, and thus lacking any real spiritual authority.

Tractarians' assertion of priestly authority often led to controversy. Some English men and women regarded such claims as threats to treasured individual freedoms, the spiritual equivalent of a return to feudalism. This reaction was, if anything, more marked in Evangelical women. Because of women's exclusion from the Anglican clergy, the assertion of priestly authority was also an assertion of masculine authority. While Evangelicalism promised both men and women unmediated access to God and freedom of individual conscience, Tractarian doctrine limited this independence, requiring a woman's relationship to God, to some extent at least, to be mediated by a male.

Tractarian clergy caused further controversy when they began to defend the practice of parish priests hearing the confessions of their parishioners and granting absolution, a practice known as "auricular confession." Traditionally, Anglican confession had been practiced as part of the worship service: the priest would call for repentance, the congregants would silently confess their sins to God, and then the priest would pronounce absolution of sins to the whole congregation. Private auricular confession, while the standard method in the Roman Catholic Church, had seldom been practiced in the Anglican Church, but the Tractarians argued that it was consistent with Anglican doctrinal statements and part of the proper duty of a priest. Detractors saw this trend as a reversal of the Protestant Reformation and a further threat to spiritual independence. The secrecy of the confessional was also regarded with suspicion, and some Protestant writers indulged in lurid fantasies about the sexual possibilities opened up by a secret confession of sin from a woman to a priest.

These sexual suspicions were aggravated by the Tractarians' support for celibacy of the clergy. The Anglican clergy had long been able to marry, and the vicar in a country parish was often expected to set the example of a well-regulated family life. Only the dons at Oxford and Cambridge were forbidden to marry, and it is not a coincidence that the support for clerical celibacy originated among these unmarried academics. While few went so far as to claim that all clergymen should remain celibate, Tractarians argued that a celibate clergyman, free from the demands of family life, is better able to devote himself to the service of God. They also led the way in founding celibate communities of Anglican monks and nuns. Other members of the Anglican Communion regarded these moves as Romanizing innovations, and women in the church could feel that they were being rejected as unclean by this encouragement of celibate clergy. Nineteenth-century novels by women, such as Margaret Oliphant's *The Perpetual Curate* (1864) and Emma Jane Worboise's polemical *Overdale* (1869), often represented the call for celibacy as interfering in an otherwise loving marriage. Other women, however, saw a celibate life of religious service, whether lived within a religious community or not, as an attractive alternative to traditional marriage, and the Tractarians offered single women a sense of purpose and importance often lacking in the larger culture, where they were branded as "superfluous women" and treated as a social problem.

Another bone of contention concerned the Eucharist and in what sense Christ was present in the elements of the Eucharist, the bread and the wine used in the ceremony. The sacrament of the Eucharist (also called Holy Communion, The Lord's Supper, and Mass) is derived from the biblical account of the Passover meal, which Jesus shared with his disciples just before his crucifixion:

> For I have received of the Lord that which also I delivered unto you, That the Lord Jesus the same night in which he was betrayed took bread: And when he had given thanks, he brake it, and said, Take, eat: this is my body, which is broken for you: this do in remembrance of me. After the same manner also he took the cup, when he had supped, saying, This cup is the new testament in my blood: this do ye, as oft as ye drink it, in remembrance of me. For as often as ye eat this bread, and drink this cup, ye do shew the Lord's death till he come.
>
> —1 Cor. 11: 23–26[12]

Nearly all Christians celebrate a ritual sharing of bread and wine based on this narrative, but denominations differ in their interpretation of "this is my body." Catholics hold to the doctrine of transubstantiation, which claims that the elements of the Eucharist, while retaining the superficial appearance of bread and wine, actually become the body and blood of Christ. Protestants in the Calvinist tradition tend to adhere to a doctrine of Spiritual Presence, but not a physical transformation of the elements, and some denominations, such as the Baptists, see the elements as merely symbolizing the body and blood of Christ and the ritual as memorializing his sacrifice. The Elizabethan Settlement deliberately fudged the issue, allowing for a variety of interpretations in the queen's religiously fragmented realm, and in the eighteenth century the Anglican Church paid little attention to the issue. Eucharist was celebrated relatively infrequently, usually four times a year, and the doctrine tended toward the Calvinist interpretation. The Tractarians, however, insisted on the centrality of the Eucharist to Christian life and on the doctrine of the Real or Bodily Presence of Christ in the elements of the Eucharist; they began to institute monthly or even weekly communion services, and through the century gradually adopted rituals that emphasized the sanctity and importance of the Eucharist.

As more and more tracts were written expounding different elements of Tractarian doctrine, concern grew over the "Romanizing" tendencies of these doctrines, the way that Tractarians seemed to be making the English Church more and more like the Roman Catholic in its doctrine and ceremonies. The controversy came to a head—and the tracts to a close—in 1841 with Tract 90, in which Newman argued that the Thirty-Nine Articles, that fundamental statement of Anglican belief, could be interpreted in a catholic, though not a Roman Catholic sense, allowing such practices as the invocation of saints, veneration of relics, and the offering of masses for the dead. The Tract inspired a storm of protest, as Newman recorded in the *Apologia pro Vita Sua* (1864): "In every part of the country, and every class of society, through every organ and opportunity of opinion, in newspapers, in periodicals, at meetings, in pulpits, at dinner-tables, in coffee-rooms, in railway-carriages, I was denounced as a traitor . . . "[13]

And detractors who claimed that the Tractarians intended to undo the Protestant Reformation thought their direst fears confirmed when, four years later, John Henry Newman, leader of the Oxford Movement, converted to Roman Catholicism, sparking a rash of conversions by fellow Tractarians. Of course, many High Churchmen continued to have faith in the Anglican Church and its *via media*, or "middle way," between the superstition of Roman Catholicism and the brash irreverence of the evangelicals. Those who remained Anglicans carried on the tradition of the Tractarians, and the new generation went even further in the revival of Catholic rituals in the Church of England, so that these Anglo-Catholics of the second half of the nineteenth century are generally known as Ritualists.

Many of their rituals were intended to give physical expression to Anglo-Catholic doctrine. Several of the revived rituals, for instance, emphasized the centrality of the Eucharist, which some Anglo-Catholics again began calling the Mass. These rituals restored from Roman Catholic tradition included the ringing of bells at the elevation of the Host, or communion bread; the use of unleavened bread in the Eucharist; and the eastward facing celebration of the Eucharist, in which the priest turns his back on the congregation to face east with them. Other rituals emphasized the sacred and mysterious nature of the church itself: the use of incense, the decoration of the church with statues and pictures of saints, the use of six candles on the high altar.

Finally, the role and authority of the priest was emphasized in many of the revived rituals, in particular through the adoption of elaborate vestments, or ceremonial clothing. Through the eighteenth century, Anglican vicars tended to perform services in, at most, a gown and surplice; Low-Church Anglican clergy often left off the surplice and conducted service in the gown alone. Identical to the preaching gowns in the Calvinist and Lutheran traditions and the doctoral gown worn by college professors today, the Anglican clergyman's gown was plain and black, with long hanging sleeves; the surplice was a simple white tunic worn over the gown. The Ritualists, however, wore much more elaborate and colorful vestments: an *alb*, or long white tunic, underneath the *chasuble*, a kind of poncho, or the *cope*, a very long cloak, which varied in color according to the time of year or the church festival being celebrated: purple for Advent and Lent, red for Palm Sunday, blue for festivals associated with the Virgin Mary, white or gold for Christmas, Epiphany, and Easter Day. They might also wear an embroidered *stole*, a wide silk band around eight feet long, worn crossed over the chest.

Ritualists were also concerned with church architecture and contributed significantly to the Gothic revival in Britain; many medieval buildings were restored to their Gothic splendor, and neo-Gothic Victorian churches sprang up

This cartoon of the Reverened Dr. James Bellamy, which
appeared in *Vanity Fair*, shows a clergyman wearing a cassock.
Vanity Fair (April 1, 1893).

to meet the needs of a growing population. Ritualists also restored the interiors
of the churches, in particular the chancel (the area between the nave, where the
congregation sat, and the sanctuary, where the priest performed the service),
and they often populated those chancels with traditional robed choirs.

Evangelical and Anglo-Catholic services both offered attractions to their congregations. More obvious, perhaps, is the multisensory appeal of the Anglo-
Catholic service, with its beautiful vestments and church decorations, its incense, and the trained voices of its choir. At the center of this service dwelt the
profound mystery of the Eucharist, in which the believer becomes one with
Christ through the real presence of his blood and body. For some, however,
these worship services, conducted strictly according to the liturgy, could seem

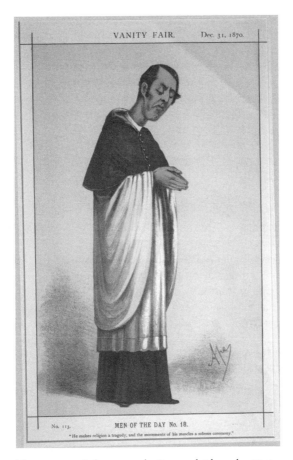

VANITY FAIR.   Dec. 31, 1870.

No. 113.   MEN OF THE DAY No. 18.

" He makes religion a tragedy, and the movements of his muscles a solemn ceremony."

This cartoon of clergyman, the Reverend Alexander Heriot
Mackonochie, which appeared in *Vanity Fair*, shows the more
elaborate garb of the ritualists. *Vanity Fair* (December 31,
1870).

overly formal and regimented. By contrast, Evangelical services, conducted in
less ornate surroundings, tended to be more emotional and spontaneous, though
still following the *Book of Common Prayer*. Extempore prayers might replace
or supplement liturgical prayers, and congregational hymn singing—rather
than or in addition to a choir—promoted a sense of individual participation and
community solidarity in religious devotion. At the center of these services was
the sermon, generally explication of Scripture and its application to the moral
and spiritual lives of the congregation.

Victorian controversies over ritual can seem petty to an outsider, but the rituals represented differences in fundamental beliefs, and conflicts over ritual could
have serious consequences: in some cases they even led to legal prosecution of

Ritualist innovators, especially after Parliament, in an attempt to achieve more
uniformity within the Anglican Church, passed the Public Worship Regulation
Act of 1874. Some Anglo-Catholic practices, however, gradually became uncontroversial and were widely adopted, and eventually the issues that divided the
Low Church and the High Church were eclipsed by the shadow of secularism
that threatened the whole of the church and, indeed, all Christianity. But these
two parties still represent major divisions in the Church of England, even in
the twenty-first century.

The Broad Church

The term "Broad Church" apparently first appeared in print in 1850 in an
article by A.P. Stanley in the *Edinburgh Review*, where he claimed that the
Church of England was "by the very conditions of its being, not High, not
Low, but Broad" and that "it was meant to include, and that it has always
included opposite and contradictory opinions."[14] The Broad Church was not a
well-organized or unified party, but rather a group of liberal, educated, theologically progressive men who shared a vision of the Church of England as
tolerant of dissenting opinions and open to new ideas. These Broad churchmen
included Thomas Arnold, theologian and famous headmaster of Rugby School;
Charles Kingsley, clergyman and novelist; F.D. Maurice, theologian and Christian socialist; A.P. Stanley, Oxford academic; and Thomas Hughes, author of
the popular novel, *Tom Brown's School Days*.

While the Evangelicals stressed the Protestant past of the Church of England,
and the Tractarians and their successors stressed its Catholic past, the Broad
Church stressed the church's diverse and evolving present. Dedicated to the
preservation of the church, they believed that it could only survive by meeting
head-on the challenges of the modern world. Their preferred responses to those
challenges determined the shape of the movement.

To the challenge of religious pluralism in Britain, the Broad churchmen had
an obvious response: a church broad enough to encompass almost all Christians
in Britain. The only exceptions tended to be the Roman Catholics, who owed
allegiance to the Pope and could not recognize the English monarch as legitimate
head of the church, and the Unitarians, who denied the divinity of Jesus Christ.
This second exclusion was somewhat ironic, since in many ways the Broad
Church had much in common with Unitarianism, and Maurice, one of its most
prominent members, was the son of a Unitarian minister. Services in parishes
with a Broad Church incumbent tended to be eclectic, and could include elements
characteristic of Low Church and/or High Church worship.

Broad churchmen welcomed the knowledge offered by science and by novel
methods of biblical criticism, and they were willing to reconsider and reformu-
late Christian doctrine in the light of this new knowledge. Theologically liberal,
they early acknowledged the admixture of myth in the Bible, and they sought
to disentangle the myth from the timeless truth revealed by God. Their vision

of the church was one that was broad-minded enough to tolerate the kind of liberal theology that they themselves espoused, but the actual church was not always so forgiving, and controversies swirled around them, culminating in the controversy over *Essays and Reviews* (1860), discussed in the final chapter of this book.

Broad churchmen were also concerned that the Anglican Church had not adequately responded to the challenges of industrialization and social injustice. As a result, the church had lost nearly all influence with working-class men, who saw it as indifferent to their social position and their rights; some joined one of the dissenting sects, but many others rejected religious teaching altogether. Many Broad churchmen—and some High churchmen who worked in the slums of major cities—became Christian Socialists, preaching an early kind of liberation theology and working for the education and political rights of the working class. F.D. Maurice, who helped to found the Working Men's College in 1854 and served as its first principal, was the major prophet of the movement. With John Malcolm Ludlow and Charles Kingsley, he published penny journals dedicated to spreading Christian Socialism, the short-lived *Politics for the People* (1848) and the *Christian Socialist* (1850–1852). These journals represented the Christian message as one of equality and social justice. Writing as Parson Lot in the earlier journal, Kingsley argued that the Bible itself was on the side of the working man: "Instead of being a book to keep the poor in order, it is a book, from beginning to end, written to keep the rich in order."[15]

Closely allied to this attempt to reclaim working-class men for the Church of England was a movement known as "muscular Christianity," which tried to reconcile Christian and heroic values in a new definition of masculinity. Victorian Christianity tended to identify Christian values with virtues traditionally defined as feminine: meekness, patience, compassion, and self-sacrifice. In particular, the figure of Christ, the model for all Christians, was significantly feminized in Victorian devotional poetry and hymns, such as F.W. Faber's "Sweet Saviour, Bless Us Ere We Go"; H.W. Baker's "The King of Love My Shepherd Is"; Henry Collins's "Jesu, Meek and Lowly"; and George Rundle Prynne's "Jesu, Meek and Gentle."[16] Moreover, Victorian literature was full of self-sacrificial female Christ-figures, from Gaskell's *Ruth* to Christina Rossetti's Lizzie in *Goblin Market*, and even male Christ-figures, such as George Eliot's Mr. Tryan in *Scenes of Clerical Life*, often seem significantly feminized. While this identification with Christ could benefit women, as we will see in Chapter Seven, it posed problems for men's self-definition. Did becoming more Christ-like mean becoming more feminine? Did traditional masculine virtues of valor, self-assertion, and physical prowess no longer matter? Also, while Christian virtues might make a woman into an ideal Victorian wife and mother, how could they contribute to men's success in the competitive Victorian marketplace or in ruling an empire? The High Church, with its asceticism, its advocacy of clerical celibacy, and its (allegedly) feminine interest in aesthetics posed a further problem, a devaluing of male sexuality and the man's role in the family.

Muscular Christianity sought to attract men back to the church and to rede-fine Christian manliness in a way that affirmed the value of traditional mas-culine virtues and of the male body. In practical terms, this vision of Chris-tian manliness had its greatest effect in the curriculum of boys' education, where muscular Christianity combined an emphasis on Christian character with an emphasis on physical fitness and competitive sports and represented them as mutually reinforcing. Thomas Hughes's novel *Tom Brown's School Days* (1857) presents a fictionalized version of just such a muscular Christian education at Rugby. The novelist Charles Kingsley, however, whose robust interest in heterosexual activity is abundantly clear in his frank letters to his wife, became the writer most closely associated with this branch of the Broad Church movement, and his writing did much to popularize its teachings. His major contribution was his novel *Alton Locke*, based on the life of Chartist leader Walter Cooper, a forceful statement of Christian Socialist ideas.

The three major parties in the Church of England battled throughout the nineteenth century for dominance in the church and beyond, each fighting for its position with an earnest belief in the truth and importance of its doctrines and in the deleterious effects of those of its rivals.

Broad churchmen regarded Evangelicals and High churchmen as narrow and blinkered. They were particularly hostile to the Evangelicals' view of Biblical inspiration, which they saw as contradicted by scientific advances. Any belief-system that clung to such outmoded views would inevitably be destroyed by advancing knowledge, and the Broad Church feared that the eternal truths of Christianity would be discarded along with its untenable mythologies. The High Church they tended to brand as effeminate and too much tied to Roman Catholicism—"unmanly and unEnglish." Tractarians, in their turn, saw the Evangelicals as dangerous in their denial of the authority of the church, the only sure bulwark against a secular onslaught, and the Broad Church as dangerous in their vision of a church broadened, yes, but weakened by abandonment of essential doctrines. Finally, the Evangelicals saw the High Church as a threat to the religious liberty of the individual and as a way station on the journey toward Roman Catholicism. They viewed the liberal theology of the Broad Church as gutting Christianity of its fundamental truths.

But the diversity and controversy within the Church of England was only a part of religious life in Victorian Britain: outside the church were Protestant Dissenters, Roman Catholics, and Jews, whose influences and beliefs will be discussed in the next chapter.

2

Variety in Victorian Religious Experience

Not all Victorian Christians were Anglicans, and not all Victorian subjects were Christians. While the range of opinion within the church was great, there still remained a large number of people outside it. Just how large a number became clear in 1851, when a religious census asked churches and chapels to report on attendance at all services on Sunday, March 20, 1851. When returns were published, the growth in non-Anglican denominations became clear: according to the original figures, 47.4 percent of worshippers on that Sunday attended Anglican services—less than 50 percent. In addition, only around 60 percent of "eligible attenders" (total population minus about 30 percent assumed to have legitimate excuses of illness or infirmity) had attended any service at all. Anglican attenders were clearly a minority of the British population.

But who were all these non-Anglican worshippers? How did they worship on that long-ago Sunday morning? They were known collectively as Dissenters or Nonconformists, for their failure to conform to Anglican doctrine as expressed in the Acts of Uniformity (1559, 1662), establishing the English Church. The terms are generally applied only to Protestant Christians, not to Roman Catholics or Jews, whose positions in Victorian England were considerably different from those of non-Anglican Protestants, and who are considered separately here. Dissenting places of worship were known as "chapels," the term "church" being reserved for Anglican places of worship. ("Chapel" could also refer to places of worship in hospitals, schools, or prisons; to private spaces for worship established for noble families, either within the manor house or in a separate building on the estate; and to smaller buildings for worship, "Chapels of Ease," constructed for the convenience of worshippers whose parish church was too distant. In Victorian England, all these chapels would usually be Anglican.)

Many times English Protestant sects are divided into categories of Old Dissent and New Dissent. Old Dissent consists of the denominations recognized in the Act of Toleration of 1689, which gave Dissenters freedom to worship: these included Presbyterians, Baptists, Congregationalists (Independents), and Quakers. New Dissent covers the denominations founded in subsequent years, particularly Wesleyan Methodism and the smaller groups that it spawned. A more useful distinction for Victorian England, however, is that between evangelical Dissenters—Methodists, Baptists, and Congregationalists—and non-evangelical Dissenters, such as Quakers and Unitarians.

Table 2.1 records the number of places of worship and the total attendances on Census Sunday for all the major British denominations. Because worshippers in some denominations attended more than one service on that day, historians often use another figure, the total number of worshippers at the best-attended service of the day, to gauge the relative significance of each group. Figures cited in the following discussion will represent numbers at the best-attended services for each denomination.

Because of the significant differences between dissenting groups, few generalizations about the whole of Dissent can be made, except ones concerning the legal disabilities of non-Anglicans. Instead, to understand the variety of Victorian religious life, each major group—its distinctive doctrines and practices, its social status, and its contributions to Victorian life—must be considered separately. I will begin with the denomination that the census revealed to have the largest Sunday attendance after the Anglican Church, with over one quarter of English and Welsh worshippers: the Methodists.

METHODISTS

The origins of Wesleyan Methodism can be dated to 1739, when John Wesley, an Anglican vicar, began preaching in the fields, delivering a message of salvation and assurance to the increasing crowds that gathered around him. Originally, Wesley wanted merely to reinvigorate the life of the Church of England; he did not intend to form a new denomination. Those who had religious experiences during Methodist revivals were organized into local societies that met together regularly, but Wesley insisted that they also attend their parish church. As the movement developed, many Wesleyans would attend Anglican services in the morning and Methodist services in the evening, and the evening service remained especially important for Methodist chapels, even after this custom lapsed. But Methodism grew quickly, and it gradually began acting more like an independent denomination. Wesley established the Methodist Conference in 1784 to ensure continuity of leadership after his death, and this group of 100 men became the governing body for the Methodist Church, setting policy for all local congregations in the Connexion. Wesley also worked independently of the Anglican Church, at one point defying the Bishop of London by ordaining Methodist ministers for missionary work in America

Table 2.1 Summary of Results of Religious Census of 1851 for Major Denominations in England and Wales

Denomination	Number of Places of Worship	Total Attendances
Church of England	14,077	5,292,551
All Methodists	11,835	2,681,465
Wesleyan Methodist	6,579	1,544,528
Primitive Methodist	2,871	511,195
Welsh Calvinistic Methodist	828	264,112
Methodist New Connexion	297	99,045
Wesleyan Methodist Association	419	94,103
Wesleyan Reformers	339	91,503
Bible Christian	482	73,859
Independent Methodist	20	3,120
Congregationalists (Independents)	3,244	1,214,059
All Baptists	2,772	928,160
Particular Baptists	1,947	740,752
New Connexion General Baptists	182	64,321
General Baptists	93	22,096
Other Baptists	550	100,991
Roman Catholics	570	383,630
All Presbyterians	160	80,510
Presb. Church in Eng.	76	37,124
United Presb. Synod.	66	31,628
Church of Scotland	18	11,758
Unitarians	229	50,061
Lady Huntingdon's Connexion	109	44,642
Mormons	222	35,626
Quakers (Society of Friends)	371	22,478
Plymouth Brethren	132	17,592
Moravians	32	10,874
New Church	50	10,352
Catholic and Apostolic Church	32	7,542
Jews	53	6,030
Other Denominations	539	104,675

Source: Data from K.D.M. Snell and Paul S. Ell, Rival Jerusalems: The Geography of Victorian Religion (Cambridge: Cambridge University Press, 2000), p. 423.

after the bishop had refused to do so. The final break with the Anglican Church, however, did not come until 1795, after Wesley's death.

Unlike the Protestants of Old Dissent, most of whom were Calvinists, Methodists held Arminian doctrines of salvation. Calvinists believe that Christian salvation is available only to the "elect," those whom God has chosen to save. Arminians, however, believe that Christ's atonement is universal, that

salvation is offered to everyone. This doctrinal difference has a significant impact on the commitment to missions, with Arminians feeling a much stronger
vocation to preach the gospel to everyone, since everyone can reap its benefits.
Under the influence of evangelicalism, the Calvinism of Old Dissent in many
denominations was moderated and the idea of who might be included in the
"elect" significantly broadened, and even many Anglicans adopted a largely
Arminian position.

Wesleyan Methodist congregations tended to come from the lower middle
and artisan classes. Their chapels were generally simple, their services emotional
and enthusiastic and full of hymns. In fact, inspired by Moravian Christians,
John Wesley introduced congregational hymn singing into the English church,
compiling a hymnal in 1780, *A Collection of Hymns for the Use of the People
Called Methodists*. Many of the hymns were written by Wesley or a member of
his family: in the 1831 edition of the hymnal, 668 of the 769 hymns were written
by John Wesley, his father Samuel Wesley, and his two brothers Charles and
Samuel, Jr. Many of those hymns were sung throughout the Victorian period,
across denominations, including in the Anglican Church.

Many smaller groups were spin-offs from the original Wesleyan Methodists,
including the Kilhamites, the Wesleyan Association, the Bible Christians (in
Cornwall and the west of England), and, most importantly, the Primitive
Methodists. The Primitive Methodists split from the Wesleyans in 1808 over
issues that included the commissioning of women evangelists. In the beginning
of the movement, Wesley had approved women's preaching, but as Methodists
moved into the mainstream, they became more conservative and the Methodist
Conference banned women preachers in 1804. The Primitive Methodists under
Hugh Bourne continued to promote women preachers, and they were excluded
from the Methodist communion. The Primitive Methodists were also called the
Ranters because of their outdoor preaching and singing: they would hold prayer
meetings at race courses, preach in the fields, and sing hymns on the streets,
much like the later Salvation Army. They came from a lower social stratum
than did their Wesleyan brothers and sisters; they were strongest in Norfolk,
Lincolnshire, and Yorkshire, and among miners in Durham and Northumber-
land. Unlike the Wesleyan Methodists, the Primitive Methodists were strongly
involved in the temperance movement in the second half of the century. While
their numbers did not rival those of the Wesleyan Methodists, on that fateful
March Sunday, 229,646 people across Britain attended their evening services,
their best-attended of the day.

CONGREGATIONALISTS/INDEPENDENTS

That same morning, around 515,000 British Congregationalists—about
11 percent of worshippers that day—attended services in their own chapels.
The Congregationalists or Independents were one of the denominations of Old
Dissent. The most distinctive thing about the Congregationalists was their
system of church government. Unlike the Methodists, who were governed

centrally by the Methodist Conference, each Congregational chapel governed itself, choosing its own minister and administering all its own affairs; as one Congregationalist minister put it in 1831, "It is our glory that hitherto we have been no sect. We subscribe no creed. We submit to no synod or conference."[1] Predictably, this system led to great diversity among Congregationalist chapels, and a great difficulty in establishing a Congregational Union, which nevertheless came into being in 1831. Independent congregations were generally drawn from the lower middle classes, including shopkeepers and tradesmen; the clergy of these chapels tended to be well educated and long-winded, preaching without notes on complicated biblical and theological topics. Prayers were extempore and could last half an hour. Victorian Congregationalists were evangelicals and moderate Calvinists, and their Calvinistic doctrines moderated further through the century. They were active in charity and reform organizations, and they took the lead in the London Missionary Society, one of the leading foreign missions groups in Britain.

The most prominent Congregationalist writer was Elizabeth Barrett Browning, and their emphasis on individual conscience and theological understanding informs much of her work, from her early hymns—some inspired by extempore Congregational sermons—to her masterpiece *Aurora Leigh*.

BAPTISTS

Like the Congregationalists, Baptists were Old Dissenters fired by the new enthusiasm of evangelical doctrine. Their system of church governance was also like that of the Congregationalists, each chapel being entirely self-governing, without a set creed or a central controlling organization. Their most distinctive practice was adult baptism by complete immersion; they rejected infant baptism, maintaining that a person should be baptized only after a profession of faith as a symbol of a new spiritual birth, what was called "believer's baptism." Parents could not make a profession of faith on behalf of their children. Baptists insisted on complete immersion because they read the Bible as teaching that Jesus himself was baptized in that way.

Although there was much cooperation between Congregationalists and Baptists—including exchanges of preachers and sharing of chapels—Baptists came from a significantly lower social stratum than did the Congregationalists, and their pastors were generally less educated, though they could be fine popular preachers. The most dynamic and successful of these preachers was undoubtedly Charles Spurgeon, a man with no formal training, who, beginning in 1855, preached each Sunday to a congregation of thousands, first in Exeter Hall, and then in London's Metropolitan Tabernacle, built specifically to house his enormous Baptist congregation.

There were three main Baptist sects. The General Baptists adhered to Arminian theology; the Particular Baptists, the most numerous group, were moderate Calvinists, and the Strict and Particular Baptists were strict Calvinists. As might be expected, Baptists had an even more difficult time forming

This drawing shows the Metropolitan Tabernacle in London, where Charles Spurgeon preached to huge crowds. Edward Walford, *Old and New London: A Narrative of Its People, and Its Places* (New York: Cassell, 1880, 6: p. 52).

a union than did Congregationalists, but the Baptist Union, initially founded in 1813 and reorganized in 1832, struggled on through the century. Altogether, the religious census recorded that these groups accounted for a little less than 9 percent of the worshippers, with 366,000 in attendance on Census Sunday.

PRESBYTERIANS

In the religious census of 1851, which covered only England and Wales, the Presbyterians made a poor showing. Although in the eighteenth century Presbyterians had been the dominant denomination of Old Dissent, by the mid-nineteenth century most English Presbyterians had become Unitarians, with the decisive break between Unitarians and Trinitarian Presbyterians coming in 1836. Had the census included Scotland, however, the numbers would have been significantly different, for the Presbyterian Church was the established Church of Scotland (the Kirk), and it still attracted a large share of the Scottish attenders. The results of the Scottish religious census were published in 1854, and although they are generally considered less reliable than those of the English and Welsh census, they showed that most Scottish attenders (83 percent) belonged to a Presbyterian sect. About a third of worshippers went to the Church of Scotland,

and just under a third to the Free Church, the denomination founded by a group of evangelical Presbyterians who had split from the state church in 1843 because they objected to the state exercising power over church matters; the rest were United Presbyterians. Less than 17 percent went to a non-Presbyterian church or chapel.

The fact that Britain was made up of two regions with different established religions led to unlikely alliances and to paradoxical patterns of church attendance. Anglicans going north of the border often attended Presbyterian services, rather than Episcopal (Anglican) ones, demonstrating a loyalty to the idea of Establishment rather than to a set of theological doctrines. For similar reasons, the Church of Scotland Presbyterians were reluctant to ally themselves with the remnant of English Presbyterians, because *those* Presbyterians were Dissenters from their state church.

Presbyterian theology was Calvinist, emphasizing God's sovereignty and the necessity of God's grace to achieve salvation. The Calvinist heritage, with its focus on the elect and the need to establish oneself as among the elect, contributed to the reputation of the Scots as dour and moralistic. Church governance was carried out by Presbyteries, groups of people made up of representatives of the local congregations; the decisions of Presbyteries were binding on the congregations. At the local level, laymen could wield significant power within the church by becoming elders, who exercised leadership within the churches and helped in ministering to the congregation.

Scottish immigrants to England gradually reconstituted the moribund Presbyterian churches in England, but in the Victorian mind, Presbyterianism remained closely associated with Scotland.

UNITARIANS

Deriving from the Presbyterian tradition, Unitarians were nonevangelical Dissenters, and their numbers seem very small in comparison with those of the evangelical denominations. On the Sunday of the census, only 27,612 people in England and Wales attended morning service, the largest service of the day, in Unitarian chapels, compared with 654,349 at the Wesleyan Methodist evening service (their largest) and 515,071 at the Congregationalist morning service. Moreover, their numbers remained steady through the Victorian period, with no significant growth. But their congregations consisted of well educated and often socially prominent Whigs or radicals, so they had a cultural influence stronger than their numbers would suggest.

The doctrine that set them apart from other Christian denominations was their denial of the Trinity and their insistence on the unity of God. Because this entailed denying the divinity of Christ, many Victorians did not consider Unitarianism a Christian denomination at all. Victorian Unitarians were the heirs of Enlightenment deism, with its rationality and its suspicion of enthusiasm. Unitarian sermons tended to be aimed at the intellect rather than the emotions, and charitable endeavors eschewed evangelization in favor of social reform and the education of the working classes. Its leader through much of the century was James Martineau, an unusually dynamic preacher. Because of the Unitarians' progressive ideas about women's education, it produced some notable women writers, including Elizabeth Gaskell, wife of a Unitarian minister, whose novels offer as a solution to the problems of industrial society Christian compassion and human understanding, and Harriet Martineau, sister of James Martineau, who wrote books about economics and theology as well as fiction.

Harriet Martineau's first publications appeared—anonymously—in a Unitarian periodical, but over the course of her life she moved away from her early faith and eventually came to see Unitarianism as a last stand for people who had lost their Christian faith but could not bear to abandon their childhood beliefs altogether:

> I now see the [Unitarian] comrades of my early days comfortably appro-
> priating all the Christian promises, without troubling themselves with
> the clearly specified condition—of faith in Christ as a Redeemer...
> Unitarianism is a mere clinging, from association and habit, to the old
> privilege of faith in a divine revelation, under an actual forfeiture of all
> its essential conditions.[2]

For many, however, Unitarian beliefs offered a religious faith reconcilable with reason and a religious community that acknowledged human spirituality and sought social improvement.

QUAKERS (SOCIETY OF FRIENDS)

Quakers remained a relatively small group in Victorian society, numbering about 16,000. This was partly because they did not seek converts and because they required anyone marrying a non-Quaker to leave the congregation. Despite their small numbers, however, their radical differences made them conspicuous, and their reform work made them significant.

Quakers believed in a doctrine of divine inspiration known as the Inward Light; all worship, all activities of life, should be conducted according to the will of God as communicated through the Inward Light. For this reason they rejected all formal religious ceremony, all sacraments including baptism and the Lord's Supper, and even the jurisdiction of human laws. They were pacifists and political quietists, focused on the centrality of the inner life. They often engaged in civil disobedience with regard to taxation, refusing to provide monetary support for the Established Church or the armed forces. Because Inner Light was given to everyone, they rejected hierarchy in all forms, refusing to have paid ministers, to bow or curtsey to their social "superiors," to use titles such as "Sir" or "Lord," and even to remove their hats as a sign of respect.

At their worship services, the congregation would sit in silence until someone felt moved by God to speak. Any member of the meeting, male or female, was welcome to speak. The Quakers did recognize that some of their number felt a particular vocation to preach, and such ministers were sometimes in attendance at meetings. If they had traveled far in order to attend a meeting, their expenses were paid, but they were not remunerated for their service. There might be several ministers in attendance at a given meeting, or none at all. Women were also eligible for this kind of ministry; in fact, by 1835, they outnumbered men in Quaker ministry two to one. Quaker houses of worship, generally called Meeting Rooms, were deliberately simple, without the trappings necessary for more liturgical forms of worship. Generally, men and women would sit separately in rows of seats facing a raised platform or gallery, where the ministers (if there were any) sat, together with the elders of the congregation, who could also be male or female.

Quakers were conspicuous in Victorian society for their very plain dress and their unusual speech. In addition to their antiquated use of "thee" and "thou," they refused to use the standard names for the days of the week, because of their pagan origins, referring instead to Sunday as First Day, Monday as Second Day, and so forth. Though some Quakers achieved economic success in business and banking, their style of living was unostentatious, and they disapproved of most secular pastimes, including novel reading and music. Of course, for some Quakers, wealth brought a loosening of restrictions and a greater conformity with general societal norms, but these lax Quakers were frowned upon in their meetings.

Quakers tended to come from the ranks of middle-class businessmen and tradesmen. The silence and simplicity and political quietism of the movement had limited appeal for the working classes, who generally remained unchurched or gravitated toward evangelical forms of dissent.

The Quaker sense of human equality before God led them to support the education of women, and Quakerism produced some remarkable women reformers and authors, including Elizabeth Fry, well-known for her work in prison visiting and reform; poet Mary Howitt; and Sarah Stickney Ellis, (in)famous author of *The Women of England, The Wives of England,* and *The Daughters of England.* (Ellis married a non-Quaker and, consequently, at her marriage converted to Congregationalism.)

Quakers of both sexes participated in other important nineteenth-century reform movements, including abolition of slavery, reform of lunatic asylums, and repeal of the Corn Laws. Quaker John Bright was one of the two leaders of the Corn Law League (with Richard Cobden), and although his political involvement was controversial among his coreligionists, it was motivated by his fundamental Quaker convictions.

OTHER DISSENTING SECTS

We have surveyed the most popular and the most influential dissenting denominations in Victorian Britain: the Methodists, the Congregationalists, the Baptists, the Presbyterians, the Unitarians, and the Quakers. The religious census of 1851, however, recorded statistics for thirty-five Christian religious groups in Britain, and dozens of other, much smaller and geographically confined groups, undoubtedly existed. Most of the rest of these thirty-five—other than the Roman Catholics, who are considered below—were breakaway groups from the major denominations. Two denominations founded in the nineteenth century, however, do merit further attention: the Plymouth Brethren and the Mormons.

Despite the name, the earliest Brethren groups originated not in Plymouth, but in Dublin in the 1820s. The first English group of what also came to be called the Assembly Movement did form at Plymouth in 1830 under the leadership of John Nelson Darby; consequently, Brethren were sometimes called Darbyites. The doctrine of these groups was generally that of conservative evangelicals. They stressed the sole authority of the Bible and recognized only two sacraments, the Lord's Supper and baptism; they usually practiced believers' baptism by complete immersion, like the Baptists. Also like the Baptists, they were non-credal, requiring allegiance to no particular set of doctrines, with no hierarchy or central governing organization. But they went further than the Baptists: they also had no ordained clergy or salaried ministers, only a "presiding elder" to keep order at services. They were also notable for their millenarianism, or interest in the imminent end of the world. Darby, in fact, predicted the end would come in 1842, but later was able to explain away his apparent error. On census Sunday in 1851, there were 7,272 worshippers at the best-attended service of the day. Edmund Gosse in his autobiographical work, *Father and Son* (1907), wrote a fascinating account of his father's beliefs and practices as a member of the Plymouth Brethren, Edmund's own religious upbringing, and his eventual loss of faith.

Mormonism, which was founded in America in 1830, also made inroads in mid-Victorian Britain through a concentrated focus on missions work. The first Mormon missionaries arrived in 1837, the year of Victoria's accession; in 1840, another group of missionaries crossed the Atlantic, led by Brigham Young himself, who would become the Mormons' second leader. They founded a periodical in Liverpool, the *Millennial Star*, to promote Mormon belief. Mormon founder and prophet Joseph Smith, hoping for wide-scale and eminent conversions, even sent copies of the *Book of Mormon* to Queen Victoria and Prince Albert.

The missionaries encouraged converts to immigrate to Illinois, where they said the promised kingdom of Christ on earth was soon to be established. Many of the poor and hungry of England—especially Liverpudlians—took up the offer of immigration: Mormon records indicate numbers of immigrants exceeding 17,000. Some converts, however, stayed in Britain, and on March 20, 1851, 16,628 were present at the best-attended Mormon service. But in 1852 Brigham Young revealed that Joseph Smith, before his martyr's death in 1844 at the hands of an armed lynch mob, had had a revelation from God enjoining polygamy on Mormons, and Britons were alternately amused and horrified. Thereafter, Mormonism in Britain began to decline steadily and did not start to recover until the twentieth century.

DISSENTING GRIEVANCES

Whatever their specific doctrines and practices, all Dissenters in nineteenth-century Britain were second-class citizens, denied legal privileges enjoyed by Anglicans. These "dissenting grievances" were only gradually relieved over the course of the century, as the relationship between the church and the state underwent significant changes.

The first improvement in the Dissenters' status was the repeal of the Test and Corporations Act in 1828. Under the Act, anyone holding public office, including an officer's commission in the army or navy had to affirm the Thirty-Nine Articles of the Anglican Church. In practice, Parliament had routinely passed "acts of indemnity," which legalized the positions of Dissenters elected to office, including a small number of dissenting members of Parliament, so the change in practice was not so great. It did, however, represent a significant shift in the idea of the proper relationship of church and state: now, non-Anglicans could participate fully in government.

But they were still disadvantaged in other ways. The ancient Universities of Oxford and Cambridge had been founded to provide higher education for the clergy—after Henry VIII, the Anglican clergy—and both required subscription to the Thirty-Nine Articles. Cambridge required it only before taking a degree, so Dissenters could pursue an education at Cambridge, but they could not conscientiously take a BA or an MA. Oxford actually required students to sign the articles at matriculation and again before taking a degree, so Dissenters could not even enroll. University College, London, had been founded in 1826 to offer higher education to non-Anglicans, but it was not allowed to give degrees. Partial relief from this grievance came in 1836, when University College was officially chartered and the University of London was founded to give degree examinations for University College and King's College, London, for the first time allowing Dissenters to earn university degrees without renouncing their beliefs. Degrees from Oxford and Cambridge were slower in coming; Dissenters were excluded from taking degrees until 1854 in Oxford and 1856 in Cambridge. Even then, they were still barred from holding fellowships or participating in the governance of the ancient Universities until 1871.

Three of the other grievances concerned rites of passage over which the Church of England exercised a kind of monopoly. Births could be registered only in the local Anglican Church, and marriages—except those of Jews and Quakers, who had special dispensations—could only be conducted in the Anglican Church. Finally, burials had to take place in churchyards, either by Anglican rites or in total silence; Dissenters could not be buried according to the ceremonies of their own faith. The first two were taken care of in 1836 by the Registration Act and the Marriage Act. The first required local registrars (originally appointed to oversee the Poor Laws of 1834) to register births, marriages, and deaths beginning July 1, 1837; the second allowed them to perform marriages in the registrar's office or to oversee marriages conducted in dissenting chapels. Dissenting funeral rites took longer to achieve. In the 1850s, as a result of overcrowding and concerns about hygiene in churchyards, major cities established municipal graveyards, outside the city limits, where Dissenters could hold their own services. It wasn't until the 1880 Burial Act, however, that Dissenters throughout Britain were guaranteed the right to be buried in Anglican churchyards by their own ministers and according to their own rites.

The most divisive grievance, however, was the payment of church rates, taxes to support the maintenance of the local Anglican Church. Dissenters resented their money going to support the competition—or even, depending on theological stance, the enemy. And, of course, Dissenters were simultaneously supporting their local chapels with voluntary donations. After Parliament passed the Irish State Temporalities Act of 1833, which abolished the church rate in Ireland, many English Dissenters expected that their own church rate would soon follow. But they were disappointed. Not until 1868 was this serious grievance, and the major bone of contention between local churches and chapels, abolished.

By 1880, dissenting grievances had been gradually relieved; legally, Dissenters were no longer second-class citizens. Popular prejudice against Dissenters remained, but it, too, was waning. Although the Church of England remained the state church, Britain had come a long way toward becoming a religiously pluralistic society.

ROMAN CATHOLICS

Nevertheless, social acceptance for Roman Catholics in Britain was much harder to achieve: British anti-Catholicism was deeply engrained, partly because Catholicism itself seemed to many essentially foreign to British identity. Partly this resulted from the association of Roman Catholics with continental Europe. But, more significantly, the Anglican Church had been formed in explicit opposition to the Roman Catholic Church, and to be Protestant had become an essential element of Britishness. Moreover, many people believed that, because of their allegiance to the Pope, Catholics could not be loyal subjects of the English monarch; indeed, an earlier Pope had excommunicated the monarch and released Catholics from their vows of loyalty to the English Crown. Finally, the memory of Catholic conspiracies against the English government, such as the Gunpowder Plot, remained fresh in the minds of many English Protestants. In fact, at times of particular conflict, November 5, Guy Fawkes Day, which commemorated the foiling of the plot, often brought anti-Catholic demonstrations and even violence.

In addition, particular Catholic doctrines aroused Protestant fears. The most serious was the supreme authority of the Pope, which British Protestants represented as a kind of tyrannical and arbitrary power that an enlightened Britain had rejected. Anti-Catholics thus often referred to Catholicism as "Popery" and Catholics as "Papists," picking out this particular element of Catholic belief for opprobrium. They regarded other Catholic doctrines—the Real Presence of Christ in the Eucharist, the veneration of saints, the use of relics—as little more than retrograde superstitions. Other practices and emphases, including some that the Tractarians adopted, struck the Protestant British as undermining the traditional family, especially priestly celibacy and authority: the Catholic Father seemed to usurp the position of the Victorian father. The growth of Catholic religious orders during the Victorian era did nothing to relieve such anxieties, since convents allowed women to abandon traditional family life and live instead under the direct authority of the church.

Anti-Catholic prejudice was particularly strong among Evangelicals, and some Evangelical periodicals, including the *Record* and the *Christian Lady's Magazine*, filled many pages with "No Popery" rhetoric. Tractarians were, predictably, more sympathetic, but they could not afford to be too closely identified with Roman Catholicism. Many of the tolerant Broad Christians in the Broad Church nevertheless drew the line at Roman Catholicism.

At the end of the eighteenth century, the Catholic population in Britain was small, amounting to about 1 percent of the total population, and they were still living under the Penal Laws, a set of parliamentary acts that prevented them from holding government office and limited their property rights. This population included some old and aristocratic Catholic families who had suffered through many years of persecution. But in 1800, the number of Catholics under the British Parliament's jurisdiction multiplied overnight. The Act of Union with Ireland added about five and a half million Catholics to the total. This influx of Catholics made relief from the Penal Laws a priority. Irish voters were certain to elect Catholic parliamentary representatives, none of whom could be seated in Parliament, and this would undoubtedly inflame an already tense Irish population. Still, more than a quarter of a century passed before Catholic Emancipation, as it was called, became a reality in 1828.

Catholic Emancipation finally gave Roman Catholics in Britain and Ireland the right to hold government offices, but the new rights came hedged round with conditions, known as "securities." One of these, aimed particularly at the much-distrusted Jesuits, prevented the growth of Roman Catholic religious orders in Britain by forbidding them to take in new members; though it was passed, it was never seriously enforced. Another "security" barred Roman Catholic officials from advising the monarch on matters relating to the Church of England. The act also raised the property qualification for voting in Ireland, which disenfranchised a large number of Irish voters and limited the impact of the Roman Catholic vote in Ireland. Most relevantly, Catholics entering Parliament were required to take an oath swearing allegiance to the reigning monarch, denying the jurisdiction of the Pope over British law, and promising "never . . . to disturb or weaken the Protestant religion or Protestant government in the United Kingdom."

Peers from old Catholic families, including the Duke of Norfolk, long barred from the place in the House of Lords to which they were entitled, took the oath—and took their seats. The Duke of Norfolk's son, Henry Howard, was elected as the first Roman Catholic member of the House of Commons since the Reformation and took his seat on May 15, 1829.

Catholic Emancipation rectified an obvious injustice, but it did not do much to calm the tensions in Roman Catholic Ireland. It did nothing to benefit the poverty-stricken peasants and actually hurt those small landholders who lost their votes as "security." Resentment over tithes to the Church of Ireland (the Anglican Establishment in Ireland) continued to erupt violently. In Britain, the act caused tremendous national controversy and awakened fears of Catholic resurgence, temporarily exacerbating anti-Catholic sentiment. It was the first of many such crises in the nineteenth century, as Britain's Roman Catholic population expanded and the Roman Catholic Church in Britain gained strength.

The next episode of national anti-Catholic panic was sparked by the rise of the Oxford Movement and intensified by the conversions of leading Tractarians to Rome. Unlike the generally conservative and reserved old Catholics, these new converts were more militant and expansionist. J.H. Newman even published a book, *Lectures on Certain Difficulties Felt by Anglicans in Submitting to the Catholic Church* (1850), attempting to win more converts and further alarming many Victorian Anglicans.

Despite their high-profile conversions, though, Tractarians did not add significantly to the number of British Catholics. The most significant source of growth in population came instead from Irish immigrants. In the decade 1841–1851, as many as 400,000 Irish immigrants entered England, and on Sunday, March 1, 1851, over a quarter of a million people in England and Wales attended Mass. Protestant Englishmen, already imbued with anti-Irish and anti-Catholic prejudice, could easily see these immigrants as a Catholic invasion force. To make things worse, the Catholic Church in Britain, in order to cope with the huge numbers of new parishioners, had to bring in foreign priests, some Irish, but many Italian as well, increasing the sense that Catholics were essentially un-English. Irish immigration also created divisions within the Roman Catholic population itself, between native English Catholics, with their higher birth and quieter traditions developed through years of persecution, and the working-class immigrants with their own different religious traditions.

But fears of Catholicism reached their height with the restoration of the Catholic hierarchy in England. Since the Reformation, England had had the status of a Roman Catholic mission; Catholics in England were governed not by an established hierarchy of bishops and archbishops, but instead by vicars apostolic. In 1850, however, Pope Pius IX (Pio Nono) restored the Catholic hierarchy, establishing twelve bishoprics and an archbishopric at Westminster. He made Nicholas Wiseman, the controversial vicar apostolic for London, a cardinal and appointed him the first Archbishop of Westminster. Unwisely, Wiseman fanned the flames of English anger by his triumphalist announcement of the Restoration: "Your beloved country has received a place among the fair churches, which, normally constituted, form the splendid aggregate of Catholic communion; Catholic England has been restored to its orbit in the ecclesiastical firmament, from which its light had long vanished."

Papal Aggression, as it was called, was regarded as a challenge to the authority of the Archbishop of Canterbury, the Church of England, and even the Queen herself, as Defender of the Faith. There was a strong upsurge in anti-Catholic feeling among all classes of society. In some places, this resulted in "No Popery" riots and even violence against Irish immigrants and Catholic clergy. Parliament quickly passed some largely ineffectual legislation criminalizing the Pope's recent declaration.

After the early 1850s, anti-Catholic feelings among most of the population gradually subsided into what Cardinal Manning called "a more civilised hostility." This hostility was fed by a series of papal proclamations issued by Pius IX during the second half of the nineteenth century. His declaration of the doctrine of the Immaculate Conception of the Virgin Mary, which asserted that Mary's mother conceived her through miraculous means rather than through sexual intercourse, promoted the resurgence in Marian devotion across Europe even as it further alienated British Protestants: to them, it seemed to place Mary on a level with Christ himself as one born without sin. The Pope's 1864 declaration (an encyclical *Quanta Cura* and the *Syllabus Errorum*) set the Catholic Church against the modern world, condemning, among other things, socialism, rationalism, liberalism, freedom of the press, freedom of religion, and separation of church and state. This papal pronouncement seemed to confirm British prejudices that Catholicism was retrograde religion, irrational and superstitious. And the declaration of Papal Infallibility in 1870 reemphasized the one point that the British found most objectionable in Roman Catholicism, its submission to papal authority.

The nineteenth century was a tumultuous period in the lives of Roman Catholics in Britain. On one hand, their numbers increased manyfold, and they gained significant civil rights that they had been denied; moreover, the restoration of the hierarchy gave them a securer and more visible place in English society. On the other hand, English Catholicism underwent sometimes wrenching changes, and native English Catholics found themselves struggling to fit into the new order represented by converts and immigrants. And anti-Catholic prejudice, though no longer enshrined in English law, continued to play a significant role in English society.

JEWS

By modern standards, the level of prejudice against Jews in Victorian England—the casual stereotyping, the limited civil rights—would be considered shocking. Compared to the much more violent anti-Semitism in continental Europe in the nineteenth century, however, it was relatively mild, and English Jews enjoyed a good measure of peace and security. Unlike the Roman

Catholics, their "otherness" seemed to pose little threat to English identity or the religious Establishment.

Through much of the century their numbers remained small: at the start of the century, there were around 20,000 Jews in England, and by mid-century that number had grown to about 35,000. Although there were important Jewish communities in Birmingham and Liverpool, most English Jews lived in London, concentrated in the east end of the city, though wealthier Victorian Jews began to move to other neighborhoods, including Westminster and Hyde Park. The center of religious life for London Jews was the Great Synagogue in Duke's Place, which had been founded in 1690 and rebuilt in 1790. (The synagogue was destroyed by a German air raid in 1941.) By the 1870s, however, synagogues had multiplied, as Charles Dickens's son wrote in *Dickens's Dictionary of London* (1879): "Independently of the great synagogue there are nearly a dozen Jewish places of worship in the metropolis; the principal ones being situated in Bevis Marks, Fenchurch-street, Portland-road, Berkeley-Street, Barnsbury, Bayswaters, &c."

Dickens, Jr., also testified to the vibrancy of Jewish life and charitable work in the capital:

> [T]he community of London Jews support a Convalescent Home, a Ladies' Benevolent Society, a Home for the Deaf and Dumb, a house for the distribution of "cosher" [sic] food to the poor, an Orphan Asylum, and three separate free schools for boys and girls... There are shops for the sale of Hebrew books... in Bevis Marks and Bloomsbury. The Jews of London support two newspapers, *The Jewish Chronicle* and *The Jewish World*.

While many East-End Jews were poor, a group of Jewish businessmen and bankers gained wealth and social prominence: Sir Moses Montefiore, knighted by Queen Victoria; Sir Isaac Lyon Goldsmid, the first Jewish baronet; Sir David Salomons, the first Jewish Lord Mayor of London; and Lionel de Rothschild, the first Jewish MP who had not converted to Anglicanism. (Benjamin Disraeli, a converted Jew, was already an MP when Rothschild took his seat.)

Nineteenth-century Jews suffered civil disabilities similar to those of Dissenters and Roman Catholics, although special arrangements had already been made for Jewish weddings and funeral services. In addition, at the beginning of the century, Jewish men were denied voting rights. As with other non-Anglican groups, these legal inequities were gradually eliminated over the course of the Victorian era.

In the wake of Catholic Emancipation in 1828, there began a struggle for Jewish emancipation. This cause was supported not only by prominent Jews and their associates, but also by many MPs, including Thomas Macaulay, and ordinary Londoners, 14,000 of whom signed a petition supporting the "Jew Bill" in 1833. Dissenters, themselves the victims of unequal laws, were also vocal

This drawing shows the interior of the synagogue in Great Portland Street, London. Edward Walford, *Old and New London: A Narrative of Its People, and Its Places* (New York: Cassell, 1880), 4: p. 457).

in their support of Jewish Emancipation. The Bill passed in the Commons, but failed in the House of Lords, and in the end reforms came piecemeal. The right to vote was granted in 1835; the right to hold municipal office came ten years later. Jewish students had been welcome at University College, London, from its foundation, in which Sir Isaac Lyon Goldsmid played a major role, and they were finally allowed to attend Oxford in 1854 and Cambridge in 1856, at the same time that Christian Dissenters became eligible. Also like the Dissenters, they had to wait until 1871 before they could hold Oxford and Cambridge fellowships.

The struggle for Parliament was much harder fought. Having given up the ideal of an Anglican governing body, some Conservatives were reluctant to give up the ideal of a Christian one. Lionel de Rothschild was elected MP for the City of London in 1847 and again in 1850, but each time was unable to take his seat. Only in 1858 did Parliament provide a form of oath that Jewish members could swear—on the Hebrew Bible—and at that point Rothschild was able to take his rightful place in the House of Commons.

In addition to Jewish emancipation, three other major issues occupied the attention of Anglo-Jewish society in the nineteenth century. First, the community was split over the advent of Reform Judaism in Britain. The movement had originated in Germany, and at its inception involved a new, more critical attitude toward sacred texts; an abandonment of certain parts of Jewish law, particularly dietary law; and changes in liturgy. Some parts of the service were shortened, in other parts the vernacular language was substituted for Hebrew, and choirs and musical instruments were introduced. The first Reform congregation in Britain was the West London Synagogue of British Jews, founded in 1840, and it sparked several decades of controversy within the Jewish community.

The second major issue was Zionism, the movement for the establishment of a Jewish homeland in Palestine, which was at that time under the control of the Ottoman Turks. Support for Zionism in the Jewish community was fueled by the nationalism that was part of European Romanticism, and Moses Montefiore, the wealthy Anglo-Jewish philanthropist, was one of the leaders in the early Victorian period, repeatedly visiting Palestine and offering financial support for Jewish settlements. There was also considerable support among British Protestants for the restoration of Jews to Palestine. Some were motivated by a pro-Semitic strain in Evangelical thought, which regarded the Jews as still God's chosen people; others saw the restoration of the Jews to Israel as one of the preconditions for the return of Christ to earth. Lord Shaftesbury, an MP and Evangelical leader, was particularly enthusiastic and in the late 1830s seriously considered the practicability of promoting agricultural settlements there. But although settlement increased after the Treaty of Paris (1856), which ended the Crimean War, no large-scale government effort to restore the Jews to Palestine would be made until the Balfour Declaration in 1917.

Finally, just as Irish immigration produced complications for British Catholics, so Russian immigration created problems for British Jews. Pogroms in Russia in 1881 caused an influx of Russian Jews to Britain. The Jewish community struggled to provide for these largely penniless immigrants, and their foreignness and poverty increased anti-Semitic sentiment in the general population, as the total number of British Jews shot up to somewhere between 180,000 and 250,000 by the turn of the century. This wave of immigration significantly changed the face of Anglo-Jewish society.

Nineteenth-century novels portray a range of Jewish characters, from minor characters embodying negative stereotypes to strongly sympathetic protagonists. The negative characters are perhaps the most memorable: the wicked, greedy Jew Fagin who exploits young boys in Dickens's *Oliver Twist* (1838) and George du Maurier's mesmerizing Svengali in *Trilby* (1894). But Dickens, stung by accusations of anti-Semitism, later created the virtuous moneylender Riah in *Our Mutual Friend* (1864–1865). Jewish writers, too, attempted to influence the perception of Jews in British culture. Converted Jewish writers such as Grace Aguilar and Benjamin Disraeli stressed the close relationship between Judaism and Christianity and portrayed positive Jewish characters in order to enhance the understanding and sympathy of Christian readers. Jewish poet and novelist Amy Levy worked toward a more realistic portrayal of the Jewish community in her novel *Reuben Sachs* (1888), though she was criticized by some for representing her own people in a negative light. The most fully developed and sympathetic Jewish character in mainstream literature is George Eliot's Daniel Deronda, who, in the course of this pro-Zionist novel discovers and embraces his Jewish identity, marries a Jewish woman, and immigrates to Palestine.

Over the course of the nineteenth century, Jewish population grew, synagogues multiplied, Jewish authorship and publishing thrived, and Jews came to play an ever-larger role in British life and politics. Victorian Jews, like Dissenting Christians and Roman Catholics, gained important civil rights and became more fully integrated into mainstream culture as Britain gradually came to terms with becoming a religiously pluralistic society.

3

A Clergyman's Life

Imagine that you are a young Victorian man, and you have decided that you want to be a clergyman in the Church of England. But why? What motivated Victorian men to choose a clerical career?

CAREER CHOICE AND VOCATION

For some, a clergyman's life seemed to offer "an elegant, leisured, and gentlemanly style of life . . . with sizeable prizes for the lucky, the talented, and the well-connected."[1] This could be particularly attractive for the younger sons of the gentry who needed a gentlemanly source of income to supplement what provision their fathers could make for them. R.L. Edgeworth, the father of Maria Edgeworth, saw clerical positions as almost providentially designed for such men of good family: "Church benefices may thus be considered as a fund for the provision of the younger sons of our gentry and nobles."[2] And if their parents had sufficient influence with a patron or sufficient wealth to buy the next presentation of a living (see "Introduction"), they could expect a respectable clerical career. For those of a lower social class, the relatively low costs of entry and relatively good prospects in the church, as compared with law, medicine, and the armed forces, made it the most attractive way of moving into the professional class.

Increasingly, however, as a result of Evangelical seriousness about religious duty and Tractarian emphasis on the exalted role of the clergy, Christians began to feel that a clergyman should have a vocation to Christian ministry, and more young men choosing a clerical career did so, at least in part, because they felt a strong desire to serve God, their church, and their fellow men.

EDUCATION

Whether you are choosing a clerical career because you feel a sense of vocation or merely because it seems to offer a socially respectable career path, you have to decide whether you can afford to obtain a university degree. It was possible at this time to be ordained without a degree. At the lowest level, you could seek ordination without any formal training as a "literate"; this was a path often chosen by dissenting ministers who sought ordination in the Church of England. Alternatively, you could study for a couple of years at one of the theological colleges that sprang up to meet this need. St. Bees in Cumbria and St. Aidan's in Birkenhead prepared students for ordination and granted theological diplomas. Some universities, including Trinity College, Dublin, and the University of Durham, offered courses of study for nongraduates seeking ordination. While all these alternatives were cheaper than the universities, which could cost upward of £400, they were also much less prestigious; some bishops required a university degree for ordination in their diocese, and it certainly increased chances of promotion within the hierarchy. Any young man who wanted to make a good career in the Anglican Church would be well-advised to take his degree, preferably from Oxford or Cambridge, though the University of Durham, Trinity College, Dublin, and King's College, London, also offered reasonably respectable degrees. A large majority of ordinands throughout the period were university graduates, most of them Oxford and Cambridge men. In the 1830s and 1840s, for instance, over 80 percent of the Anglican clergy came from one of the ancient universities, though this percentage would decline through the rest of the century.

Since your family can afford it, you will go to either Oxford or Cambridge. But which one? The two ancient universities had divergent reputations during the period. From the late 1830s Oxford became associated with the Tractarian movement and subsequently with the High Church party in the Anglican Church. Later in the century, after the publication of *Essays and Reviews*, which was dominated by contributors from Oxford, it became associated with the Broad Church and its attempts to demythologize Christian texts and doctrine. Thus, nineteenth-century Oxford was theologically active and theologically controversial; there one would be in touch with the latest developments in English theology and with important figures such as Edward Pusey, J.H. Newman, and, later, Mark Pattison and Benjamin Jowett, both of whom contributed to *Essays and Reviews*. Both universities tended to side with the conservative Tory party, which supported the authority of the Church of England, the king, and the aristocracy. Oxford, however, was more conservative than Cambridge; at Cambridge there flourished a small but active group of more politically liberal students, who supported the opposing party, the Whigs (later called the Liberal party). So if you have Whiggish sympathies, perhaps Cambridge would be the better choice. Also, Cambridge had a reputation for strength in the natural sciences, so if you have an interest in geology or mathematics, Cambridge might again be preferable.

For you will probably not be seeking a degree in theology. No such degree was offered until 1869 at Oxford and 1873 at Cambridge. A degree in any subject would do, and many Victorian clergymen were trained primarily in Greek and Roman literature and history—that is, in pre-Christian cultures. Undergraduates who planned to seek ordination would normally attend lectures given by the professor of divinity at their university, and they would also be expected to read a few central Anglican classics, usually including William Paley's *Natural Theology* and Joseph Butler's *Analogy*. In the middle of the century, they could also choose to take a theological examination after graduation, the Cambridge Voluntary or the Oxford Voluntary, but, as their names imply, neither was required.

Your degree program will last three or four years, during which time you will meet with a tutor at your college, attend university lectures, and prepare yourself through reading and study for examinations to be taken in your final term. If you fail your exams, you will not receive a degree. If that happened, you could still pursue ordination, though with reduced career prospects. The theological colleges, such as St. Bees and St. Aidan's often trained men who had attended university but failed to graduate, either because they could not afford to complete a degree or because they could not pass their exams. If you pass your exams, you will receive your degree, and you will be ready to take the next steps toward ordination.

First, though, the education offered at Oxford and Cambridge raises a question: if for much of the century the universities offered little theological teaching and no practical training in pastoral care, why should clergymen go to university at all? The ancient universities had been founded, of course, to train clergymen, and in the early part of the Victorian period over half of the students enrolling at these institutions intended to seek ordination. But the course of study until the later nineteenth century was in no way vocational; most students, whatever their intended career, undertook a gentlemanly liberal arts education, and if extra training was needed for a particular profession, it was sought after graduation. Thus, even early Victorian medical men who trained at Oxford and Cambridge knew more about Greek literature than about human anatomy. What was important for a clergyman, in particular, was that he be a gentleman and share the background of gentlemen to whom he would minister. In *Directorium Pastorale*, J.H. Blunt argued that clergymen

> should be capable, from education and social training . . . of taking their place without embarrassment to themselves or offence to others on those higher levels of society which are occupied by their rich parishioners, that their office may be respected through the respect won also by their persons.[3]

This kind of education would also enable them to exercise influence on behalf of the church and of Christianity with the cultural and political elites. Novelist Anthony Trollope clearly preferred the clergymen of good social background and education, and in *Clergymen of the Church of England* (1866), he bemoaned the increasing numbers of clergymen who had not been to university, characterizing the nongraduate as "the man who won't drink his glass of wine, and talk of his college, and put off for a few hours the sacred stiffness of the profession and become simply an English gentleman."[4]

The nineteenth century, however, saw a professionalization of law, medicine, and the clergy, as well as the development of more specialized training for these professions. Some graduates entering the clergy, therefore, would seek additional theological training before ordination. Graduates under the age of twenty-three, the minimum age for ordination, were especially likely to fill in the time with such additional training. Many studied informally under the supervision of a willing clergyman, who could use such teaching to supplement his income. Later in the century, graduates could choose to attend residential colleges such as Chichester Theological College, Wells Theological College, and Cuddesdon College, near Oxford, which offered graduates specifically theological training, something like an American seminary; all these institutions were founded by High churchmen, who desired better training for men who were to undertake the crucial role of an Anglican priest.

ORDINATION AND TITLE FOR ORDERS

Having completed your university degree and, possibly, some further theological training, you now must look for clerical employment. Before you can request ordination, however, you need to have a "title for orders" in hand— that is, the promise of a clerical position that will follow ordination. Such a title could be difficult to obtain, since competition for eligible entry-level positions was stiff, though less eligible positions in Wales or in the industrial areas of the North of England were generally available for the willing candidates. (These positions were often filled by nongraduates, either students from the theological colleges or "literates.") Some new graduates might have family connections to help them find a position, but others would resort to using clerical agents or advertisements to locate a suitable job. If you performed particularly well in your university career, you might be offered a teaching fellowship at an Oxford or Cambridge College, and ordination would follow. Many of the fellowships, in fact, required ordination, but fellows were also often forbidden to marry, which might reduce your willingness to accept the fellowship if it is offered to you. Alternatively, you can try to obtain a position as a schoolmaster at an Anglican school, which could serve as your "title for orders." You can also apply to be chaplain to a college, a school, an asylum, or a unit of the armed forces, all of which could be used as titles for orders. But the most common title for orders—and the one you will pursue—was a curacy.

The role of the curate changed over the course of the century. In the early part of the Victorian period, curates served as substitutes for nonresident vicars or rectors, doing all or nearly all the parish work in exchange for a portion of the senior clergyman's remuneration. After the Pluralities Acts of 1838 and 1850 tightened the restrictions on the holding of multiple clerical positions, however, the number of nonresident clergymen fell, and curates were more frequently hired as assistants by resident clergymen. Clergymen in parishes, especially growing urban ones, might employ several curates to help perform the extensive and exhausting parish work.

Salaries for curates tended to be low, only £50–£120 per annum. The 1813 Stipendiary Curates Act set a notional minimum salary of £80, or the full value of the benefice, but there were exceptions for those curates and/or incumbents who held their positions before the law was passed, and some incumbents simply violated the law. In 1832 in Lincolnshire, 62 percent of curates were still paid less than £80.[5] While this salary might be adequate for a single man, it will be difficult to start a family unless you are able to supplement your salary with private funds.

Moreover, curates had little job security. If an incumbent clergyman who had hired a curate as substitute died or decided to come back into residence, the curate lost his job. The incumbent who hired an assistant curate paid him out of his own income, and he could fire him if he did not give satisfaction.

Once you have found a position to serve as your title for orders, you must write to the bishop in whose diocese you plan to serve, indicating your intention to apply for ordination. The bishop will reply with a letter of instruction, listing all requirements, sometimes including a list of required readings; the receipt of the letter will be followed by a personal interview with the bishop. About a month before the bishop's examination, you have to provide the following documents:

1. a baptismal certificate, to establish your church membership and your age;
2. evidence that your intention to apply for ordination has been announced in your home church. This announcement would allow anyone with well-founded objections to your ordination to make them public;
3. nomination to your curacy, chaplaincy, or teaching position, your "title for orders";
4. evidence of your academic preparation, whether from a university or theological college;
5. "testimonials" to your moral fitness, either a letter from your Oxford or Cambridge college or three letters from beneficed clergymen, signed by their bishops. Generally, these testimonials were a formality, especially at the colleges, and tutors were often criticized for not taking their testimonial duties more seriously.

Though later in the nineteenth century efforts were made to standardize the process, the examinations that bishops gave to candidates for ordination varied greatly in depth and difficulty. Groups of candidates for positions within the diocese would be examined at the same time. The period of examination usually ran Thursday through Saturday, with ordination ceremonies on Sunday. Candidates would be put up for the long weekend in lodgings, or with church families, or, often, with the bishop himself. The exams consisted of both written and oral ("viva voce") sections, set and evaluated by the bishop. The exams were often relatively easy, but candidates could and did fail and had to be rejected as ordinands. Those who succeeded would officially sign the Thirty-Nine Articles and be ordained by the bishop as deacons of the Church of England in a Sunday service. The man who placed top in the exams was known as the "Gospeller," and he was given the privilege of reading the Gospel passage at the ordination service.

After the service, you will be a deacon, occupying the lowest level of holy orders, and, like other deacons and priests, whether curate or vicar or rector, you will assume the honorary prefix, "the Reverend." (Proper Victorian usage decrees that the prefix be used with the clergyman's whole name—the Reverend Septimus Harding—or with title and last name—the Reverend Mr. Harding—but never with the last name alone; referring to an ordained clergyman merely as Mr. Harding is also correct.) You will have to serve one year as a deacon before becoming eligible to be "priested," or ordained as a priest. During this year, which serves as a probationary period, you can perform many of the usual duties of the clergyman, but you cannot administer the Eucharist until you are a priest. If you fail to perform adequately or exhibit moral laxity during your probation, however, you can still be refused the further ordination. Ordination to the priesthood will involve another set of oral and written exams similar to those for diaconal ordination.

Most clergymen regarded a curacy as merely temporary, a first step on the way to becoming an incumbent—a rector, a vicar, or a perpetual curate. Some were too sanguine: approximately one-third of ordained clergymen never became incumbents or waited more than fifteen years for their first incumbency. And even those who eventually succeeded might spend a long time in this temporary post: in 1874 (admittedly, a difficult period), it was calculated that the average time a curate waited for his first incumbency was twelve years.[6]

INCUMBENCY

Nevertheless, especially since you have a university degree, you will probably eventually become a vicar, a rector, or at least a perpetual curate, of your own parish. Here, you have job security: the position is regarded as a freehold, and neither the patron nor the bishop can force you to relinquish it. You can also generally expect a higher salary, though the variations in salary were tremendous. Although £200 was the amount Bishop Kaye in 1834 regarded as "the absolute minimum which a clergyman needed to discharge his parochial duties,"[7] in 1830, 37% of benefices were worth £200 or less. Sixteen percent were worth between £201 and £300; £300 is sometimes cited as the minimum amount necessary for giving one's mid-Victorian family a comfortable—but not at all luxurious—middle-class life.[8] The remaining 49 percent were worth over £301, with the top 4 percent worth between £1,000 and £2,000.

The house of Mr. Crawley, the pepetual curate of Hogglestock in Trollope's *Last Chronicle of Barset* is a classic representation of genteel clerical poverty on the lower end of the salary range:

> It was a wretched, poverty-stricken room. By degrees the carpet had disappeared, which had been laid down some nine or ten years since, when they had first come to Hogglestock, and which even then had not been new. Now nothing but a poor fragment of it remained in front of the fire-place. In the middle of the room there was a table which had once been large; but one flap of it was gone altogether, and the other flap sloped grievously towards the floor, the weakness of old age having fallen into its legs. There were two or three smaller tables about, but they stood propped against walls, thence obtaining a security which their own strength would not give them.... It was not such a room as one would wish to see inhabited by an beneficed clergyman of the Church of England; but they who know what money will do and what it will not, will understand how easily a man with a family, and with a hundred and thirty pounds a year, may be brought to the need of inhabiting such a chamber. When it is remembered that three pounds of meat a day, at ninepence a pound, will cost over forty pounds a year, there need be no difficulty in understanding that it may be so. Bread for such a family must cost at least twenty-five pounds. Clothes for five persons of whom one must at any rate wear the raiment of a gentleman, can hardly be found for less than ten pounds a year a head. Then there remains fifteen pounds for tea, sugar, beer, wages, education, amusements and the like. In such circumstances a gentleman can hardly pay much for the renewal of furniture![9]

Meanwhile, some incumbents had a more than sufficient income and were able to provide their children not only food and clothing but excellent education and good marriage prospects. The differences in clerical income were not based on the size of the parish or the difficulty of the duties involved, but on custom and the peculiar history of each parish. So, depending on your connections, your luck, and, to some extent, your merit, as an incumbent you may struggle to maintain middle-class living standards or may live a quite luxurious life.

Another important difference between incumbents was the location of their parishes in rural or urban areas. The mid-Victorian ideal was a quiet, rural parish, preferably in the south of England. In the lax old days, a clergyman in such a parish might do little more than deliver the sermon and officiate at the service on Sunday, administer the Eucharist four times a year, and perform requisite church ceremonies for christenings, weddings, and funerals as needed. The remainder of the time could then be spent in gentlemanly fashion, socializing, writing academic papers, and pursuing hobbies. In George Eliot's *Middlemarch*, set in the 1830s, each clergyman has a favorite pastime:

the comfortably wealthy Mr. Casaubon hires a curate to do the duty of the parish and spends his time writing a *Key to All Mythologies*, the vicar Mr. Farebrother collects natural history specimens, and the rector Mr. Cadwallader goes fishing.

But under the influence of the clerical revival inspired by the Evangelicals and later the Tractarians, the clergyman's responsibilities became much broader. As a dedicated rural incumbent, you would spend most of your week seeing to the physical, mental, and spiritual welfare of your flock. You will visit the sick and, perhaps with volunteer help, distribute charity to the poor—some of it out of your own shallow pocket. You will also oversee the education of the local children at the parochial school and Sunday school. You will be expected to visit your parishioners in their homes, attending teas and dinner parties, as well as meetings of church-related organizations. Communion services will also be more frequent—at least monthly, and in some places weekly.

If you are married, your wife, too, will be expected to participate actively in the social life of the village, distribute charity, teach Sunday school, and lead women's organizations dedicated to the work of the church, as well as oversee the household and bear and rear the children.

Despite this somewhat daunting set of duties, many still aspired to the position of rural clergyman. But the life of such a clergyman, often one of the only educated men in the parish, could also be lonely and monotonous, and later in the century, young clergymen gravitated toward urban parishes, where the social challenges seemed greater and the pace of life more exhilarating. Bishop John Gott, in his book, *The Parish Priest of the Town* (1885), makes clear this sense of excitement and mission:

> As it runs through our streets, the stream of life grows into a river. In large towns the good is better than elsewhere for three reasons; it resists more temptation, calling out its whole strength and endurance; it is surrounded with misery, developing its charity and sacrifice; and its environment of means of grace, and the Communion of Saints, is fuller and richer. In large towns the bad also is worse, its environment too is congenial and very fertile. So on both sides life is more intense.[10]

The number of people in a town parish was larger than in a country parish, and the incumbent generally oversaw a large organization of clerical and lay workers that ministered to the needs of the parish. Many more church-related activities and organizations would consume his time: Sunday schools, day schools, night schools, clubs, guilds, Bible classes, and charities of all descriptions. While the clergyman in a rural parish was sometimes underworked, the urban clergyman was constantly busy, and while the rural clergyman suffered from isolation, the urban clergyman had to balance constant social demands with study and meditation. Urban congregations also had higher expectations, both about the quality of the sermons and the frequency of services: by the end of the century, the urban clergyman would probably be offering daily services and weekly communion.

Table 3.1 Anglican Bishoprics/Cathedral Cities in England and Wales

1. Canterbury (Archbishopric)	19. Peterborough
2. York (Archbishopric)	20. Ripon (established 1836)
3. Bangor	21. Rochester
4. Bath and Wells	22. Salisbury
5. Carlisle	23. St. Asaph
6. Chester	24. St. David's
7. Chichester	25. Winchester
8. Durham	26. Worcester
9. Ely	
10. Exeter	New Bishoprics/Cathedrals
11. Gloucester (Bristol) (amalgamated 1836)	27. Manchester (established 1847)
	28. Truro (1876)
12. Hereford	29. St. Albans (1877)
13. Lichfield (and Coventry until 1837)	30. Liverpool (1880)
14. Lincoln	31. Newcastle upon Tyne (1882)
15. Llandaff	32. Southwell (1884)
16. London (St. Paul's Cathedral)	33. Bristol (split from Gloucester 1887)
17. Norwich	34. Wakefield (1888)
18. Oxford (Christ Church Cathedral)	

You need to think carefully about your first incumbency, because it will probably be your last as well. The majority of Victorian clergy spent their whole career serving their first parish as incumbent. There was no career ladder, no means of promotion by merit, though merit in a well-placed parish might catch the eye of the bishop and lead to a better position. Later in the century there was more mobility, with clergy moving to more desirable livings, but for most clergymen, a position serving as rector or vicar was the extent of their ambition. Only a very few went on to higher office.

BEYOND THE PARISH CLERGYMAN

Diocesan Clergy

The next step up the hierarchy was the bishop, who oversaw all the parishes in his diocese or "see," from his headquarters (the "palace") in a Cathedral city; bishops assumed the title "the Right Reverend"—the Right Reverend John Smith or the Right Revered Mr. Smith or, if he holds a higher degree, the Right Reverend Dr. Smith. There were twenty-six Anglican bishops in Britain at the start of the Victorian period, including the Archbishop of Canterbury, the head of the Church of England, and the Archbishop of York (see Table 3.1). (The proper prefix for the archbishops is "the Most Reverend.") These twenty-six bishops were known as the Lords Spiritual, because they were entitled to seats in the House of Lords, so the appointment of a bishop was more political than spiritual. Bishops were nominated by the prime minister and appointed by the queen, and then approved by vote of the dean and chapter of the cathedral in their diocese. (The chapter is the governing body of the diocese, consisting of the cathedral clergy of the see: the dean, the canons, and sometimes others, including minor canons.) Though some prime ministers tried to rise above political considerations and appoint men of intelligence, holiness, and demonstrated ability, Tory prime ministers tended to appoint conservative bishops, while Whigs looked for more liberal ones. This explains the anxiety at the beginning of Trollope's *Barchester Towers*, when the government is tottering and the Bishop of Barchester dying: if he dies with the current government in place, the prime minister will nominate the bishop's son, Archdeacon Grantly, to be the new bishop; if, however, a new government takes over, the nomination will go to someone else, in the event, Dr. Proudie.

The Queen could not absolutely refuse to appoint a nominated clergyman, but Victoria took an active role in the process; she kept abreast of church matters, she sometimes made suggestions of likely candidates herself, and she argued with her prime ministers when she disapproved of their selections. Victoria opposed both Evangelical and excessively High Church candidates, preferring moderate churchmen.

The duties of the bishop included performing confirmations both at the cathedral and at churches within his see; examining and ordaining clergymen for his parishes, and sometimes appointing new clergy; and providing help and counsel to clergymen, as well as overseeing their performance as incumbents. These, combined with the correspondence necessary for their political and administrative duties, kept bishops very busy. Owen Chadwick records figures for one bishop, Boyd Carpenter of Ripon, who traveled at least 12,000 miles a year, preached or made speeches 190 times each year, and in 1895, wrote 4,936 letters.[11]

In large and populous sees, there was so much work that bishops required assistance. Archdeacons were generally chosen by the bishop to help with the oversight of the parishes in his diocese, and the prefix associated with their office was "the Venerable," as in the Venerable Theophilus Grantly or the Venerable Mr. Grantly. An archdeacon visited and inspected each parish in his archdeaconry, serving as the "eye of the bishop" and as his local representative. He was charged with checking on the behavior of the incumbent, the state of the church property, and the provision of education through church schools and Sunday schools. The visits of archdeacons were often a source of anxiety for parish clergy, and conflicts were common. Before 1840, stipends for archdeacons tended to be low, and most archdeacons were generally pluralists, holding other ecclesiastical appointments to make ends meet. After the Dean and Chapters Act of 1840, though, the stipend of new archdeacons was considerably enhanced, to £500 plus fees, allowing them to devote themselves entirely to the work. Archdeacons were often aided by rural deans. This was an ancient office revived in the nineteenth century to meet the demands of a growing population. An incumbent would be appointed rural dean within the area where he was serving, responsible for inspection of the churches and church property of the neighboring clergymen. Rural deans also took the lead in school inspections and in arbitrating disputes among local clergy. They were generally appointed by the bishop on the recommendation of his archdeacon, and they would continue to serve as incumbents in their parishes while performing the additional duties of rural dean.

While the archdeacons and rural deans helped relieve some of the bishops' excessive workload in the first half of the century, they could only help with oversight, not with confirmation, ordination, or correspondence, and they proved to be insufficient. From the 1870s, suffragan bishops were nominated by the bishop himself to help him with his ecclesiastical work; the bishop of a diocese sent two names of clergymen to the Crown, and one was chosen. These assistants could substitute for the bishop in performing any of his duties.

At the start of the century, bishops' stipends varied even more than the benefices of ordinary clergy; in the wealthiest dioceses, such as Canterbury and Durham, they could amount to more than £19,000 each year; in the poorest, the Welsh see of Llandaff, the bishop's stipend was only £924. In 1836, the Established Church Act went some way toward equalizing bishops' stipends, providing most bishops with between £4,500 and £5,500, although the five most important sees (Canterbury, York, London, Durham, and Winchester) still enjoyed much more: the Archbishop of Canterbury, for example, got £15,000, the Archbishop of York and the Bishop of London £10,000.

Your chance of achieving a bishopric, even with your Oxford or Cambridge degree, is not good, despite the expansion in the number of bishops later in the century. Though you may be an exemplary incumbent, without good political or family connections, you have little chance of such promotion.

Cathedral Clergy

The traditional role of the cathedral was worship: the daily cathedral services, with their beauty and majesty, glorified God and showed forth his praise. With their choirboys and choral services, they maintained the high traditions of church music. Each Anglican cathedral was headed by a dean styled "the Very Reverend" and appointed by the Crown. He was assisted by a group of resident canons, appointed by the bishop; in the early part of the century the number of canons could vary significantly from one cathedral to another. The dean and the resident canons made up the governing body of a cathedral, the chapter, which was responsible for all operations of the cathedral, including maintenance, finances, and worship services; they also had to confirm certain diocesan decisions and appointments made by the bishop and could serve as an advisory body for him.

But in practical-minded nineteenth-century Britain, the function of worship alone seemed insufficient to justify the cathedrals' large endowments and their legions of clergymen. In 1840, the Ecclesiastical Commission reformed the cathedrals, abolishing many cathedral offices and regularizing salaries of cathedral clergymen. The dean's stipend was set at £1,000; the resident canons would receive £500 each. The number of canons was also standardized: most cathedrals were allowed four resident canons, with only a few exceptions, which were allowed five or six.

The benefice held by a canon is called a "prebend" so that canons are sometimes known as "prebends" or "prebendaries." Prior to 1840, there were many nonresident prebends, which were held by pluralist clergymen. In 1840, these positions were abolished, and instead each cathedral could appoint twenty-four nonstipendiary canons; these positions were honorary ones that the bishop could confer on particularly worthy incumbents in his diocese. Still, the "resident" canons were usually only in residence three months of the year, spending the remaining nine months in other clerical employment, as incumbents in the parishes or professors in the universities.

In seeking new roles in Victorian Britain, some cathedrals once again took up their traditional role in education, founding schools or theological colleges. In addition, most cathedrals eventually became more closely integrated with the work of the diocese, so that cathedral clergy might work with the bishop in his ministry. Individual canons often had specific duties within the cathedral or diocese. The "precentor" was a canon in charge of the worship services, particular the music in the choral services. Another canon might be lecturer at the cathedral's theological college. A third might lead the cathedral school and oversee the education of the choirboys. The archdeacon, too, might hold a canonry in the cathedral. Other clergymen attached to the cathedral included the "minor canons" or "priest-vicars," whose function was to sing the cathedral services.

The bishops, archdeacons, and cathedral clergy, all concentrated in the great cathedral cities of England and Wales, might be considered the aristocracy of the church, men of wealth and influence—and, often, ambition. Trollope explores this world of the church aristocracy in the *Chronicles of Barsetshire*, especially in *Barchester Towers* (1857), where he defends clerical ambition:

> A lawyer does not sin in seeking to be a judge, or in compassing his wishes by all honest means. A young diplomat entertains a fair ambition when he looks forward to be the lord of a first–rate embassy; and a poor novelist when he attempts to rival Dickens or rise above Fitzjames, commits no fault, though he may be foolish.... If we look to our clergymen to be more than men, we shall probably teach ourselves to think that they are less, and can hardly hope to raise the character of the pastor by denying to him the right to entertain the aspirations of a man.[12]

Most nineteenth-century clergymen, however, were freed from the temptations of excessive ambition by the unreachability of such high offices. Most would live and die incumbent clergymen, whether in a village or an industrial city, quietly serving their parish.

4

Religion and Daily Life

Victorian religion was both manifestly public and intensely private. While it is relatively easy to explore religion's public face by reading parliamentary papers, published sermons, and religious periodicals, it is more difficult to understand the private side of religion: how it affected ordinary believers in their daily lives. One problem is that many writers of the Victorian era took it for granted that their readers already had such an understanding, so the material fades into the background of a novel or biography, difficult to recover. Another problem is the sheer diversity of individual experience across different denominations, decades, and geographies. But the subject is so crucial—and so interesting—that it is worth exploring this little discussed territory, even if such exploration cannot possibly map the full range of private religious experience in the nineteenth century.

This chapter is divided into three sections, each addressing how religion affected ordinary people at particular times in their lives: Sundays, weekdays, and special occasions.

SUNDAYS

For many Victorians, attending a religious worship service on Sunday was more a matter of custom than a matter of deep faith, so the experience of Sunday worship was common to much of the British population. But what was that experience? When would it occur? Where would it occur? What would the services have been like?

Time of Services

In many parishes in the early part of the century, and in some rural parishes through the century, worshippers would have attended service whenever it was

William Holman Hunt's painting, "The Light of the World,"
became the most familiar image of Christ in the Victorian era:
It became a part of people's daily lives. Reproduced thousands
of times, it hung in homes across Britain and throughout the
Empire. This image comes from W. Shaw Sparrow, ed., *The
Gospels in Art* (New York: Stokes, 1904), p. 174.

offered. There might be a morning service at 10 AM or 10:30 AM, an afternoon service at 2 PM or 2:30 PM, or an evening service beginning sometime between 4 PM and 7 PM. (If the main service of the day was held in the afternoon or evening, morning service might occur earlier, at 9 AM or 9:30 AM.) Through the Victorian era, bishops strongly encouraged their clergy to offer two services on Sunday, but many found that this only split their congregation into two parts, rather than increasing its size or encouraging attendance at both services. The repetition in the Anglican Morning Prayer and Evening Prayer services (see below) tended to discourage parishioners from attending a second service.

When given a choice of services, Anglicans tended to go to church in the mornings, and so did Unitarians and Congregationalists. Other dissenting sects, including the Methodists and Baptists, had their largest services in the evening. In fact, Methodists had begun emphasizing the evening service before their break with Anglicanism, so that their members could attend an Anglican service in the morning and a Methodist one in the evening, and some Victorian Methodists maintained this custom. In general, only the most serious of Victorian Christians attended more than one service on Sunday.

Order of Service

All Anglican services would be based on the *Book of Common Prayer* (1662). Sunday morning services would usually be Morning Prayer (also called Matins), followed by a sermon, then the litany and part of the communion service, even when communion was not taken. Later in the century, Morning Prayer and the Communion service were more often separated. The morning service was structured as follows:

1. A general collective confession of sins and absolution, followed by the Lord's Prayer (Matthew 6:9–13) and the doxology, which could be said or sung: "Glory be to the Father, and to the Son: and to the Holy Ghost; As it was in the beginning, is now, and ever shall be: world without end. Amen."
2. Psalm 95 (said or sung), together with the other Psalms—usually two or three—allotted to that Sunday in the church lectionary (a schedule of readings that divided up the Scripture through the year), followed by the doxology.
3. The Old Testament reading for the day as specified in the lectionary, and then "Te Deum Laudamus" or the Canticle "Benedicite, Omnia Opera" (Daniel 3:57–88 in the Apocrypha) both of which are songs of praise, followed by the doxology.
4. The New Testament reading for the day, then either "Benedictus" (taken from Luke 1:68–79) or "Jubilate Deo" (Psalm 100), followed by the doxology.
5. Recitation of the Apostles' Creed, or, on special occasions, the Creed of Saint Athanasius. (The Athanasian Creed, with its emphasis on the doctrine of eternal punishment, caused some late Victorian Christians discomfort, especially since it was recited on major Christian holy days.)

6. Prayers: first, another recitation of the Lord's Prayer, then responsory prayers, and then the "Collects"—first the Collect for that particular Sunday in the year, then the Collect for Peace and the Collect for Grace.

   The shortest version of Morning Prayer would not include hymns or a sermon, and the congregation would move onto the final prayers (under number 9 below), and that would end the service. If hymns and a sermon were added, they would occur here as follows; if sermon and hymns were to be included in the Communion Service to follow, they would be omitted here.

7. A choir anthem or the singing of hymns.
8. A sermon, which could vary in length from about 10 minutes to 90 minutes or more; more hymns might follow.
9. More prayers—A Prayer for the Queen's Majesty, A Prayer for the Royal Family, A Prayer for the Clergy and People, a Prayer of St. Chrysostom, and a benediction (2 Corinthians 13:14).

Sometimes after the Collects and the choir anthem, the Litany, a lengthy responsory prayer, would also be said; in that case only the Prayer of St. Chrysostom and the benediction would be said at the end of the service.

For a Sunday morning service, Morning Prayer would often be followed by part of the communion service. If communion was not being taken, only the first part of the service, through the Prayer for the Church (number 11 in the list below) would be performed, with prayer and final blessing. The Communion service in the Anglican Church proceeds as follows:

1. The Lord's Prayer.
2. The Collect (a communal prayer).
3. Minister reads the Ten Commandments, and after each commandment, the congregation responds: "Lord, have mercy upon us, and incline our hearts to keep this law."
4. Prayers: A Collect for the Queen and the Collect of the Day.
5. The Epistle (a passage from the Bible) appointed for the day, as specified in the *Book of Common Prayer*. While "Epistle" generally refers to the letters written by St. Paul and others and included in the New Testament, in fact the passages in the Prayer Book are taken not only from the Epistles (including Romans, I and II Corinthians, Galatians, Ephesians, Philippians, Colossians, I Thessalonians, II Timothy, Hebrews, James, I Peter, I John, and Jude), but also from Acts, Revelations, and even some Old Testament prophets—Isaiah, Jeremiah, Joel, and Malachi.
6. The Gospel passage appointed for the day, drawn from one of the four New Testament gospels: Matthew, Mark, Luke, or John.
7. Recitation of the Nicene Creed.
8. Announcements and blessing.
9. Sermon and hymns.
10. Offering for the poor.

11. Prayer for the Church (Great Intercession).
12. General Confession and Absolution.
13. "Comfortable Words" from Scripture followed by Prayers.
14. Prayer of Consecration in which the minister blesses the bread and wine that will be used in the Eucharist
15. Administration of communion: first, the minister consumes both bread and wine, then gives it to other ordained men present, then to the congregation individually, first, the bread, and then the wine.
16. The Lord's Prayer.
17. Post-Communion Thanksgiving.
18. Gloria in Excelsis—a prayer of praise to God.
19. Benediction.

At the start of the nineteenth century, most parish churches celebrated Eucharist only four times a year, at Easter, Whitsunday (a celebration of the coming of the Holy Spirit at Pentecost as related in the Bible in Acts 2, seven weeks after Easter), Michaelmas (September 29—sometimes omitted), and Christmas. The Evangelicals began and the Tractarians continued the trend toward more frequent Eucharist. By the late nineteenth century, while some village churches still had communion services only quarterly, most city churches offered monthly communion, and a few were offering it weekly.

Evening services would usually consist of Evening Prayer, with or without a sermon, as follows:

1. General Confession and Absolution, followed by the Lord's Prayer and doxology, as in Morning Prayer.
2. Psalms for the day.
3. The Old Testament lesson, followed by the Magnificat (the song of the Virgin Mary in Luke 1:46–55) or Psalm 98 ("Cantate Domino"), either followed by the doxology.
4. The New Testament reading and "Nunc Dimittis" (Luke 2:29–32) or "Deus Misereatur" (Psalm 67) with doxology.
5. Recitation of the Apostles' Creed.
6. Prayers: the Lord's Prayer, responsory prayer, and the Collects: the Collect for the Day, the Collect for Peace, and the Collect for Aid against all Perils.
7. A choir anthem or hymns, if desired.
   If Evening Prayer was the main service of the day, a sermon would usually be included here.
8. More prayers—A Prayer for the Queen's Majesty, A Prayer for the Royal Family, A Prayer for the Clergy and People, a Prayer of St. Chrysostom, and a benediction (2 Corinthians 13:14).

Dissenting services would differ significantly from Anglican services. Though some Methodist churches continued to use the Anglican Prayer Book, most dissenting services were nonliturgical: that is, they did not follow a particular liturgy or prayer book, and significant variation was allowed from service to service. Dissenting services would generally include extemporaneous prayer rather than the fixed liturgical prayers; more hymn singing; and a greater focus on the sermon itself, which could be quite long. The sermon might also be given extemporaneously (see discussion of sermons below).

Parts of the Service

Music

English cathedrals offered services in which most of the words were sung or chanted rather than said, and they maintained choirs, though the quality of such choirs varied enormously and generally improved over the course of the century. In the early nineteenth century, few parish churches would have had their own choirs or organs; some would have boasted a country band, made up of whatever instruments the local talent could offer: one band might have two clarinets, a bassoon, a cello, and a small flute; another might consist of a bassoon, two violins, and two clarinets; and still another parish might make do with just a cello and a pair of violinists. Later in the century, organs and choirs, often with choir members wearing surplices, became more common. Thomas Hardy came from a "church-band" family, and in his novel *Under the Greenwood Tree* he narrates with nostalgia the replacement of a country band with a new-fangled organ.

Until the last half of the eighteenth century, the tradition of congregational singing in British churches was "psalmody." This tradition held that the only songs appropriate for worship services were the inspired songs recorded in Scripture, especially the Psalms; nonbiblical hymns were allowed only on important church holy days. The Psalms had to be transformed, however, to make them appropriate for congregational singing: they were metricized—turned into English poetry—and set to music. Two versions of the Psalms were traditionally used: the 1562 psalter by Sternhold and Hopkins, commonly called the Old Version, and the 1696 psalter by Tate and Brady, the New Version. In 1719, Dissenter Isaac Watts offered much freer paraphrases of the Psalms in *Psalms of David Imitated in the Language of the New Testament,* as well as writing many original hymns. Watts' hymns and metrical psalms became the foundation of the English hymn tradition, and many of his hymns are still sung today, including "Alas, and Did My Savior Bleed" and "When I Survey the Wondrous Cross."

John Wesley and his Methodist congregations first popularized the singing of original hymns in English worship, and hymn singing spread fairly quickly among dissenting denominations, such as the Baptists and Congregationalists, and more slowly within the Anglican Church, beginning in Evangelical congregations. Anglican Churches sometimes felt they had to introduce hymn singing if they were to compete with the lively music offered at dissenting chapels. There were a huge number of hymnals printed in the nineteenth century, and ministers and their congregations could usually choose to use the one that suited them best. Individual congregations and schools might compile their own hymnals; denominations rushed to put together hymnals for their congregations, though beloved hymns from other denominations were almost always included; and publishers competed to have most inclusive and most popular collections. The Church of England did not have an official hymnal, but *Hymns, Ancient and Modern*, first compiled in 1861, soon became the most popular collection in Anglican churches. Some Anglican churches continued to use a different hymnal, such as *The Hymnal Companion to the Book of Common Prayer* (1870), edited by Evangelical E.H. Bickersteth; or *Church Hymns* (1870), published by the Society for the Promotion of Christian Knowledge (SPCK). These three hymnals had their own emphases, but they shared many hymns in common.

Some hymns were written for particular collections, and others lifted from previous hymn collections, but many hymns, especially early in the century, were taken from books of devotional poetry. Baptist writer Anne Steele's hymns, for example, were originally published in her large volume, *Poems on Subjects Chiefly Devotional* (1760), and John Keble's *The Christian Year* (1827) provided the church with several popular hymns. Other hymns were translated either from ancient languages, especially by the High Church, or from German hymns sung by Lutherans or Moravians. Hymns tended to be printed without music and sung to whatever hymns tunes the congregation already knew. Only later in the century did particular hymn texts become strongly linked with particular music.

Editors of hymnals felt free to use previously published material and to alter it as they saw fit to fit the doctrinal or aesthetic preferences of their market. Such alterations were generally uncontroversial, though controversy did spring up when Unitarians, compiling their first hymnal, altered hymns from other denominations to omit references to the Trinity and to the divinity of Christ. Still, objections were rare, and hymn writers in the early part of the century seemed to regard their work as the property of the whole church, refusing to enforce copyright, even when that was possible. *Hymns, Ancient and Modern* was the first hymnal to observe and enforce copyright, and this assertion of private intellectual property in the religious sphere caused significant controversy in the world of religious publishing.

Hymns were not just intended for singing at religious services: hymnals were produced with a variety of functions in mind. Some were aimed at Sunday schools, others at revival meetings. The hymnal of American revivalists Dwight L. Moody and Ira D. Sankey, *Sacred Songs and Solos*, was popularized, particularly in dissenting chapels, by their first British tour in 1873–1875. Still other hymnals were designed for domestic consumption and private reading; they were particularly popular reading for Sundays in households where secular reading matter was forbidden. Some of the most interesting of these private hymnals are the many hymnbooks designed for invalids: these include two books entitled *The Invalid's Hymn Book*, the most popular published in 1834 by its hymnist editor Charlotte Elliott, author of the invitational hymn "Just As I Am," and another published in 1866 by prolific High Church hymnist John Mason Neale. Invalids' hymnals provided hymns of comfort and sometimes explicitly identified the situations in which particular hymns might be useful: when you feel useless, when you are in great pain, when you are in fear of death. But these were not the only specialized hymnbooks: in fact, that same year Neale also published another collection for a niche market: *Hymns for Use during the Cattle Plague*.

Some hymns became popular only within particular denominations, but often popular hymns would transcend their specific denominational origins and be sung in churches and chapels across England—and even in America. Table 4.1 provides a list of the most popular hymns sung in Victorian England according to the frequency of their appearances in hymnals.

Sermons

Victorian sermons varied enormously in content, style, and length. At one extreme, some were marathon fire-and-brimstone sermons calling for repentance and threatening punishment. At the other, there were university-style lectures analyzing abstruse doctrinal points or difficult translations from ancient languages. Some generalizations about the majority of sermons, however, are possible. Most sermons were based, however loosely, upon a biblical text. J. Robinson, writing in 1805, explained it this way: "Preaching is the taking of a portion of Scripture, and explaining it; raising some useful doctrine from it, and applying it to the edification of the hearers, to instruct and to reform."[1]

One of a clergyman's primary duties was to provide the sermon for the Sunday service. Some clergymen labored mightily, writing an original sermon each week. Others took advantage of the many volumes of published sermons, selecting a ready-made sermon to deliver to their congregation on Sunday. Older clergymen often had a stock of sermons appropriate to different times of the year that they wrote in their early days and then thriftily recycled for the rest of their career. Mary Hughes recalls the sermons she heard during her visits to her Aunt Tony's house in the 1870s, where they attended the village church: "The dear old parson was a survival of the eighteenth-century type, who took his duties lightly. His sermons were so few that Tony said she knew them all by heart and needn't attend to them."[2] Extempore preaching, popular in many dissenting chapels, was not much practiced in Anglican Churches, though sometimes if the vicar failed to finish writing his sermon, as the Reverend Francis Massingberd confessed to having done, improvisation would be forced upon him.[3]

Popular preachers could attract attendance from outside the parish, especially in large cities like London. In the 1870s Henry Parry Liddon, declared the best preacher in England in 1884 by readers of *Contemporary Pulpit*, drew people to St. Paul's Cathedral, while F. W. Farrar, also renowned as a preacher, could be heard at St. Margaret's Church in London. A decade earlier F. D. Maurice's

Table 4.1 Twenty-Five Most Popular Hymns in the Anglican Church (1885)

	First Line	Author	Number of Hymnals
1	All Praise to Thee, my God, this night	Thomas Ken	51
2	Hark! The herald angels sing	Charles Wesley	51
3	Lo! He comes with clouds descending	Charles Wesley/ Martin Madan	51
4	Rock of Ages, cleft for me	Augustus Toplady	51
5	Abide with me: fast falls the eventide	Henry Francis Lyte	49
6	Awake, my soul, and with the sun	Thomas Ken	49
7	Jerusalem the golden	John Mason Neale	49
8	Jesu, Lover of my soul	Charles Wesley	49
9	Sun of my soul, Thou Saviour dear	John Keble	49
10	When I survey the wondrous cross	Isaac Watts	49
11	Holy! Holy! Holy! Lord God Almighty	Reginald Heber	48
12	Jesus Christ is risen to-day	Anon.	47
13	Nearer, my God, to Thee,	Sarah F. Adams	47
14	Hark! The glad sound, the Saviour comes	Philip Doddridge	46
15	How sweet the name of Jesus sounds	John Newton	46
16	Jerusalem, my happy home	Francis Baker?	46
17	From Greenland's icy mountains	Reginald Heber	45
18	Great God, what do I see and hear	B. Ringwaldt	45
19	O, God, our help in ages past	Isaac Watts	45
20	Saviour, when in dust to Thee	Robert Grant	45
21	All people that on earth do dwell	William Kethe	44
22	Brief life is here our portion	John Mason Neale	44
23	Come, Holy Ghost, our souls inspire	John Cosin	44
24	My God, my Father, while I stray	Charlotte Elliott	44
25	Hail the day that sees Him rise	Charles Wesley	43

Source: In *Anglican Hymnody* (London: Hatchards, 1885), James King analyzed fifty-two hymnals used in Anglican churches to determine which hymns appeared most frequently and ranked them in order of frequency of appearance.

sermons brought people to Lincoln's Inn, and Henry Melvill enthralled from the pulpit of St. Paul's. Meanwhile, the Baptist preacher Charles Haddon Spurgeon drew crowds of up to 10,000 at his Metropolitan Tabernacle in London. Some Londoners became "sermon-tasters," sampling the wares of a different preacher every week. Most Victorians, however, had to make do with the preaching in their local church or chapel, whatever its kind or quality.

Places of Worship

While Anglicans living in a cathedral city might choose to attend the cathedral services, most Victorians would worship in their local parish church or in a

This photograph of the church at Old Shoreham comes from Ralph Adam Cram's *English Country Churches* (Boston, MA: Bates and Guild, 1898). Courtesy of the Division of Special Collections, Archives, and Rare Books, University of Missouri at Columbia.

dissenting chapel nearby. Parish churches varied significantly in size, design, and ornamentation.

Because they tended to be made of local materials, a church in East Anglia might be made of flint, one in the Cotswolds of a rich, golden limestone, one in Devon of red sandstone; in Essex, timber and brick were often used. Some parish churches were built by the Saxons or Normans, originally as Catholic churches; others were built after the Reformation, with the Protestant liturgy in mind. Some were thick-walled, small-windowed, Romanesque buildings; some were ornate, pointed-windowed, and Gothic; some were elegantly neoclassical, light, spacious, and tranquil. Only the very newest English churches, however, adhered to just one architectural or decorative style; the others had been repeatedly expanded, restored, and redecorated, always in the latest style. So a Romanesque church might include a Gothic tower, Elizabethan pulpit and pews, and Victorian stained glass.

Parish churches tended to be laid out according to one of two plans: the basilican or the cruciform. The basilican plan was the simplest. At its most basic, the church would be a rectangle divided into two cells: a *nave*, where the congregation would gather, and a *sanctuary* on the eastern end, where the altar was located and where the clergy would perform the service; a semicircular area in the sanctuary would be called an *apse*. Sometimes there would be *aisles* on either side of the nave, separated from it by *colonnades*; sometimes there would be an additional vestibule area on the western end of the

This photograph of Holy Trinity Church at Stratford-upon-Avon comes from Ralph Adam Cram's, *English Country Churches* (Boston, MA: Bates and Guild, 1898). Courtesy of the Division of Special Collections, Archives, and Rare Books, University of Missouri at Columbia.

This photograph of the church at Totnes, comes from Ralph Adam Cram's *English Country Churches* (Boston, MA: Bates and Guild, 1898). Courtesy of the Division of Special Collections, Archives, and Rare Books, University of Missouri at Columbia.

This photograph of the church at Hawarden, Wales, comes from Ralph Adam Cram's *English Country Churches* (Boston, MA: Bates and Guild, 1898). Courtesy of the Division of Special Collections, Archives, and Rare Books, University of Missouri at Columbia.

nave, corresponding to the sanctuary on the eastern end: that would be called the *narthex*. There could also be an area between the nave and the sanctuary, called the *choir*, where the choir would sit; sometimes there would be a tower above this area. Cruciform churches would add *transepts* on either side of the choir, forming the "arms" of the cross.

Interior decoration also varied enormously, from churches with the simplest wooden table for an altar and bare, whitewashed walls, to churches that mirrored the ornate decoration of the European Catholic tradition, with carved chancel screens, paintings, embroidered altar cloths, and gorgeous stained glass windows. The rise of ritualism in the latter half of the century contributed to a trend toward more elaborate decoration of church interiors.

The naves of Anglican churches contained seating for the congregation, usually bench-like pews in the back of the nave for the ordinary parishioner, and at the front of the nave, nearest the altar, box pews, enclosed with high back and sides and entered through a door, where the gentry or aristocracy would sit. Well-to-do and well-born local families would pay pew rents for these reserved seats, and only they and their guests could sit there; the pew doors were sometimes fitted with locks. Pews caused controversy throughout the century: while pew-rents could be an important source of income for the churches, they reinforced social inequality and implied an inequality before God, which

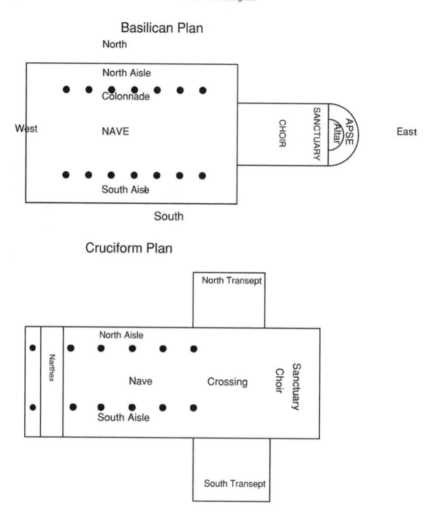

Basic church plans.

Christian doctrine rejected. New churches tended to be built without box pews, and more and more clergy had existing box pews removed.

The nineteenth century saw many new churches built as the establishment struggled to accommodate the quickly expanding population, especially in the flourishing industrial cities. The most popular architectural style for these Victorian churches was neo-Gothic. This style was promoted by architect A.W.N. Pugin, who argued in his book *Contrasts* (1836) that Gothic was the only true Christian architecture, as opposed to the paganism of neoclassical styles. The

High Church, with its dreams of pre-Reformation ritual, strongly favored new Gothic churches and Gothic renovations in existing churches.

Dissenting chapels were generally much simpler than Anglican churches, sometimes little more than wooden or brick boxes with benches and a podium. In *Hard Times*, Charles Dickens describes the utilitarian chapels of Coketown with their lack of ornamentation: "If the members of a religious persuasion built a chapel there—as the members of eighteen religious persuasions had done—they made it a pious warehouse of red brick, with sometimes (but this is only in highly ornamented examples) a bell in a birdcage on the top of it."[4] Later in the century, as they became well established, some dissenting denominations—particularly the Methodists—built new chapels in the Gothic revival style. These had open seating rather than reserved pews, in keeping with their generally more egalitarian ethos.

The Roman Catholics were struggling to keep up with the immigrant population, so their new places of worship had to be constructed quickly and cheaply. As a result, some Roman Catholic churches constructed in the nineteenth century were scarcely more ornate than the dissenting chapels. Pugin, however, a Catholic convert, designed many beautiful neo-Gothic Catholic churches throughout Britain and set the aesthetic standard for churches that would follow.

Beyond the Church Service

How Christian families spent the rest of their Sunday varied enormously. As we have seen in the discussion of Sabbatarianism in Chapter 1, some families strictly observed the commandment to "keep the Sabbath day holy" by eschewing all secular pursuits. In these families, Sundays might involve a morning service followed by a family dinner at which the sermon would be discussed; then a quiet afternoon including, perhaps, a family walk, private reading of religious literature, and meditation or prayer. The day could end with another service or with a family devotional. Other Victorians felt that after attending one religious service on Sundays, they had done their duty for the day, and spent the rest of the day in recreation: an outing in the country, a game of cricket or rugby, or even an afternoon with the latest sensation novel.

Social commentators often lamented the irreligious nature of the working classes, and certainly many did not attend Sunday services on their one day of freedom from the drudgery of daily work. Their children, however, might well attend Sunday school, using their day of rest to achieve literacy and religious education. And some working families would sleep in on Sunday morning, but later attend evening service at a dissenting chapel, seeking both physical and spiritual refreshment before beginning another week of work in the factories.

WEEKDAYS

Formal weekday services were rare in the Victorian period, but they became more common later in the century, especially among High churchmen; these were sparsely attended by the most pious and the least busy members of the population, often older women.

More pervasive were "cottage meetings" or other gatherings for Bible study and prayer. Originating in the Methodist church, such meetings became important in the Anglican Church as well as other dissenting denominations. They were sometimes led by the local clergyman, especially when he belonged to the High Church, but often by local laymen and women. As the name implies, they were often held in the home of one of the parishioners rather than in the church itself. There were also many organizations and groups that would gather for religious or charitable purposes—groups to support foreign missions, to produce warm clothing for the poor, to embroider new altar cloths for the church, to distribute Bibles or food or both. Village social life often revolved around the church and its various functions.

But, as Lord Melbourne was said to lament, religion also invaded the sanctity of private life. From early in the century, Evangelicals promoted daily family devotions: each morning or evening, the head of the household would gather his family and servants around him, read the Bible, and pray. The practice of family prayers caught on among the Evangelicals and gradually became more widespread. In her account of her London childhood, Mary Hughes recounts visits to her uncle's house in Cornwall, Reskadinnick:

> One Victorian custom which my father (God bless him!) had never even contemplated, was always observed at Reskadinnick. Family prayers, which my dear old grandfather had treated sketchily, were carried out by Uncle Bill with relentless thoroughness. Instead of mumbling a few simple requests to the Almighty, as grandpapa did, he acquired a book which covered the whole nation in its petitions, and even, on Fridays, went the length of praying for foreigners. All the servants were assembled, and it was morning *and* evening.[5]

Many books of the kind Uncle Bill had were published to guide family devotions, and some Bibles were divided up so that they could be read over the course of a year in family devotions of twenty to thirty minutes.[6]

While the paterfamilias would generally—though not invariably—lead family devotions, it was the mother who was responsible for her children's religious education, a duty that conduct books urged her to treat with the seriousness it deserved. Sentimental pictures of a mother reading the Bible aloud to her children gathered round her reflect this fact of child rearing, as well as the emotional and cultural significance it held for the Victorians. It was partly through this kind of early training that the Victorian mother was expected to exercise her nonauthoritative influence over British society. Children would also receive religious education at school: most schools in nineteenth-century England were still Anglican schools, where religious instruction was a regular part of the curriculum. This often included Scripture memorization and sometimes classes on the catechism as well (see below).

In addition to—or instead of—communal devotions or services, many Victorians set aside time for private devotions. It is difficult to know how each individual spent this most private spiritual time. Certainly, the many devotion books on the market provided Scripture readings and daily meditations. Some Anglicans may have used the Prayer Book services as the foundation for private devotions. Some may have read sermons or hymns in addition to Bible readings; others may have spent the whole time in prayer and meditation. A few kept a kind of moral and spiritual diary, chronicling their temptations and triumphs, as well as counting the blessings bestowed upon them by Providence. Though seldom discussed in public documents, such daily devotions deeply informed the experience of many Victorians and influenced the shape of their daily lives.

SPECIAL OCCASIONS

Baptisms

The Anglican doctrine of infant baptism was a source of considerable controversy. Almost all Victorian Anglicans believed that, as a result of the sin of Adam and Eve (Genesis 3), human beings are, as the baptismal service in the Prayer Book puts it, "conceived and born in sin." The controversial question was whether infant baptism entirely erased the taint of original sin, a doctrine known as "baptismal regeneration." Evangelicals regarded regeneration as a spiritual process, which was outwardly represented by the ritual of baptism but could not be effected by such a ritual, but Tractarians insisted on the doctrine of baptismal regeneration, and the language of the Prayer Book tended to support their case: after the baptism, the minister declares, "Seeing now, dearly beloved Brethren, that this Child is regenerate, and grafted into the body of Christ's Church, let us give thanks unto Almighty God." Evangelicals interpreted the Prayer Book's use of "regenerate" broadly and did not feel committed by its language to the full doctrine of baptismal regeneration. This dispute eventually led to the Gorham Controversy, in which a judicial committee determined that the Evangelicals' views were consistent with Anglican doctrine.

Such disputes meant little to most Victorian churchgoers, though some feared that an unbaptized infant would go to hell: in a harrowing scene from Hardy's *Tess of the D'Urbervilles*, Tess, terrified, baptizes her dying illegitimate baby herself, christening him Sorrow. For most, though, baptism was important mainly as a way of giving their infant a public identity.

Most Victorians preferred a private baptism conducted in their homes over a public baptism in the parish church. Though the Prayer Book makes allowances for private baptism, it specifies that "The Minister . . . shall warn the people that without great cause and necessity they procure not their Children to be baptized at home in their houses." Many clergymen attempted to do as the Prayer Book instructed them, but it was hard to overcome the custom of private baptism, with the family at home gathered round and a small party to follow.

The public baptism service would usually be performed as part of a regular Sunday service, often the evening service, which tended to be shorter. The parents and two or three godparents (one godparent of opposite sex, one or two of the same sex as infant) participated with the minister in the service. Godparents were chosen from among the friends and relations of the parents and nominally accepted responsibility for the child's religious education, though relatively few took these duties seriously. Some parents used the choice of godparents to honor much-loved friends, as a way of incorporating them into the family. Others, more socially ambitious, might try to obtain wealthy or influential friends for their newborns by inviting them to become godparents.

For the baptism, the parents, godparents, and the minister would gather at the *font*, the basin that held the baptismal water. If the parents were well off, the baby would be dressed in a long white cotton gown decorated with embroidery, lace, and ribbon. After prayers, exhortations, and Scripture reading, the minister would ask the godparents "in the name of this Child" to "renounce the devil and all his works, the vain pomp and glory of the world, with all covetous desires of the same, and the carnal desires of the flesh" and to make a declaration of faith and obedience on his or her behalf. Then the minister would tell the godparents to "Name this Child, " and, repeating the name, would either dip the child into the water in the font or pour water from the font over his head saying, "I baptize thee In the Name of the Father, and of the Son, and of the Holy Ghost. Amen." The baptism, or "christening," would generally be followed by a small family party.

Anglican infant baptism was so much a rite of passage that even some Dissenters would have their children baptized into the Anglican Church, though they could register the birth with the parish without undergoing the rite.

The Anglican Prayer Book also provided a service of "Baptism for those of Riper Years," but adult baptisms of new converts to Anglicanism remained rare.

Churching of Women

After the birth of a child, a woman would participate in this ceremony of Thanksgiving for "deliver[ance] from the great pain and peril of Childbirth." Its popularity may also have testified to a remaining sense that childbirth made a woman "unclean" and that she needed to be blessed before resuming her place in religious worship. The ceremony was sometimes carried out on a weekday; on these occasions, although the churching was performed in the church, it was essentially a private ceremony. Often, though, it was part of a regular Sunday service. In either case, the woman to be "churched" would sit at the front of the church. The ceremony included the reading of Psalm 116 or Psalm 127, the recitation of the Lord's Prayer and a responsive prayer, and a prayer of Thanksgiving. Then the new mother would bring offerings and, sometimes, take communion.

Mothers of illegitimate children and those who married contrary to church law were sometimes denied "churching." As the century progressed, middle-class and upper-class mothers increasingly objected to the public nature of the ceremony and often did not participate. But among working class and rural women, it remained a significant social recognition of a female rite of passage.

Confirmation

Confirmation was a ceremony in which a young person, having "come to years of discretion" affirmed the promises made on his or her behalf at baptism. Nineteenth-century Anglicans were generally confirmed between the ages of fourteen and nineteen. Before being confirmed, the young men and women had to prepare by learning the Prayer Book catechism, which incorporated the Ten Commandments, the Apostles' Creed, and the Lord's Prayer. They would attend catechism classes, usually with the local clergyman, where they were instructed in the fundamentals of Anglican belief and given help to memorize the necessary answers to the catechetical questions. Only when they had satisfactorily mastered this material would the clergyman certify them as ready for confirmation.

Confirmations were performed by the bishop, who generally visited parish churches for the purpose, although large-scale confirmations at the cathedral for the diocese were also common. For many young people, confirmation was a celebration of their entry into adulthood, and it was often accompanied by treats and festivities. In fact, some contemporary commentators noted disapprovingly that young men and women would often go straight from the church to the pub to continue the celebration.

After having been confirmed, the young person was allowed to take communion and become a full part of the Anglican Church, but many confirmation candidates never did. Among ordinary people, communion was regarded with awe and not a little fear. Clergymen had successfully conveyed to ordinary Christians the import of St. Paul's warning: "For he that eateth and drinketh unworthily, eateth and drinketh damnation to himself, not discerning the Lord's body" (I Corinthians 11:29). Many people feared that postcommunion sin would render them unworthy and thereby damn them, so they put off taking communion until they were close to death. Attitudes changed under Evangelical and Tractarian influence, and regular communion became an accepted part of most Anglicans' worship, but such reluctance remained in country districts through the century.

Weddings

As the Thirty-Nine Articles make clear, marriage was not considered a sacrament in the Anglican Church as it was in the Roman Catholic. It was, however, governed by church law, and marriages in England and Wales—except those of Jews and Quakers—had to be performed in an Anglican Church until 1837, when civil marriages became legal.

Traditionally, for three Sundays before a wedding was to take place, an announcement of the bride and groom's intention to wed, known as the banns, had to be read out during Sunday service in the parish or parishes where the two resided: the minister would say, "I publish the Banns of Marriage between Mary Jones of Grimsby and Christopher Johnson of Stickford. If any of you know cause, or just impediment, why these two persons should not be joined together in Holy Matrimony, ye are to declare it. This is the first [or second or third] time of asking." Couples could dispense with the banns by paying a few pounds for a license from a local clergyman, which would allow the couple to marry in any parish where at least one of them had been living for fifteen days, or, for a more princely sum (around £28), they could get a special license from the Archbishop of Canterbury, which allowed them to marry in any parish. In Hardy's *Tess of the D'Urbervilles*, the heroine is relieved when Angel Clare gets a license to allow them to marry, since she dreads someone forbidding the banns on the grounds of her previous relationship with Alec D'Urberville.

The reading of banns could also be avoided by going to Scotland, where marriage laws were different. An "irregular marriage" in Scotland required only the declaration of the couple that they wished to marry in the presence of two witnesses, with no waiting period. Moreover, while in Victorian England and Wales those under the age of twenty-one needed parental permission to marry, in Scotland the legal age of marriage was twelve for girls and fourteen for boys, with or without parental consent. Eloping couples from south of the border often went to Gretna Green, a Scottish town very near the English border, to avoid the restrictions of English law.

In England and Wales, weddings could take place any day of the week except Sunday. Through most of the period, by church law, they had to be held before noon; in the late 1880s, the period was extended to 3 PM. An Anglican wedding had to be attended by the local clergyman and the parish clerk (a layman who assisted the incumbent with parish administration), as well as at least two witnesses, though usually guests were also invited. The service was conducted as specified in the marriage ceremony in the Book of Common Prayer. Afterwards, the bride and groom would sign the church register, the bride signing her maiden name for the last time.

The bride's family generally bought her new clothes—a trousseau—as part of the wedding preparations, and one of the dresses in the trousseau would be her wedding dress. Unlike most modern brides, however, Victorian brides would expect the dress to become part of their wardrobe after marriage. Decorations of flowers and ribbons were often added to the dress for the wedding itself, then removed to allow the dress to be worn on less grand occasions. In the early nineteenth century, brides chose wedding dresses of several traditional colors: white, with its connotations of purity, was always popular, but gray was often preferred by lower middle and working-class brides because it was more practical for later wear. Blue, traditionally associated with loyalty and with the Virgin Mary, was also often chosen. But in 1840, when Queen Victoria married Prince Albert, she wore a white satin dress decorated with orange blossoms, with a wreath of orange blossoms on her head and a long veil. Thereafter, white became the overwhelmingly preferred color for Victorian brides.

Bridesmaids might wear their best dresses or might have new dresses for the occasion that resembled the bride's; they would wear flowers and ribbons in their hair, and occasionally a short veil. Some couples had all-white weddings, where bride and bridesmaids were dressed in white, the bridesmaids wearing colored ribbons or accessories to differentiate them from the bride. The men in Victorian weddings—groom, best man, and ushers—dressed in their best morning suits, which varied by class, generally with a flower in the lapel.

During the ceremony, the groom presented his bride with a plain gold wedding ring, sometimes engraved with their initials and the date of the wedding; men did not generally receive or wear wedding rings.

Because church law required weddings to occur in the morning, the ceremony was followed by a "wedding breakfast," usually held at the home of the bride, sometimes outdoors in good weather. The wedding cake would be a dark, rich fruitcake with stiff white frosting and elaborate decorations. This hearty cake ages well, and sometimes portions were sent to relatives who could not attend the event; other portions were put away for the first wedding anniversary or the christening of the couple's first child.

Couples who had the means would generally go on a wedding journey or honeymoon. Working-class couples who could afford it would travel to a British resort: Scotland, the seaside, or the Lake District. For couples in the upper middle class, the wedding journey usually involved travel in Europe—to Paris, Rome, or the Alps. Aristocratic couples would often use the honeymoon to introduce the new bride to the outlying branches of the groom's family—or vice versa.

Death and Funerals

Clergymen often visited the sick and dying in their parishes, and the Prayer Book offered specific services for the bedside. While there were no last rites to perform, as in the Roman Catholic tradition, Anglican clergymen were understandably anxious to assure themselves that the dying man or woman had faith in Christ and would be going to heaven. To confirmed Christians on their deathbeds, a visit from the vicar was likely a source of comfort, but to those with less certain faith, it could be painful and disturbing, as the vicar urged the necessity of a saving faith. The ideal Victorian deathbed, however, described repeatedly in memoir and fiction, involved a calm assurance of salvation and anticipation of heavenly life after death.

Most Victorian Christians continued to believe in Hell, though after mid-century some became increasingly uncomfortable with the doctrine of eternal punishment, and Broad Church thinkers went as far as denying that a good God could condemn souls to Hell. Heaven, however, was a much more palatable doctrine, and it maintained its hold on the Victorian imagination. But these were not the only options. While Anglicans rejected the Catholic doctrine of Purgatory, some High Anglicans, including Christina Rossetti, believed in the doctrine of "soul sleep." According to them, the souls of the dead would not go directly to hell or heaven but would instead remain in suspended animation until the Day of Judgment, when their eternal destiny would be pronounced. Whatever happened to the soul, however, Victorians had rules and customs about how to deal with the earthly remains.

In most places in England and Wales, the only legal cemeteries were the Anglican churchyards, and until 1880, people had to be buried according to Anglican rites or in total silence. The funeral service in the Book of Common Prayer began with two Scriptures, one from the New Testament (I John 11:25–26) and one from the Old (Job 19:25–27), which promise life beyond the grave, followed by sterner verses about this earthly life: "We brought nothing into this world, and it is certain we can carry nothing out. The Lord gave, and the Lord hath taken away; blessed be the name of the Lord" (I Timothy 6–7; Job 1:21). Then Psalm 39 and/or Psalm 90 were said or sung, with a doxology, and I Corinthians 15 was read. At this point, if the early part of the service was held in the church, the minister and mourners would accompany the body into the churchyard where the grave had been prepared. After a prayer, during which the body would be lowered into the grave, the mourners would cast soil onto the casket, and the priest would say, "Forasmuch as it hath pleased Almighty God of his great mercy to take unto himself the soul of our dear brother here departed, we therefore commit his body to the ground; earth to earth, ashes to ashes, dust to dust; in sure and certain hope of the Resurrection to eternal life, though our Lord Jesus Christ . . . " This was followed by prayers, particularly for the perseverance of the mourners in the faith.

Despite the focus on the happier condition of the deceased in the afterlife, the rituals were mournful rather than celebratory. Everyone at the funeral was expected to dress in black, and as the century progressed, widows and other close relatives were expected to remain in mourning for an extended period of time.

Because the Anglican Churches held a monopoly over burial sites, they could not easily deny burial to anyone. But the bodies of executed criminals, the unbaptized, and suicides were not supposed to lie in consecrated ground. Suicides posed a particularly difficult problem. Even into the nineteenth century, a person whom the coroner declared guilty of "self-murder" was ritually buried at the crossroads with a stake through his or her heart, a remnant of popular superstition about evil spirits. Most Victorians who committed suicide, however, were humanely declared *non compos mentis*, which saved them from such ignominious burial—but still did not allow them to lie in consecrated ground. Their bodies, along with those of the criminals and the unbaptized, were usually buried in unconsecrated ground on the north side of the churchyard.

Christmas and Easter

Christmas and Easter are the most important holidays on the Christian calendar, Christmas celebrating the incarnation of God as a man and Easter the atoning death of that God-man and his resurrection. Each one involves a season of preparation—the four weeks of Advent before Christmas, and the forty days of Lent before Easter. In spiritual terms, Easter was probably most important for pious Victorian Christians. It was a holiday of darkness as well as light: the Christian had to contemplate the suffering and death of Christ before experiencing the triumphant joy of the resurrection. The Prayer Book specifies services for each day of the week before Easter, and many Christians would attend at least Good Friday services. Evangelicals placed special emphasis on the atoning death of Christ, so this holiday was the most central to their faith.

Christmas, however, was the more important holiday for the less religious culture. It was a holiday with little darkness and much light at a dreary time of the year, and it was able to incorporate pagan midwinter customs with little trouble. Instead of having at its center a violent death, however temporary, it concerned birth, and its imagery was easily conflated with that of Victorian domesticity, the mother holding her baby, with the (nonbiological) father looking on benevolently.

The Victorian Christmas was only in inspiration a religious holiday. Its much-beloved customs were social and familial—the traditional parties with wassail and mince pies, the exchanging of gifts, the Christmas trees that Prince Albert introduced from his German cultural traditions, the family dinner with roast goose or turkey—or in the north of England, even roast beef—and Christmas pudding. The season was personified not by St. Nicholas, as in Europe, but by Father Christmas, who embodied the spirit of the season and appeared in many traditional mumming plays; in the nineteenth century, he adopted from St. Nicholas the custom of bringing gifts to children. Despite all these secular trappings, anyone who ever attended church would expect to go to service on Christmas morning, with the church specially decorated for the celebration, before returning to Christmas dinner. And in Dickens, of course, Christmas—rather than Easter—became associated with moral regeneration, as much for its social as for its religious significance.

5

Religion and Reform

The Victorian period saw itself as an age of improvement and reform, and much of the impetus toward reform came from religious faith. There were, of course, humanitarian as well as explicitly religious motivations for charity and reform: human sympathy operated as well as divine command. But Christians, especially Evangelicals, took the lead in charitable and reforming organizations throughout the century. Some of their causes, such as Sabbath keeping and temperance societies, can seem petty and illiberal to modern readers—and to many Victorians. But other reforms they championed led to fundamental improvements in individual lives and often in the larger society. They wanted to meet both the spiritual and the material needs of their society, and they pursued their goals with enthusiasm and energy. The list of organizations formed is overwhelming and sometimes comic: the London Society for Superseding the Use of Climbing Boys, the Waifs and Strays Society, Flower and Watercress Girls' Mission. Organizations such as these inspired Sir James Stephen to write: "Ours is the age of societies. For every redress of every oppression that is done under the sun, there is a public meeting. For the cure of every sorrow by which our land or our race can be visited, there are patrons, vice-presidents, and secretaries. For the diffusion of every blessing of which mankind can partake in common, there is a committee."[1] But these societies represent the recognition of social problems and the determination to solve them through direct action or through campaigns for legislation, as well as the expression of personal religious commitment. This chapter will outline a few of the most influential Victorian reform movements.

THE ANTISLAVERY MOVEMENT

The movement to abolish slavery originated among the Quakers. In 1783, 300 Quakers signed a parliamentary petition against the slave trade, but with little result. In 1787 a group of Quakers, together with three Anglican Evangelicals (Granville Sharp, Thomas Clarkson, and William Wilberforce) formed the Committee for the Abolition of the Slave Trade. The committee launched a campaign to turn public opinion against the slave trade, collecting evidence of the atrocities of the slave trade, publishing pamphlets detailing the horrors of life aboard slave ships, and sending speakers across Britain to spread the word. One of the most persuasive speakers was Olaudah Equiano, a former slave, who became actively involved in the abolition movement. His autobiography, published in 1789, caused a sensation; it is one of the earliest works published by an African writer and the first autobiography of a slave to gain a significant readership.

One of the most effective and enduring symbols of this public relations campaign was its "logo": the committee approved the design of a seal showing a naked African man in chains "in a supplicating posture," surrounded by the motto: "Am I Not a Man and a Brother?" Josiah Wedgwood, a Quaker himself, made this seal into cameos, which were worn as a political fashion statement by abolitionists in Britain and America. The seal also appeared on the cover of pamphlets and books dedicated to the cause.

A second major goal of the committee was to pass parliamentary legislation banning the slave trade: this goal proved much harder to achieve. Because Quakers were Dissenters and thus banned from serving in Parliament, William Wilberforce, who had been elected MP for Hull in 1780, became the parliamentary leader of the movement. He introduced the first bill for the abolition of the slave trade in 1791; it was soundly defeated. Thereafter, he introduced the same motion every year, only to be defeated again and again. Incremental gains, however, were being made: in 1788 and 1799 legislation was passed to improve the conditions on slave ships, and in 1804 the House of Commons actually passed Wilberforce's motion, but it failed to pass in the House of Lords. It was only in 1807 that the slave trade in Britain and its colonies was finally abolished, and carrying slaves on British ships became illegal.

The antislavery activists then turned their attention to the total abolition of slavery itself, holding meetings across the country. This campaign gained momentum in 1823. That year, Wilberforce published his *Appeal to the Religion, Justice and Humanity of the Inhabitants of the British Empire in Behalf of the Negro Slaves in the West Indies*, and the Society for the Mitigation and Gradual Abolition of Slavery was formed. Wilberforce lived to see the House of Commons pass the Slavery Abolition Act in 1833, though he died before the decision was confirmed by the Lords. From August 1834, when the law took effect, slavery was illegal in Britain and its dominions.

The antislavery movement engaged the attention of many different groups, including some essentially secular humanitarians, but the impetus behind the movement and the enthusiasm that sustained it was religious conviction. Many people, including Quakers and Evangelicals, came to believe that slavery was a violation of God's will and that tolerance of slavery was a national sin, and they worked tirelessly to put an end to it.

THE SUNDAY SCHOOL MOVEMENT

The provision of education in eighteenth-century Britain was haphazard at best, and it was particularly difficult to obtain for working-class children. There were fee-paying day schools that provided rudimentary training in reading, writing, and arithmetic, but many families could afford neither the fees nor the loss of the children's labor on the farm or in the factory. The charity school movement, founded in 1698, provided some free schooling for the children who could be spared from work, but it died away in the early part of the eighteenth century because of lack of funding.

The creation of Sunday schools seemed an obvious solution to the problem: these new schools could provide free education to the poorest children on the one day when they did not work. In the second half of the eighteenth century, Sunday schools sprang up independently in many English towns and villages, founded and financed by concerned individuals and groups. The motives of these founders were varied and often mixed. In his first public announcement about the founding of new Sunday schools in Gloucestershire in 1783, Robert Raikes, the man who did more than anyone else to publicize and spread Sunday schools across England, appealed to many different motivations:

> Some of the clergy in different parts of this county, bent upon attempting a reform among the children of the lower class, are establishing Sunday Schools, for rendering the Lord's day subservient to the ends of instruction, which has hitherto been prostituted to bad purposes. Farmers, and other inhabitants of the towns and villages, complain that they receive more injury to their property on the Sabbath than all the week besides: this in a great measure, proceeds from the lawless state of the younger class, who are allowed to run wild on that day, free from every restraint. To remedy this evil, persons duly qualified are employed to instruct those that cannot read; and those that may have learnt to read are taught the catechism and conducted to church. By thus keeping their minds engaged, the day passes profitably, and not disagreeably. In those parishes where the plan has been adopted, we are assured that the behaviour of the children is greatly civilised. The barbarous ignorance in which they had before lived being in some degree dispelled, they begin to give proofs that those persons are mistaken who consider the lower orders of mankind incapable of improvement, and therefore think an attempt to reclaim them impracticable, or, at least, not worth the trouble.[2]

Here Raikes appeals to Sabbatarian concerns and a desire for law and order, as well as to humanitarian and specifically religious motives.

During this period, religious education was regarded as a central part of the curriculum in all British schools, whether charity schools, day schools, or boarding schools for the middle classes, and the fact that Sunday schools met on the Sabbath increased the proportion of religious teaching deemed proper. In the early days of the Sunday school movement, in the late eighteenth century, Sunday school teachers were hired, often from the ranks of day school teachers, to teach poor students basic reading and religious knowledge; some schools also included writing, though in others writing and arithmetic were forbidden as a breaking of the Sabbath. Sunday schools were accommodated in various places: in private homes, rented rooms, schools or factories closed for the day, or in church buildings. Students would usually have class in the early morning, then be conducted to worship services, then resume study for the afternoon, sometimes attending an evening service as well. Sunday schools were financed entirely by voluntary contributions, with many supporters of the charity schools giving generously to the new Sunday schools. Between 1780 and 1814, 140 Sunday schools were founded, some by individuals, others by groups; some of them were Anglican, others dissenting—Baptist, Methodist, or Congregationalist—still others interdenominational.

The Sunday school movement is sometimes accused of being designed as an institution of social control, attempting to keep the working classes in their place by teaching them religious submission and obedience. Certainly, a desire for an ordered society was among the motivations of some Sunday school founders, but it was not the only or even the primary motivation. Many were genuinely moved by humanitarian concerns and hoped to improve the lot of the poor—both in life and in the afterlife—by providing free education. Moreover, as Philip B. Cliff reminds us, "Sunday Schools were not compulsory; children did not have to attend, and indeed a lot did not. Children could come or go, or join another school, as many did over the writing issue, and it should be noted that when day schools emerged, many children—a very large number of them—attended both day and Sunday School."[3] And while Sunday schools were sometimes "marketed" by an emphasis on the social benefits accruing to their middle-class sponsors, contemporaries were far from seeing them as necessarily conservative in their effect. In fact, at the time of the French Revolution, Sunday schools came under attack for spreading a potentially dangerous literacy to such a large number of working-class people, who could use their skills to read Tom Paine's *Common Sense* (1776) as well as the New Testament.

In the first third of the nineteenth century, the Sunday school movement changed significantly. First, it became more organized: the Sunday School Union, an interdenominational organization founded in 1803, worked to offer support to Sunday schools and improve the standard of teaching. Second, it became much larger: although figures are hard to come by, Thomas Laqueur estimated that the enrollment in English Sunday schools grew from around 200,000 in 1801 to over one million in 1831.[4] Also, Sunday schools began relying on volunteer teachers rather than the paid teachers of the early movement. Queen Charlotte's interest in founding a Sunday school at Windsor and the involvement of her ladies in teaching seem to have been key in making Sunday school teaching respectable for the middle and upper middle classes. Volunteer teachers made the operation of a Sunday school much cheaper and enabled schools to offer places to a greater range of children—no longer just the poorest of the poor, but any working-class child.

The Sunday School Union promoted standardized plans for Sunday schools, and these plans were adopted across the country. Most followed the pattern of this Newcastle version:

> The children are expected to be in their places by 9 o'clock when a teacher begins by singing with them one of the Watt's hymns, he then delivers a short address, and spends a few minutes in prayer. The three exercises occupy only twenty minutes, five for singing, ten for the Address, and five for prayer . . . after the opening service the children immediately go to their classes, with their monitors and teachers. . . .
>
> They read half an hour from twenty past nine till ten minutes before ten o'clock, when a bell is rung as a signal for them to leave their books. Every child who is capable of reading hymns should learn one, or some part of the catechism, each week, which should now be repeated to one of the teachers. Meanwhile those who are not so advanced in reading as to be able to learn off a book, should be employed in repeating Watt's first set of catechism to monitors, who will both ask the questions and give the answers. At twenty minutes past ten the bell is again rung for them to leave their classes and go to their seats for public worship, some of the teachers sitting among them, to observe their behaviour.[5]

The afternoon lessons were to follow the same pattern as the morning. Children were generally taught in sex-segregated classes, the boys' classes taught by men, the girls' classes by women, though the greater availability of women volunteers often led to women teaching boys' classes as well. On average, children received three to five hours of instruction a week, and most were enrolled for a period of three to five years.

In the mid-Victorian period, from 1831 to 1870, Sunday school attendance continued to increase, rising to about three and a half million. Teachers were generally drawn from the members of the sponsoring church; senior scholars were often encouraged to stay on as trainee teachers. More and more churches began to construct buildings to house their Sunday schools, and sometimes day schools as well. The Anglicans formed their own separate Sunday school organization, the Church of England Sunday School Institute, separate from the interdenominational Sunday School Union. In the 1860s a few Sunday schools were formed for middle-class children, but the purpose of Sunday schools continued to be the provision of basic literacy and religious instruction for working-class children until the 1870 Education Act provided for universal education. At that point, Sunday schools began to focus exclusively on their religious teaching and gradually began to include more middle-class children. Though attendance continued to rise with a burgeoning population through the end of the Victorian period, it fell dramatically after the end of the century and, as the Sunday school's *raison d'etre*, the provision of education for the working classes, came under state control, the movement went through a period of revision and readjustment.

During the nineteenth century, however, Sunday schools contributed both to the spread of literacy in the working classes and to the creation of a "respectable" working-class culture, even as they provided opportunities for laypeople, especially women, to contribute to a worthwhile cause and to develop skills of public speaking and leadership.

One fascinating example of a dissenting Sunday school is described in *A Working Woman's Life*, an autobiography by Mary Anne Hearne, who wrote under the pseudonym Marianne Farningham. In 1867 Hearne, a Baptist schoolteacher of relatively humble origin, started a girls' Sunday school class with a small group of young women who worked at the local shoe factory in Northampton. The class soon began to meet on weekday evenings as well as Sundays, for discussion and mutual support; freedom from the restraints of the Sabbath Bible lessons allowed for fuller discussion of members' lives and problems. The class became what we would now describe as a support group for young, single, workingwomen. But when members grew older or married, they refused to "graduate," so membership grew to include between 180 and 200 single and married women of all ages. The women of the class established a strike-fund to support members in case of a strike or a lockout at the shoe factory, as well as a thrift society where women could invest their savings at 5 percent interest or take out loans at similar rates. Thus women without access to conventional banks could borrow money for emergencies and, if they wished, for capital investment. But money was not only available on the terms of the capitalist economy: the class also used its money to support sick and indigent members. Members even took their annual holiday together, departing *en masse* for their furnished cottage in the country. In 1887, still going strong, they had a classroom built for their use and, aided by donations from James Clarke, a Christian publisher, established a class library. As teacher of this class Hearne honed her speaking and administrative skills, eventually finding success as a public speaker, as a writer of poetry and fiction, and as editor of the *Sunday School Times*.[6] While these results were not typical of the movement as a whole, they do testify to the potential of the Sunday school movement to encourage the development of women's skills and of working-class culture.

TEMPERANCE MOVEMENT

While the temperance movement, with its reputation for moral absolutism and its calls for prohibition, is for many modern readers the least attractive face of Victorian religious reform, it is important to bear in mind that the problem the movement sought to solve—drunkenness in the working classes—was a real one with serious consequences for society.

Employers clearly regarded drunkenness in their employees as a problem. While in an agricultural economy, a hungover worker could often take time to recover, the tighter schedules of factory work—not to mention the dangers of working around heavy equipment—made it important that workers remain awake and alert on the job.

Moreover, excessive drinking exacerbated poverty. Antidrink campaigners regularly told stories of men who drank up their wages on the way home, leaving their families with no money for groceries, rent, or medical care, and, though these temperance workers were sometimes guilty of exaggeration, they weren't indulging in fiction. Even those who sympathized with the conditions under which the men lived—the overcrowded housing, the mind-numbing work, the need for escape—saw that drink tended in the long run to increase their misery rather than relieve it.

Temperance also became a feminist issue. Until the passage of the Married Women's Property Act in 1870, a married woman had no rights over the marital property or even her own wages: an alcoholic husband could spend his wife's earnings on drink, and even sell the household furniture, and she had no legal right to object. Moreover, as police departments even today note, drinking tends to increase the prevalence and severity of domestic violence. So women often became avid campaigners to control the destructive drinking habits of men, and eventually organized themselves in the British Women's Temperance Association.

Finally, many people claimed that the direst consequences of excessive drinking were suffered by the drinkers themselves. Drinking tended to sink them deeper in poverty, undermine their health, and discourage the active pursuit of a better life, whether through individual effort or through political reform.

The earliest stage of the temperance movement, beginning in 1830, actually called for temperance, the use of alcohol in moderation, rather than abstinence; it promoted the drinking of beer and wine rather than hard liquor, and encouraged individual self-control. It was led by religious middle-class men who saw themselves as promoting the welfare of the working classes by fostering in them the middle-class values of self-regulation and delayed gratification. Many of these first-stage reformers were dissenting or Anglican Evangelicals from the north of England. While they did not preach total abstinence, some became teetotalers themselves in order to set a good example for the working classes. Drinking became for them what was generally called a "weaker brother" issue; the biblical support came from Romans 14, where Paul enjoins the early church, "Let us not therefore judge one another any more: but judge this rather, that no man put a stumbling block or an occasion to fall in his brother's way.... It is good neither to eat flesh, nor to drink wine, nor any thing whereby thy brother stumbleth, or is offended, or is made weak" (Romans 14:13, 21). While these reformers saw nothing wrong with drinking in moderation, they saw that drinking had terrible consequences for others and refrained themselves in order not to hinder those "weaker brothers" in their attempts to live better lives. In 1830 alone, twenty temperance societies were founded.

The move to total abstinence came originally not from the middle classes but from Dissenters in the working classes. Joseph Livesey was a Preston weaver turned cheese-merchant. Raised a Baptist, he remained all his life a dedicated Christian, and one deeply concerned with the welfare of the working classes. Seeing drink as one of the major problems bedeviling working men and preventing them from improving their lives, he and seven Preston workers took a pledge never again to drink alcohol and in 1835 formed the British Association for the Promotion of Temperance. Temperance societies dedicated to total abstinence proliferated, many of them initiated and sustained by Dissenters, especially Baptists and Congregationalists. The Wesleyan Methodists opposed this extreme approach, forbidding the use of their chapels for temperance meetings, but the Primitive Methodists and Bible Christians were early adopters, becoming active in the temperance movement. The Church of England was also reluctant to join with the advocates of abstinence, and no Anglican temperance organization existed until 1873, when the Church of England Temperance Society was founded, albeit with accommodation for moderate drinkers as well as teetotalers.

Temperance groups promoted abstinence by publishing tracts and magazines, providing alternative alcohol-free places of recreation for the working classes, and encouraging people to sign pledges to refrain from all alcohol. The Band of Hope, founded in Leeds, focused on persuading children as young as six to take the pledge; members of the Band would then meet once a week and participate in organized activities, sometimes including outings and trips to the seaside.

In Ireland, a Catholic priest, Theobald Matthew, was a one-man temperance league, traveling across the country and convincing hundreds of thousands of people to sign the pledge.

Some of these many temperance organizations were founded by workingmen and women specifically concerned with the conditions and social position of their class. There were even Chartist temperance groups that saw drunkenness as a barrier to the achievement of full political rights for the working classes, both because it cast doubt on working-class respectability and responsibility, and because it was an "opiate of the people," numbing them to their situation rather than helping them improve it.

The final stage of the Victorian temperance movement was inaugurated in 1853 with the founding of the United Kingdom Alliance. While earlier temperance workers, whether middle-class or working-class, focused mainly on encouraging individuals to change their ways, these new organizations fought for legislation to limit and, ideally, eliminate alcohol altogether. While prohibition was never a serious threat in Britain, these groups did manage to pass the Licensing Act of 1872, which cut opening hours for pubs significantly, and attempted to close pubs altogether on the Sabbath, though this provision was defeated.

This drawing from the *Illustrated London News* shows a gathering of the Bands of Hope (the children's temperance organizations) in Exeter Hall, an event organized by the London Temperance League (*Illustrated London News*, February 21, 1852).

These activists tended to be middle-class, and the working classes generally resented the imposition of laws that restricted their freedoms. The middle-class reformers also left themselves open to charges of hypocrisy and double standards, since the Alliance did not require members to abstain from alcohol.

By the turn of the twentieth century, the temperance movement in Britain had lost much of its momentum. In many ways, it was clearly a failure: it never came close to achieving prohibition, and it probably failed even to reduce the overall levels of drinking. It did, however, manage to pass some milder legislation and to alter social attitudes toward drinking and public drunkenness. But it also left its mark on Christianity in Britain, increasing the reputation of evangelicals as killjoys and, late in the century, further alienating working-class men from religious practice. In addition, some religious groups, including the Methodists, remained linked with abstinence through much of the twentieth century.

FACTORY REFORM: LORD SHAFTESBURY

After William Wilberforce became ill, his place as leader of the Evangelicals in Parliament was assumed by Lord Ashley, later the seventh Earl of Shaftesbury. Shaftesbury approached legislation on moral issues with the same fervor and determination as Wilberforce had. Although he worked tirelessly on a variety of causes, including the education of the poor, reform of working conditions for young chimney sweeps, and the opium question, his most lasting legacy is the factory legislation he championed during his time in Parliament.

After their successful campaign to abolish slavery, Evangelicals in Parliament turned their attention to the sufferings of the nominally free industrial workers of Britain, particularly in the textile industry. Working conditions were often harsh and dangerous, working hours were long, and children as young as six were employed: the case for better regulation might seem strong. But the dominant economic theory urged that government leave the economy alone—*laissez faire*—and Parliament was reluctant to infringe upon the freedom of the factory owners or the workers.

Nevertheless, the Evangelicals under Shaftesbury managed to pass the Factory Act of 1833, which limited the employment of children and regulated child labor practices. It forbade the employment of children under nine in almost all textile factories; limited children eleven and under to a forty-eight-hour work-week and a nine-hour workday and required the provision of some schooling for these workers; limited young workers eleven to eighteen years old to a sixty-nine-hour week and a twelve-hour day; and established inspectors to enforce the rules set out by the act. These inspectors became useful in monitoring conditions in factories for all workers.

It took more years of relentless campaigning to achieve further reforms, but eventually Parliament was persuaded to pass the Shaftesbury's Ten Hours Act (1847), which limited women and children under eighteen to a ten-hour workday. Shaftesbury also proposed and helped pass regulations on the labor of women and children in coalmines through the 1842 Mines Act. These reforms were incremental and focused on workers that Parliament saw as vulnerable (that is, women and children); no limitation was placed on adult men. But they were nevertheless important, both for their immediate effect and for the regulatory precedent they set.

Shaftesbury and his fellow Anglican Evangelicals regarded factory legislation as part of their Christian duty; as he said, "to me it appeared an affair less of policy than of religion."

HOUSING REFORM: OCTAVIA HILL

While Evangelicals in Parliament worked for humane legislation in keeping with their Christian values, some other Christian reformers remained suspicious of government interference and preferred to try to reform society through private action. Some of this suspicion may have been due to reigning laissez faire economic theory, but some stemmed from a concern that government action could relieve only material hardships, and that real social improvement required spiritual regeneration as well. For these reasons, Octavia Hill's work on housing reform began as a small-scale private charity; only later did she come to see the need for more comprehensive government action.

Hill was raised in a liberal Unitarian family dedicated to social engagement and alleviating the suffering of others. Her independent mother imbued her with a strong work ethic and no ladylike reluctance to earn money or perform physical labor. As a teenager, she began to attend F.D. Maurice's Anglican services at Lincoln's Inn, and she came under the influence of Maurice and the Christian Socialist movement. She soon converted to Anglicanism, finding in the divine figure of Christ a model of the kind of self-giving that should characterize a healthy and equitable Christian community.

As she taught and worked beside working-class women in London, Hill saw firsthand the results of inadequate and unsanitary housing in their lives. In 1864, with money loaned to her by John Ruskin, she purchased the lease on three dilapidated houses in the worst section of Marylebone and refurbished them, naming them Paradise Place. She acquired tenants, offering a reasonable rent for clean and well-kept rooms, and then set out to serve as a paradigm of a good landlord. She dealt with her tenants as individuals rather than as charity cases, collecting the rents herself every week and getting to know their lives and conditions. She helped them find jobs and offered advice. She worked to make them self-sufficient individuals, but within the context of a supportive Christian community. Soon she bought a further six houses, and then eleven more in 1869. Others began buying houses to place under her control, and even the Ecclesiastical Commissioners asked her to assume management of their tenement houses and consulted her about refurbishing them.

Through her housing reform, she believed herself to be doing God's work, and that conviction empowered her to act:

> "Break out a window there in that dark corner; let God's light and air in" or, "Trap that foul drain, and shut the poisonous miasma out"; and one has the moral power to say, by deeds, which speak louder than words, "Where God gives me authority, this, which you in your own hearts know to be wrong, shall not go on. I would not set my conviction, however strong it might be, against your judgment of right but when you are doing what I know your own conscience condemns, I, now that I have the power, will enforce right!"[7]

Her power to enforce right—and her influence in important circles—continued to increase through the end of the period. She was appointed to the Central Commission of the Charity Organization Society, which coordinated the efforts of all the London charities. The COS inevitably became involved in campaigning for government action, including involving the London authorities in the provision of low-cost housing. Hill was also consulted in the creation of the Artisans' Dwelling Bill of 1875, which gave local authorities the right to buy slum houses, demolish them, and construct improved housing in their place. Late in her life, she helped to found the National Trust. But all of this she saw as part of her responsibility as a Christian woman to do God's

Octavia Hill established Red Cross Gardens in 1887 as "an open-air sitting room for the tired inhabitants of Southwark," and built next to it six model cottages and a community hall with a reading room, a library, a concert hall, and meeting facilities. This picture appears in C. Edmund Maurice, *Life of Octavia Hill* (London: Macmillan, 1913).

work on earth, relieving suffering, preserving natural beauty for the sake of all, and creating healthy communities where Christian life was possible for everyone.

"FALLEN WOMEN"

The Magdalen Hospital at Whitechapel, London, founded in 1758, was the first English institution dedicated to the rescue and reform of prostitutes. Through the middle of the nineteenth century, most such institutions were run by either the Church of England or the Roman Catholic Church, and they were based on the "penitentiary system." As the name implies, the prostitutes in these institutions were regarded as penitent sinners, required to pray and worship multiple times a day, and sometimes housed in relatively harsh conditions. The 1840s and 1850s, however, saw increasing concern over prostitution and the wretched lives of the prostitutes themselves, and dozens of new institutions were founded: by 1885, the Church of England ran at least fifty-three penitentiaries, and there was at least one institution dedicated to the reform of

prostitutes in every city and large town. And, although penitentiaries continued to be founded, notably by new religious orders of women, there was also a
challenge to the penitentiary system. The Evangelicals disliked the institutional
setting and instead pioneered the "family home system": under this system,
small numbers of prostitutes would be housed together in an environment that
mirrored as closely as possible Victorian domesticity. All reformers, however,
sought to solve the women's economic as well as spiritual problems by training them to serve as domestic servants or to run their own households in the
future. Most refuges ran laundries that helped support the institution even as
they offered on-the-job training for inmates.

One of the most famous examples of the family style refuge was Urania
Cottage. Founded by the evangelically inclined Anglican philanthropist Angela
Burdett-Coutts, with backing and advice from Charles Dickens, Urania Cottage
sought to rehabilitate prostitutes using a regime famous for its liberality and
kindness. A small group of women—in 1861, exactly ten—lived in the pleasant
cottage, which had a flower garden and even a piano. They had worship services twice daily, and they honed their domestic skills—sewing, cooking, and
tending the garden—in preparation, it was hoped, for marriages somewhere in
the British colonies. Like many of the Evangelical institutions, Urania Cottage
stressed the importance of treating the women as individuals rather than examples of a larger social evil. High Church reformers as well, such as activist and
novelist Felicia Skene, also supported this kind of individualized and humane
refuge to help "fallen women" reenter society.

While all such institutions regarded the women as sinners who needed to
repent, many reformers also saw them as victims, both of an economic and
educational system that left poor women few options, and of a pervasive double
standard that accepted premarital sexual experience in men but harshly condemned it in women. Anger about the double standard came to a head with the
passage of the Contagious Diseases Acts in 1864, 1866, and 1869. These acts
were intended as public health measures to reduce the transmission of venereal
diseases, particularly in the armed services. The 1864 Act allowed police in
twelve specific garrison towns and ports to stop any woman suspected of being
a prostitute and subject her to a genital examination. If she refused the examination, she was arrested and imprisoned. If the exam revealed venereal disease,
she could be forced to remain in a "lock hospital" for up to three months. In
1869 the law increased the maximum period in hospital to nine months and
extended the coverage to six additional cities—and some advocates suggested
an extension to the whole of the country.

These laws infuriated Christians and feminists—and particularly Christian
feminists such as Josephine Butler, who founded the Ladies' National Association for the Repeal of the Contagious Diseases Acts. The laws endorsed the
double standard, both by imposing the forcible examination and institution-
alization on women rather than their military clients, and by tacitly accepting men's sexual exploitation of this class of women. They also threatened

"respectable" women as well as "fallen" women, since any woman suspected of being a prostitute—that is, any woman walking on certain city streets—could be subjected to such humiliating treatment. Butler saw her opposition to the Acts as a mission from God: her memoir of the battle for repeal is called *Personal Reminiscences of a Great Crusade* (1896), and she implicitly compares herself to John the Baptist in the title of her 1875 book, *The Voice of One Crying in the Wilderness*. She saw her work as ushering in a millennium of peace and justice:

> The light of day will fall upon all the dark places of the earth, now full of the habitations of cruelty, and there shall come forth, at the call of the Deliverer, the thousands and tens of thousands of the daughters of men now enslaved in all lands to cruelty and lust. There will be no more hollow virtues, no more specious and splendid crimes. None shall ever again rejoice at another's expense, or hold advantages bought by the blood and tears of his fellow; but "rising in inherent majesty, the Redeemer's Kingdom will strengthen and extend, wide as the limits of nature's boundary, far as sin has diffused its poison."[8]

Here she uses prophetic rhetoric to denounce prostitution and to align her cause with God's will. Partly as a result of Butler's own writing, public speaking, and tireless leadership of the organization she built, the Contagious Diseases Acts were repealed in 1886. She then went on to campaign against child prostitution with William Thomas Stead, a campaign that eventually convinced Parliament to raise the age of consent from thirteen to sixteen. Although she endured powerful opposition, criticism for her unfeminine public work, and even occasional physical attacks, she was inspired by her faith to continue to work toward a vision of right and justice: as she is reported to have said, "God and one woman make a majority."

EVANGELISM: HOME MISSIONS

Although many Christians sought to improve people's lives in this transitory world, they were necessarily more concerned about the fate of their souls in the next, and many Christian efforts were aimed at spreading the gospel, both at home and abroad. The Religious Tract Society and the British and Foreign Bible Society, which will be more closely examined in the next chapter, hoped to save the British population—and, eventually, the world—by distributing Bibles and other religious literature. Other organizations dedicated their efforts to evangelizing specific groups such as the armed forces (Army Scripture Reader and Soldiers' Friend Society; Royal Naval Scripture Readers' Society) or seamen (Missions to Seamen; Seamen's Mission and School). The British Society for the Propagation of the Gospel among the Jews and the London Society for Promoting Christianity amongst the Jews focused on bringing about the conversion of the Jews, a good in itself and also a step, many believed, toward the second coming of Christ. Many organizations, including the London City Mission, the London Domestic Mission, the Scripture Readers' Association, and the Christian Men's Union Gospel Mission, not to mention scores of dedicated High Church clergymen, sought to take the gospel to the unchurched working classes.

Among the longest-lasting and most successful of these missions to the working classes was the Salvation Army. The founders of the Salvation Army, William and Catherine Booth, were both raised in Methodist families as serious evangelical Christians, though they moved away from Wesleyan Methodism and its respectable conservatism as they became more radical in their evangelism. Both of them became successful gospel preachers, and in 1865 they founded the East London Christian Mission, dedicated to evangelizing the poorest people in London, including populations that other religious groups deemed unreachable. Their simple and egalitarian version of the Christian gospel met with a strong response, and branches of the mission were formed in urban slums across the country. By 1878, the organization had more than 800 workers. In that year, it was reorganized along quasi-military lines, with the local preachers as officers and Booth himself as general.

Much of the Salvation Army's success was due to its harnessing of the energy of women, who served at every level of the organization. Although the women preachers aroused opposition from more conventional religious denominations, they also provided the organization with reserves of enthusiasm and talent untapped by much of mainstream Christianity. As William Booth put it, "My best men are women!"

To reach the urban poor, the Salvation Army abandoned the decorum of middle-class church services in favor of a louder, brasher form of worship, which included the famous brass bands, street performances, and fiery open-air preaching. The Army also became active in broader reform movements, including temperance movements, Stead's campaign against child prostitution, and campaigns against "sweated labour."

Although the Salvation Army's emphasis shifted in the last decade of the century, as it began focusing more on social work and less on direct evangelism, it survived the Victorian era with much of its mission intact and, like the London City Mission, continues its work even today.

Not all efforts at home missions were homegrown, however. Dwight Moody, the American evangelist, together with Ira Sankey, the talented gospel singer who led the music for Moody's services, toured Britain twice in the second half of the nineteenth century, each time preaching to large crowds and stimulating widespread conversion. He began his first tour in 1873, preaching to relatively small groups in York: he then preached in other cities in the North of England to ever-increasing crowds before moving on to Scotland, where he was greeted with enthusiasm by enormous crowds who gathered to hear him preach. In the fall of 1874, he went to Ireland where, to the dismay of Roman Catholic clergy, he won converts from among the Catholic population. He then returned to England, preaching in Manchester, Sheffield, Birmingham, Liverpool, and finally London. At the start of his tour, he preached in chapels, but as interest grew, the services had to be moved to public halls to accommodate the crowds. Even in larger cities, local organizers struggled to find venues with sufficient capacity to hold the huge numbers of people who flocked to see him. Admission had to be regulated by the distribution of free tickets, and even so crowds would start gathering at least an hour before meetings were scheduled to begin. In smaller towns, such as Aberdeen, which lacked large public buildings, Moody would have to preach in the open air. In other places, temporary halls had to be purpose-built for the revival meetings.

Wherever they went, Moody and Sankey received support from Dissenters and from some Evangelical Anglicans. In Scotland, he was welcomed by Free Church minister Andrew Bonar; in London, one of his primary sponsors was Baptist preacher Charles Spurgeon.

His services produced thousands of new converts, and Moody conscientiously put them in touch with local congregations that could provide them continued support. He also inspired many British Christians to redouble their efforts at evangelism and charitable work. He gave particular impetus to the YMCA movement, promoting it at his meetings and helping to raise money.

By the end of his first British and Irish tour, Moody had preached hundreds of times, conducting over 285 meetings in London alone, and he had been heard by millions of people. And, though some Britons reacted to his American-style revivalism with distaste, others responded with enthusiasm. His inspirational preaching and the upbeat revival music of Ira Sankey's *Sacred Songs and Solos* had a powerful effect on British Christianity.

EVANGELISM: FOREIGN MISSIONS

At the beginning of the eighteenth century, two British organizations were promoting the spread of Christianity abroad: the Society for the Promotion of Christian Knowledge (SPCK), which encouraged the work of the Anglican Church in British colonies, particularly in North America, and the Society for the Propagation of the Gospel in Foreign Parts (SPG), which worked to send religious literature to British colonies. But mission work expanded significantly with the growth of Methodism and Evangelicalism, and in the 1790s, many new organizations dedicated to foreign missions were founded, including the Baptist Missionary Society (1792), the Edinburgh and Glasgow Missionary Societies (1796), the Church Missionary Society, which was originally called the Society for Missions to Africa and the East (1799), and, most importantly, the interdenominational London Missionary Society (1795). The founders of these groups were motivated by a desire to take Christianity's message of salvation and eternal life in heaven to people around the world, to save their souls and bring them knowledge of God. As Baptist missionary William Carey wrote in 1792:

> It must undoubtedly strike every considerate mind, what a vast proportion of the sons of Adam there are, who yet remain in the most deplorable state of heathen darkness, without any means of knowing the true God, except what are afforded them by the works of nature; and utterly destitute of the knowledge of the gospel of Christ, or of any means of obtaining it.[9]

In cooperation with missions groups on the European continent, these new missions organizations sent missionaries to Tahiti, the West Indies, Africa, Bengal (in India and also what is now Bangladesh), Canada, and New Zealand. They regarded the expansion of Britain's empire and sphere of influence as a providential opportunity to take the gospel to the newly opened areas of the world. They also saw the growth of British possessions abroad as laying upon them special responsibilities for the people of those territories. Nevertheless, in the early nineteenth century, missionaries were generally determined to remain independent of political and imperial power, and they tried to avoid political entanglements, though organizations such as the Society for the Propagation of the Gospel (SPG), which were closely tied to the Anglican Church and, consequently, to the British government, found this particularly difficult. Often, missionaries found themselves at odds with the local authorities. In the early nineteenth century many missionaries to the West Indies, especially Methodists, openly opposed the slavery practiced there, and they were hated and harassed by the slave-owning colonists and barely tolerated by the government. The East India Company effectively barred missionary activities in India for many years, fearing that their commercial interests would be hurt by controversy over proselytizing among Muslims and Hindus. In many places, missionaries felt obliged to denounce the behavior of colonists toward native populations, not only on humanitarian grounds, but also because it brought Christianity itself into disrepute and made their efforts at evangelism more difficult.

Whatever their initial intentions, however, missionaries found themselves drawn willy-nilly into imperial politics. Missionaries found that, whatever their dreams of independence, in reality they needed the support, or at least the tolerance, of imperial authorities to continue their work. In some places, such as South Africa and New Zealand, they even argued for the extension of British imperial power as a way of controlling the cruelties and injustices practiced upon the natives by the local authorities. In order to gain access to many mission fields, including India, missionaries also began to use rhetoric that appealed to British self-interest, arguing that missions was central to the "civilising" mission of the British people, which included not only religion but also commerce and empire.

Despite the friction between the nationalistic goals of empire and the universalist outlook of Christian missions, organizations continued to send missionaries and do what they could, given the conditions in each new territory. In most places, they aimed to train native ministers and set up self-supporting native churches. In some countries they supplemented their evangelical missions with medical missionaries or educational programs: in India, missionaries attempted to attract converts by offering English-language education to urbanized Indians. Gradually, as the empire expanded and transport improved, missionaries went to new mission fields, including the Middle East and China.

Many of these missionaries were women; in fact, by the last decade of the nineteenth century, most British missionaries were women. The mission field offered women opportunities for travel, work, and leadership denied them in Britain; they were valued for their work with native women and children, especially teaching and medical care. Andrew Porter reports that the work of women missionaries "significantly reinforced the trend . . . toward the practical concern with welfare,"[10] as opposed to an earlier, narrower focus on direct evangelism.

On the home front, women, men, and even children mobilized to help the missionaries in the field, feeling themselves part of an important international movement. They contributed money to the missionary societies, headed up local auxiliaries, and subscribed to missionary periodicals—the *Church Missionary Intelligencer*, the *Juvenile Missionary Herald*, *Mission Field*, *Medical Missions at Home and Abroad*, as well as avidly reading articles and books about missionary adventures. Missionaries in Britain on furlough were eagerly sought as speakers, and whether they reported success or failure, their visits galvanized supporters to new efforts. But in the minds of many Britons their work also provided moral justification for Britain's imperial mission, so that they ended up inadvertently lending support to the very imperial authorities with whom they were so often at odds.

Most Victorians did not see religion as a matter merely of individual salvation and private worship. For many, religious faith was a dynamic force that found its outlet in efforts to reshape the world, whether through individual activity, communal organizations, or legislative reform. The legacy of Victorian religious life, therefore, must be sought not only in the churches and synagogues, the hymns and sermons, but also in the parliamentary record, the minutes of countless committees, and the daily lives of thousands of charity workers, reformers, and campaigners who were inspired by their private faith to public action.

6

The Bible and Other Bestsellers

The 1611 King James translation of the Bible had long been a bestseller in Britain, but its astounding sales in the nineteenth century owed a great deal to a concerted advertising campaign surpassing the wildest dreams of authorship. Evangelicals, in particular, wanted to see a Bible in every household, preferably in every hand. They believed in the Bible as the inspired word of God, and they believed that, with the aid of the Holy Spirit, its meaning would be plain to any person exposed to it. So the distribution of Bibles—without any further missionary efforts—could effect the salvation of the world. That is why Evangelicals put so much effort into producing and distributing English Bibles, and into translating the Bible into hundreds of languages for foreign missions. Many organizations were formed for the purpose by various denominations, but the most powerful and effective was an interdenominational organization, the British and Foreign Bible Society (BFBS).

The British and Foreign Bible Society was formed in 1804 by a committee of the Religious Tract Society, "To promote the circulation of the Holy Scriptures in foreign countries and in those parts of the British Dominions for which adequate provision is not yet made, it being understood that no English translations of the Scriptures will be gratuitously circulated by the Society in Great Britain." The sale of Bibles, rather than their free distribution, was central to the society's domestic mission. Like many Victorians, they feared that handouts would "pauperize" the poor, leading to a loss of self-respect and self-reliance. They also thought that people would tend to undervalue things that cost them nothing, and they did not want the Bible to suffer that fate. So instead they sold the working classes cheap Bibles: at the beginning of the century, two shillings, which represented the cost of production plus 5 percent for handling. This amount was payable in installments of a penny per week, which was collected

In Thomas Jones Barker's painting, "The Secret of England's Greatness" (1863), Queen Victoria presents a Bible to a kneeling African chief as Prince Albert looks on (National Portrait Gallery, London).

by members of local Auxiliaries and Associations of the Bible Society, often women. The Bibles found a willing market among the working classes, and the number of Bibles distributed rose to over a quarter of a million a year. By 1835, the BFBS had 269 auxiliaries, 347 branches, and 1,541 associations spread across the country.

The BFBS was committed to distributing Bibles without notes or commentary, which allowed people of different denominations to cooperate in the effort. There was controversy, however, over the Apocrypha, the books included in the Roman Catholic Bible, but regarded as noncanonical—and thus not divinely inspired—by the vast majority of Protestants. The Anglican and Lutheran Bibles included the apocryphal books, but in a section at the back of the Bible separate from the canonical books; the Presbyterian Bible, and that accepted by most dissenters, eliminated these books altogether. The BFBS gladly eliminated the Apocrypha from Bibles designed for the British market, but Bible Societies on the Continent needed Bibles that included the Apocrypha for their European missions, and Presbyterian members of the BFBS balked, eventually leaving the organization and founding their own Bible Society.

The BFBS also distributed numerous Bibles in foreign languages, including Mohawk (a new translation), French, German, Portuguese, Dutch, Danish, ancient and modern Greek, Manx, Spanish, Ethiopic, Norwegian, Arabic, Polish, Lithuanian, Gaelic, Russian, Finnish, and Chinese. In fact, when Prince Albert turned down Lord Shaftesbury's request that the BFBS be given display space at the 1851 Great Exhibition on the grounds that the exhibition was devoted to scientific progress rather than religion, Shaftesbury argued that the fact that the society now had 170 versions in 130 languages represented exactly the right sort of human progress. Prince Albert agreed, and the BFBS displayed at the Great Exhibition a bookcase twenty-three feet long and nine feet high containing all these works.

The BFBS also gave birth to another utterly unique Bible distribution system—and, arguably, to the first corps of paid social workers. These were the Biblewomen, working-class women hired by the Bible Society to sell Bibles in working-class households and collect the weekly payments. According to the founder and organizer of the Biblewomen, Ellen Ranyard, these women were the "missing link" between the higher and lower classes, able to visit in homes where ladies and even clergymen might be intimidating: "Having observed the power of NATIVE AGENCY in Foreign Missions, it also struck her that a good poor woman, chosen from among the classes she wished explored, would probably be the most welcome visitor; while, as a paid agent, she could be kindly and firmly, though perhaps invisibly, directed as circumstances might require."[1] These Biblewomen could also offer practical help and advice that ladies, coming from such different social circumstances, could not; so the organization consisted of Lady Superintendents, who oversaw the work and handled the finances, and Biblewomen, who visited in the homes of the poor. They gave advice on hygiene and child rearing, provided recipes for cheap and nourishing soups, and sometimes distributed clothing or blankets donated for the purpose. As Leslie Howsam puts it, "The biblewomen were the first paid social workers in the history of the profession, and their work might well have been impossible without the obscuring veil of Bible distribution."[2] But for Ellen Ranyard and her workers, the Bible distribution was more than an "obscuring veil"—it was providing another, longer-lasting kind of nutrition, food for the soul in addition to food for the body.

Cheap Bibles from the BFBS, for all their popularity, were not the only Bibles in high demand. Originally intended to insure quality in reproduction, English law allowed only three presses to print and distribute the King James Bible: Oxford University Press, Cambridge University Press, and the Queen's Printer. All three did well out of this monopolistic arrangement: while orders from the BFBS occupied their presses much of the time, they also sold thousands of Bibles on their own part, in various bindings from the simplest to the most expensive. But the legal restriction applied only to Bibles published without any extra materials; Bibles with commentary or other material added could be published by anyone. Other publishers took advantage of this exception to produce Bibles for the higher end of the market—nicely bound, lavishly illustrated volumes, with commentaries, maps, concordances, and other extras. These were often designed as family Bibles, with pages designated for family records. These Bibles were used for domestic devotions and also served as a mark of respectability for those aspiring to join the middle class.

The total number of Bibles sold in the Victorian era would be hard to determine, since so many editions and publishers were involved. But figures from the three "Privileged Presses" can give some sense of the huge numbers involved. In the first ten years of the Queen's reign, from 1837 to 1847, the three presses collectively produced 5,792,770 Bibles and 5,145,727 copies of the New Testament alone—over half a million of each per year.

OTHER RELIGIOUS BESTSELLERS

While Evangelicals emphasized the centrality and uniqueness of the Bible as God's revelation, Tractarians and other high churchmen were anxious that the Bible be read alongside—and in accordance with—the *Book of Common Prayer*, which was another religious bestseller. By the nineteenth century prayer books were generally available for use in churches, but many Anglicans owned their own copy for use during services as well as for private or family devotions.

Another book often bought for use in private devotions was John Keble's 1827 collection of poetry, *The Christian Year*. The volume follows the Christian calendar and provides poems for each holy day, from Advent Sunday through Whitsunweek to St. Peter's Day. Several of the poems also became popular hymns, including "New Every Morning Is the Love," taken from Keble's poem for "Morning"; "Sun of My Soul, Thou Saviour Dear," taken from his poem for "Evening"; and "There Is a Book, Who Runs May Read," taken from his poem for Septuagesima Sunday.[3] The volume went through multiple editions and continued selling well through the century: by 1868, it had sold 265,000 copies and continued selling an average of 10,000 copies a year.

The sales of this book, aimed at a middle-class readership, were dwarfed, however, by the sales of tracts designed for a working-class audience. In 1799, the Religious Tract Society had been formed to publish and distribute these evangelical tracts—generally free of charge—among the literate of the working classes. Evangelicals handed them out everywhere—not only at revival meetings, but also in train compartments, shops, omnibuses, and prisons. They were also used by Sunday schools as easy reading material for readers not yet ready to take on the language of the King James Bible. One of the best-selling tracts, *The Sinner's Friend*, published in 1821, sold more than 800,000 copies by 1845 and was translated into many foreign languages, including 20,000 copies destined for Tahiti.[4] In general, though, these tracts were not bought by their readers but purchased for free distribution, and perhaps ought to be considered a special category of bestseller.

Collections of sermons also sold remarkably well in the nineteenth century, often outselling even novels. Some were sold to ministers wanting ready-made sermons when their own inspiration failed, but sermon collections were also popular Sunday reading material. Famous preachers such as J.H. Newman, E.B. Pusey, or Charles H. Spurgeon, could easily sell thousands of copies of their collections, but a large number of more obscure clergymen also had books on the market that generated respectable sales. Spurgeon's most impressive sales came in periodical form: his three Sunday sermons were taken down, corrected, and published weekly in the *Metropolitan Tabernacle Pulpit*, which sold 25,000 copies a week.[5]

Other religious periodicals also enjoyed large circulations. Of course, many mainstream periodicals reviewed religious books and covered religious topics, but it is relatively easy to identify those periodicals that covered only religious topics or covered all their topics from a particular religious point of view. There were huge numbers of such periodicals, including highbrow quarterlies, middlebrow monthlies, and the more popular (and cheaper) weekly periodicals. Every denomination and church party had its own periodical, and many charities and church-related organizations published their own magazines with updates on their work. Some of the more important titles include the *Christian Observer* (1802–1877), a moderate Anglican Evangelical monthly, with a moderate circulation of about 1,000; the *Record* (1828–present), a radically Evangelical anti-Catholic newspaper, with a larger circulation of 4,000; the High Church *Christian Remembrancer* (1819–1868), which became a quarterly in 1845; *The Tablet* (1840–present), the primary Roman Catholic periodical; and the monthly *Wesleyan Methodist Magazine* (1822–1914), which, starting as *Arminian Magazine* in 1778 and continuing today as *Methodist Magazine* (1914–present), is "the oldest surviving religious periodical in the world."[6] After the repeal of the Stamp Tax in 1855 made it possible to distribute periodicals much more cheaply, religious penny newspapers flourished. The Roman Catholic *Universe* (1860–present) and the High Anglican *Church Times* (1863–present) at their height reached 100,000 people per issue. James Clarke's interdenominational evangelical newspaper, *The Christian World*, eventually reached a circulation of 120,000 copies a week.

A surprising number of these periodicals were edited by women. Evangelical Charlotte Elizabeth Tonna edited the *Christian Lady's Magazine* from 1834 to 1846. For over forty years, from 1851 to 1894, High Church novelist Charlotte M. Yonge edited the *Monthly Packet*, a magazine for Anglican youth. And Emma Jane Worboise was editor of James Clarke's monthly the *Christian World Magazine* from its foundation in 1866 until 1886. These magazines not only published many articles, poems, and serialized novels by women, but also encouraged a sense of community and of empowerment among Christian readers, especially women readers.

IMAGINATIVE LITERATURE

Bibles, prayer books, sermons, even religious periodicals, are all uncontroversial examples of religious literature. But in the genres of poetry and fiction, the distinction between religious and secular literature is not so clear. After all, much of mainstream Victorian literature, from Dickens to Brontë to Meredith, uses religious language and addresses spiritual themes, and many Victorian authors were regular attenders at Christian worship services. But it is still worth making a distinction between religious and mainstream literature, even if the dividing line can sometimes be unclear. Some of the distinguishing features of religious literature will be internal to the works. For instance, sometimes the work clearly sets out to achieve a particular religious goal—salvation, moral edification, worship, or doctrinal debate; sometimes it will make much use of particular kinds of religious writing such as scriptural exegesis, homily, or hymn. But external factors can be even more decisive: Was it first published in a religious magazine or by a religious publishing house? Was the author popularly associated with a particular denomination or religious party? Do the Victorian reviewers—mainstream and religious—regard this as a religious work? All of these can enter into our judgment of whether to think of a particular novel or poem as religious literature.

Religious Novels

The Victorian novel, with its ethical focus and intrusive narrators, lent itself to religious and moral discourse. Anthony Trollope testified to this sense of the novel as a conveyer of moral and social teaching when he wrote, "I have ever thought of myself as a preacher of sermons." Though his novels were not explicitly religious, there were an enormous number of Victorian religious novels "preaching" on nearly every conceivable subject and in many different subgenres.

> *Historical novels* such as Charles Kingsley's *Hypatia* (1853) and Newman's *Callista: A Tale of the Third Century* (1855) explored Victorian conflicts through narratives set in early Christian times.
>
> *Domestic novels* such as Charlotte M. Yonge's *The Daisy Chain* (1856) or Elizabeth Missing Sewell's *The Experience of Life* (1852) applied Christian moral injunctions to ordinary life.
>
> *Social problems novels* brought Christian moral standards to bear on Victorian social problems. Examples include Charlotte Elizabeth Tonna's *Helen Fleetwood* (1841), often identified as the first industrial novel, and Felicia Skene's *Hidden Depths* (1866), which took on the sexual double standard and the reclamation of Victorian prostitutes.
>
> *Novels of doubt* record the struggles attendant on the Victorian religious unsettlement. Some of these, such as Newman's *Loss and Gain* (1848), J.A. Froude's *Nemesis of Faith* (1849), and Elizabeth Missing Sewell's *Margaret Percival* (1847) fictionalize the authors' own religious upheavals. The most famous of the novels of doubt is Mary Arnold (Mrs. Humphry) Ward's *Robert Elsmere* (1888), a weighty four-volume novel about a

young clergyman who loses his orthodox faith as a result of studies of biblical criticism. This book became perhaps the least likely of bestsellers: within a year of its 1888 publication, it had sold 40,000 copies in Britain and 200,000 in America; Ward herself estimated that one million copies had been distributed in English, without taking account of the many translations into other languages.

"Party novels" supported the views of a particular Christian denomination or Anglican party—or attacked those of a different party. These included anti-Tractarian novels such as Emma Jane Worboise's *Overdale, or the Story of a Pervert* (1869); anti-Catholic novels such as Catherine Sinclair's *Beatrice* (1852); and anti-Evanglical novels such as Frances Trollope's *The Vicar of Wrexhill* (1837).

Theological novels, which sometimes overlapped with "party novels," participated in debates over controversial theological and religious doctrine.

Novels, in fact, became an important forum for theological debate. Clergymen such as Newman, Kingsley, and F.W. Farrar used novels as well as sermons to explicate and justify their own religious points of view, but this forum was particularly important for women, who were not permitted to preach sermons or publish theological treatises. When they were children, many religious women novelists aspired to preach their own sermons. In her *Autobiography* (1903), Charlotte M. Yonge records how, on a childhood visit to the family of her clerical uncle, she shocked her female relatives: "[I]mmediately after our arrival . . . I was seen exalted on a locker with my uncle's bands on, preaching."[7] Elizabeth Sewell composed sermons in the nursery, but "her brothers, themselves destined to become clergymen—discouraged her from pursuing theological studies."[8] Instead, these women grew up to write religious novels, which might almost be thought of as the sermons Victorian women could never preach.

How seriously authors and readers took the religious teaching embodied in religious novels is demonstrated by the phenomenon of "response novels"—novels written to oppose the religious or theological positions of previous novels. Newman's autobiographical *Loss and Gain,* for instance, was written in response to Elizabeth Harris's novel *From Oxford to Rome.*[9] Emma Jane Worboise wrote several evangelical novels in response to High Church novels, using sound-alike titles: her *Hearts-Ease in the Family* is a response to Charlotte M. Yonge's *Hearts-Ease, or the Brother's Wife,* and her *Amy Wilton,* which supported the claims of Dissenters to Christian communion and salvation, was a reply to Elizabeth Sewell's *Amy Herbert,* which emphasized the importance of baptism into the established church.

Religious authors like Yonge, Sewell, and Worboise regarded their work as a kind of Christian vocation, as Worboise emphasized in her magazine:

[T]here is no profession more truly *sacred* than authorship; like the ministry, it ought to be a *vocation* rather than a profession. A bad sermon may be forgotten almost as soon as delivered; a bad book lives for generations. Authorship is *work*, work of the most serious kind, and it must be done for God if it is to command His blessing; not for fame, not for emolument, though both are quite lawful, and even praiseworthy, as secondary aims.... "Thank God for well-earned fame," wrote one of our best and noblest women-writers. Nor is money at all to be despised; in this life we cannot live respectably without it, and the labourer is worthy of his hire whether he till the soil, or preach the Gospel, or write books or magazine articles.... True and worthy authors... are dedicated to the noblest toil on earth! They rank with the ministers of God's Word, and in another way they do His work...[10]

Religion in Mainstream Novels

Religion was so pervasive a part of Victorian culture that no realist novel set in the nineteenth century could entirely ignore it. Moreover, many of the major novelists of the period themselves experienced religious upbringings that profoundly influenced their later moral and philosophical views.

Charles Dickens was largely critical of organized religion or charity—indeed, of almost all social institutions. Religious characters in his novels are often portrayed as unattractive and hypocritical, from the *Pickwick Papers*'s Mr. Stiggins to Arthur Clennam's stern and humorless mother, ensconced behind her Bible in *Little Dorrit*, to oily Mr. Chadband and ridiculous Mrs. Jellyby in *Bleak House*, with her devotion to saving the souls of people in Borriohoola-Gha. With regard to religious themes and attitudes, Dickens's novels do endorse an individual morality based upon humanistic values that are consistent with and possibly derived from Christianity, but the moral content is largely secularized. Perhaps Dickens's works seem most religious when he portrays the possibility of redemption through "conversions" of the sort experienced by Ebenezer Scrooge; these conversions, however, seem much more psychological than spiritual, and they are effected not by God or the church but by human love and sympathy.

Anthony Trollope probably wrote more about clergymen than any other novelist, particularly in his Barsetshire series: *The Warden* (1855), *Barchester Towers* (1857), *Dr. Thorne* (1858), *Framley Parsonage* (1861), *The Small House at Allington* (1864), and *The Last Chronicle of Barset* (1867). He writes about good clergymen (Septimus Harding and Francis Arabin), bad clergymen (Obadiah Slope and Dr. Vesey Stanhope), and indifferent clergymen (Bishop Proudie and Archdeacon Grantly). He is fascinated by their marriages, their politics, and their moral decision-making—but generally not by their spiritual lives. These clergymen are professional men, not much different from Trollope's doctors and politicians, except in the details of their responsibilities. That similarity accords with Trollope's ideal of a clergyman as English gentleman, as expressed in his *Clergymen of the Church of England* (1866).

Emily and Charlotte Brontë had a more vexed relationship with Christianity. Their father Patrick Brontë was an Evangelical Anglican, the perpetual curate of Haworth, a parish in Yorkshire. Their mother came from a Methodist family with strong Anglican ties. After their mother's death, they were cared for by their Aunt Branwell, who is often referred to as "strict" and "Calvinist." Strict, she might have been, and earnest in her religious convictions, but like most Methodists, she was Arminian, rather than Calvinist, believing "that God was a God of love who wanted to save all mankind."[11] The teaching at the schools they attended, however, both at the Clergy Daughters School at Cowan Bridge, the model for Lowood in *Jane Eyre*, and at Roe Head, would have been pervaded by a more Calvinist model of salvation.

Emily's novel *Wuthering Heights* reflects her rejection of the religious teaching of her youth. Religion is represented by the tyrannical and frightening Yorkshireman Joseph, who subjects the young Catherine and Heathcliff to three-hour services, and the terrifying Calvinist preacher of the narrator's dream, Jabes Branderham. The world of the novel is, instead, a vibrantly pagan world, where Christian ideas and morality are made to seem shallow and insignificant.

The treatment of religion in Charlotte's writing is more complicated. On one hand, the novels are permeated with Biblical language and allusions, particularly *Shirley* (1849). They are also noted for a strong rejection of Roman Catholicism, which Brontë associates with a surrender of self-determination. Her most famous novel, *Jane Eyre* (1847), however, bears witness to her conflicted relationship with religious ideas through characters representing different aspects of religion. At Lowood School, Jane admires the Christian stoicism and firm faith of Helen Burns, even though she knows she cannot emulate it and does not really want to. The more powerful figure, however, is Mr. Brocklehurst, the school's director and a religious hypocrite, based on the figure of the Reverend William Carus Wilson, director of Cowan Bridge. Under Brocklehurst's leadership the girls are treated harshly, poorly dressed, and underfed, while his own wife and daughters are "splendidly attired in velvet, silk, and furs."[12] When Miss Temple, the head teacher, gives the children bread and cheese for lunch to compensate for burnt porridge at breakfast, Brocklehurst upbraids her:

> You are aware that my plan in bringing up these girls is, not to accustom them to habits of luxury and indulgence, but to render them hardy, patient, self-denying. Should any little accidental disappointment of the appetite occur, such as the spoiling of a meal ... the incident ... ought to be improved to the spiritual edification of the pupils, by encouraging them to evince fortitude under the temporary privation. A brief address on these occasions would not be mistimed, wherein a judicious instructor would take the opportunity of referring to the sufferings of the primitive

Christians; to the torments of martyrs; to the exhortations of our blessed Lord himself, calling upon His disciples to take up their cross and follow Him; to His warnings that man shall not live by bread alone, but by every word that proceedeth out of the mouth of God; to his divine consolations, "if ye suffer hunger or thirst for my sake, happy are ye." Oh, madam, when you put bread and cheese instead of burnt porridge into these children's mouths, you may indeed feed their vile bodies, but you little think how you starve their immortal souls.[13]

Through Brocklehurst's lengthy tirade, Brontë emphasizes life-denying aspects of Christianity, or at least of his brand of Christianity, its glorification of suffering and privation. But hypocritical Brocklehurst is as concerned with the economic as with the moral consequences of an extra meal being served, and his use of biblical quotation to justify his own stinginess further discredits him and his religiosity.

The novel seems most ambivalent about St. John Rivers and the religious vocation that he represents. In his marriage proposal he offers Jane the possibility of meaningful work as well as travel to distant lands, which she once had desired: soon after becoming a governess, Jane would look out the window to the horizon, and she "longed for a power of vision which might overpass that limit; which might reach the busy world, towns, regions full of life I had heard of but never seen . . . I desired more of practical experience than I possessed . . . [women] need exercise for their faculties, and a field for their efforts as much as their brothers do."[14] But now she longs instead for romantic love and sexual fulfillment with Rochester, and her "vocation" comes when she hears him literally calling her name from far away. The reader approves of Jane's refusal to settle for a loveless marriage and her determination not to be subsumed by Rivers's powerful personality and sense of vocation. But, as has been often noted, after Jane and Rochester retire together from the world and its problems to enjoy a private and domestic felicity, the novel ends not with them but with Rivers's dynamism and faith:

No fear of death will darken St. John's last hour: his mind will be unclouded; his heart will be undaunted; his hope will be sure; his faith steadfast. His own words are a pledge of this: "My Master," he says, "has forewarned me. Daily he announces more distinctly—'Surely I come quickly!' and hourly I more eagerly respond—'Amen; even so come, Lord Jesus!'"[15]

St. John Rivers is literally given the last word in the novel, and it is "Jesus." Though Brontë chooses for her heroine a settled English domestic idyll, the attraction of Rivers's sense of religious meaning and evangelical mission remains potent.

Although it uses frequent biblical allusion and deals with religious themes, contemporary reviewers certainly did not view *Jane Eyre* as a religious novel or its protagonist as a Christian heroine. In 1848 Eliza Rigby wrote in the *Quarterly Review*: "It is true Jane does right, and exerts great moral strength, but it is the strength of a mere *heathen* mind which is a law unto itself. No Christian grace is perceptible upon her."[16] Several religious novelists wrote in response to Brontë. As Elizabeth Jay demonstrates in *Religion of the Heart*, Worboise's *Thornycroft Hall* is a reply to *Jane Eyre*, defending the Clergy Daughters School and its director William Carus Wilson, as well as revising some of the ethical judgments of Brontë's novel. Tractarian novelist Charlotte M. Yonge also responded to *Jane Eyre* in *The Daisy Chain*, recasting Jane's refusal of St. John Rivers's offer of missionary work and companionship in Meta Rivers's acceptance of a similar offer. When Norman May proposes to Meta—"Would you?—No, it is too unreasonable. Would you share—share the work that I have undertaken?", she accepts him and his work. When Norman later laughingly objects: "I believe you are taking a would-be missionary instead of Norman May!", Meta responds without denying the imputation. "All would-be missionaries did not make dear papa so fond of them," said Meta, very low; "and you would not be Norman May without such purposes."[17] Responding to the ending of *Jane Eyre*, Yonge insists that Christian women want vocation and meaningful work in the wider world, as well as love.

While Charlotte Brontë, though an Anglican, was not regarded as a religious writer, her friend and biographer, *Elizabeth Gaskell*, often was. The wife of a Unitarian minister in Manchester, Gaskell wrote novels that were progressive and socially engaged. Fearing that if her novels were explicitly Unitarian her readership would be limited, she wrote in more general religious terms, acceptable to a broad audience. She often portrayed positive Christian characters, notably the evangelical dissenting minister Thurstan Benson and his sister Faith from *Ruth* (1853), who offer help and forgiveness to the "fallen" heroine of the novel. But, more profoundly, her novels narrate the redemptive power of sympathy and compassion that, in her religious tradition, derive ultimately from divine sources. She believed in "the real earnest Christianity which seeks to do as much and as extensive good as it can," and she identifies this active form of Christianity as the ultimate solution to intractable Victorian problems of poverty and social injustice.

Although not herself a Christian believer, of all the canonical Victorian novelists, *George Eliot* is perhaps most deeply imbued with Christian values of moral responsibility and self-sacrificial love, values central to her own Religion of Humanity. She had an evangelical conversion experience in her youth, and for several years remained fervently and earnestly religious. But in her twenties she abandoned this early faith, which led to an estrangement from her father. Her loss of faith is connected with her growing intellectual comprehensiveness and independence, as well as with her translation of Feuerbach's *The Essence of*

Christianity, which attempted to demythologize Christianity while retaining its moral core.

Her early fiction makes use of religious characters whose most fundamental creed is really the Religion of Humanity, whatever theological doctrines they profess. Notable examples include Mr. Tryan in "Janet's Repentance" from *Scenes of Clerical Life*, and Dinah Morris, the compassionate Methodist preacher in *Adam Bede*. Even her intrusive omniscient narrator in *Middlemarch* has a homiletic character, trying to effect the moral regeneration of her readers, their conversion to a religion of humanity, as in this passage about the religious hypocrite, Bulstrode:

> He was simply a man whose desires had been stronger than his theoretic beliefs, and who had gradually explained the gratification of his desires into satisfactory agreement with those beliefs. If this be hypocrisy, it is a process which shows itself occasionally in us all, to whatever confession we belong, and whether we believe in the future perfection of our race or in the nearest date fixed for the end of the world . . .
>
> This implicit reasoning is essentially no more peculiar to evangelical belief than the use of wide phrases for narrow motives is peculiar to Englishmen. There is no general doctrine which is not capable of eating out our morality if unchecked by the deep-seated habit of direct fellow-feeling with individual fellow-men.[18]

This "fellow-feeling," a wide human sympathy, is at the heart of Eliot's non-theological creed.

Like Eliot, *Thomas Hardy* also went through a phase of deep evangelical faith in his youth before rejecting this religious worldview as untenable. Hardy's novels portray a decidedly post-Christian world, one closer to a pagan or classical pre-Christian outlook than to Victorian Christianity. Nevertheless, this world is not free of all vestiges of Christian doctrine and morality: in Hardy's world, Christianity is often identified with a narrow and judgmental morality. This negative Christian influence is clearest in *Tess of the D'Ubervilles* (1891) where Tess, having lost her sexual innocence to the machinations of Alec D'Urberville, meets a text-painter along the road. His mission is to paint biblical verses in bright red paint on the weathered wooden barns and fences of Wessex to convince people of their sin: "THY, DAMNATION, SLUMBERETH, NOT. 2 PET. ii.3." Tess feels herself condemned by the biblical messages—"I think they are horrible," said Tess. "Crushing! Killing!"[19]—and by Christianity's unnatural sexual morality, from which even her agnostic husband Angel is unable to free himself. Clergymen such as Angel Clare's High Church brothers are condemned for their narrowness and lack of compassion, and evangelical conversion itself is mocked when Alec D'Urberville reappears in the novel as a travelling preacher.

Even though Hardy sees the world as godless and essentially tragic, only made the more so by the rigidity of Christian moral doctrine, he still recognizes the existence of a Christianity of compassion, at least for "extreme cases"[20]: Angel Clare's parents, staunch Evangelicals, certainly endorse the sexual morality that condemns Tess, but, whatever their limitations, they believe in forgiveness and moral regeneration, and Hardy makes clear that, had she been able to confess her situation to them, she would have found them ready to accept and love her.

Mainstream Victorian novelists could hardly fail to engage with the religious culture of the age. The religious language and ideas of Christianity were part of the material from which their fiction was wrought, and to many modern readers this may look like a commitment to Christianity itself. But this engagement with Christianity often took the form of rejection, powerful critique or, at the least, significant revision.

Religious Poetry and Religion in Mainstream Poetry

Though it can be difficult to make distinctions between religious fiction and mainstream fiction, the distinctions are even harder to draw in poetry. Sometimes religious poetry is easy to identify: it is found in the hundreds of hymnals published, in the religious magazines of the period, and in many devotional books. This form of religious literature was particular important for the Tractarians: "For the Oxford Movement, poetry was synonymous with religious truth and offered believers the best, and most appropriate, way of communicating and understanding their faith."[21] Critics including G.M. Tennyson have identified a unique Tractarian poetics, which embodies the "doctrine that material phenomena are both the types and the instruments of real things unseen" by expressing spiritual truths through material analogies. This poetics also incarnates the Tractarian doctrine of reserve by "encoding religious knowledge in poetry."[22] It is this religious poetics that unites the work of John Keble, Adelaide Proctor, Dora Greenwell, and Christina Rossetti.

Much of the mainstream poetry in the Victorian period, however, also draws on religious images, spiritual expression, and themes of faith and doubt.

For all that T.S. Eliot claimed that *Alfred Tennyson's In Memoriam* was more remarkable for the quality of its doubt than for the quality of its faith, many Victorians found inspiration and hope in the expression of the poet's own struggle for an intellectually tenable and emotionally satisfying faith in the face of pain, death, and new scientific theories; it will be discussed in greater detail in Chapter 8. *Matthew Arnold* is equally eloquent in his poems of the loss of faith, including "Stanzas from the Grand Chartreuse" and "Empedocles on Etna," in which Arnold uses a pre-Christian philosopher on the verge of suicide to voice his own sense of life in a post-Christian world. In the famous conclusion of his "Dover Beach," Arnold records the ebbing of religious faith and the sense of loss, alienation, and meaninglessness that is left behind:

> The Sea of Faith
> Was once, too, at the full, and round earth's shore
> Lay like the folds of a bright girdle furled.
> But now I only hear
> Its melancholy, long, withdrawing roar,
> Retreating, to the breath
> Of the night-wind, down the vast edges drear
> And naked shingles of the world.
>
> Ah, love, let us be true
> To one another! For the world, which seems
> To lie before us like a land of dreams,
> So various, so beautiful, so new,
> Hath really neither joy, nor love, nor light,
> Nor certitude, nor peace, nor help for pain;
> And we are here as on a darkling plain
> Swept with confused alarms of struggle and flight,
> Where ignorant armies clash by night (ll. 21–37).

Despite the power of these familiar lines, Arnold's friend and fellow-poet *Arthur Hugh Clough*, though much less often read, should perhaps be declared the poet laureate of unbelief. He is primarily known today as the subject of Arnold's elegy, *Thyrsis*, and as the author of a pair of lyrics, "The Latest Decalogue" and "Say Not the Struggle Naught Availeth." Much of his strongest work, however, dramatizes the struggle and pain of religious doubt. His long poem, *Dipsychus* (1865), takes the form of a dialogue on faith between the doubting Dipsychus ("double-minded") and an ironic Spirit identified in drafts as "Mephisto." An earlier poem that similarly confronts the loss of faith is "Easter Day, Naples, 1849," with its seasonal refrain,

> Christ is not risen, no
> He lies and moulders low;
> Christ is not risen.

The second section of the poem spells out the consequences of this conclusion:

> Is He not risen, and shall we not rise?
> Oh, we unwise!
> What did we dream, what wake we to discover?
> Ye hills, fall on us, and ye mountains, cover!
> In darkness and great gloom

Come ere we thought it is *our* day of doom,
From the cursed world which is one tomb,
Christ is not risen!

Eat, drink, and die, for we are men deceived,
Of all the creatures under heaven's wide cope
We are most hopeless who had once most hope
We are most wretched that had most believed.
    Christ is not risen.

Eat, drink, and play, and think that this is bliss!
There is no Heaven but this!
There is no Hell;
Save Earth, which serves the purpose doubly well,
Seeing it visits still
With equallest apportionments of ill
Both good and bad alike, and brings to one same dust
The unjust and the just
With Christ, who is not risen.

Eat, drink, and die, for we are souls bereaved
Of all the creatures under this broad sky
We are most hopeless, that had hoped most high,
And most beliefless, that had most believed.
Ashes to ashes, dust to dust;
As of the unjust, also of the just—
Yea, of that Just One too.
It is the one sad Gospel that is true,
Christ is not risen (ll. 64–94).

Like Matthew Arnold, Dissenter *Robert Browning* ventriloquized characters from earlier times—as well as from English literature—to explore Victorian religious issues. "Caliban upon Setebos, or Natural Theology on the Island" is a dramatic monologue in which the subhuman monster Caliban develops a theology based on his observation of the natural world and his own nature, as natural theologians claimed to do. But Caliban's God, the Setebos who could create such a monster, turns out to be a kind of monster himself, most closely resembling the sovereign and arbitrary God of the Calvinists who saves the elect and condemns the others, just as Caliban will kill one crab in a group on a whim: "not loving, not hating, just choosing so" (l. 103).

In "Cleon," Browning uses the Roman poet's recognition of mortality and longing for immortality to make a case for Christianity. Creon answers a letter from the king about the meaning of life and its ends. Near the end of the poem, Creon considers for a moment the possibility of an afterlife that would satisfy the deepest of human longings:

I dare at times imagine to my need
Some future state revealed to us by Zeus,
Unlimited in capability
For joy, as this is in desire for joy (ll.324–327).

But he rejects it almost immediately: "But no!/Zeus has not yet revealed it; and alas,/ He must have done so were it possible!" (ll. 334–335). In the final stanza, however, Browning implies that it is Cleon's own pride and sense of cultural superiority that excludes him from knowledge of the afterlife; Cleon rebukes the king for sending a letter to St. Paul:

... And for the rest,
I cannot tell thy messenger aright
Where to deliver what he bears of thine
To one called Paulus; we have heard his fame
Indeed, if Christus be not one with him—
I know not, nor am troubled much to know.
Thou canst not think a mere barbarian Jew,
As Paulus proves to be, one circumcised,
Hath access to a secret shut from us?
Thou wrongest our philosophy, O king,
In stooping to inquire of such an one,
As if his answer could impose at all!
He writeth, doth he? Well, and he may write,
Oh, the Jew findeth scholars! Certain slaves
Who touched on this same isle, preached him and Christ;
And (as I gathered from a bystander)
Their doctrine could be held by no sane man (ll. 337–353).

Cleon's rationalism, as well as his racial and class prejudice, prevents him from accepting the doctrines that would give him what he longs for.

Perhaps the most moving of the monologues is "An Epistle of Karshish," in which an Arab physician-scientist, committed to material explanations of the world, meets the resurrected Lazarus (see John 11), hears the message of Christ, and finds his rational terms inadequate to describe what he experiences. Clearly, Browning is vividly dramatizing a Victorian conflict between scientific explanation and spiritual experience through his Arab narrator. Like Cleon, near the end of the poem he experiences a moment of self-doubt in which his experience with Lazarus tempts him to accept the truth of Christianity, as he writes to his teacher:

The very God! Think, Abib; dost thou think?
So, the All-Great, were the All-Loving too—

So, through the thunder comes a human voice
Saying, "O heart I made, a heart beats here!
Face, my hands fashioned, see it in myself!
Thou hast no power nor mayst conceive of mine,
But love I gave thee, with myself to love,
And thou must love me who have died for thee!"
The madman saith He said so: It is strange (ll. 304–312).

In 1850, urged by his wife and fellow poet, *Elizabeth Barrett Browning*, to abandon his masks temporarily and write in something closer to his own voice, Browning also wrote a pair of long poems, *Christmas-Eve* and *Easter-Day*, which explore Victorian religious themes more directly, addressing the central problem set at the start of the second poem: "How very hard it is to be/A Christian!" (ll.1–2). In these poems Browning struggles manfully with the problems presented by German Higher Criticism, lack of material evidence for Christianity, and the failure of natural theology, and finally relies upon intuition to conclude (as Karshish could not) that there must be a loving God.

The most important mainstream women poets of the period, Elizabeth Barrett Browning and Christina Rossetti, are even more closely tied to religion and religious themes.

Barrett Browning was a Congregationalist, and her poetry is permeated by that independent and individualistic brand of Christianity. Her piety had deep roots in the home of her childhood, where her father would come in to pray with her every night; in fact, a sermon that she wrote in her teens and apparently delivered to her family at Christmas has been discovered. Throughout her life, whether she was in England or abroad, she sought out Congregational worship services. Her early poetry in *The Seraphim and Other Poems* (1833) and *A Drama of Exile* (1844) is her most orthodox and most explicitly religious. The first volume, in fact, contains five poems that were in common use as hymns in the United States. The long title poems of both these volumes are ambitious attempts to render Christian subjects in the manner of Greek drama: *The Seraphim* narrates the story of Christ's crucifixion through the perspective of two angels, while *A Drama of Exile* portrays the Fall of Adam and Eve.

Throughout her career, though, Barrett Browning continued to be committed to the view that poetry is a vocation from God, and that poets are, as she writes in *Aurora Leigh* (1856),

... the only truth-tellers, now left to God,
The only speakers of essential truth,
Opposed to relative, comparative,
And temporal truths; the only holders by
His sun-skirts ... (I: 859–863).

This is particularly clear in the Prologue to "A Curse for a Nation" (1855), where an angel commands her to write political poetry denouncing America's hypocrisy in countenancing slavery:

> I heard an angel speak last night,
> And he said "Write!
> Write a Nation's curse for me,
> And send it over the Western Sea." (ll. 1–4).

In Barrett Browning's view, the poet is the one who must tell God's truths and curse God's curses.

Christina Rossetti, too, saw her poetry as a divine calling. Deeply religious, her religious beliefs and struggles were expressed in her poems. She was a High Church Anglican and was a tertiary in the Anglican convent where her sister Maria became a nun. (A tertiary is an associate of the religious order who participates in its work without taking religious vows.) Religion in the Rossetti household was divided along gender lines: her father and brothers Dante and William took little notice of religion, though they used much religious imagery in their work, while her mother, her sister Maria, and Christina herself were fervent Christians. Her early books of poetry are divided into two sections, one for secular poems and one for religious. But even the secular poems are often permeated by Christian themes. *Goblin Market*, for instance, with its tale of self-sacrifice and redemption through a female Savior, is marked as a "secular" poem. Her later career is dominated by the writing of three devotional books for publication by the SPCK (Society for the Promotion of Christian Knowledge): *Called to Be Saints: The Minor Festivals Devotionally Studied* (1881); *Time Flies: A Reading Diary* (1885); and *The Face of the Deep: A Devotional Commentary on the Apocalypse* (1892). These books welded together poetry and prose for the purpose of worship and spiritual growth. As with Elizabeth Barrett Browning, some of Rossetti's poetry was set to music and sung as hymns: her Christmas poem, "In the Bleak Midwinter" remains a popular seasonal hymn in many churches.

The most profound and original religious poet of the period, however, had little effect on Victorian poetry or culture. *Gerard Manley Hopkins* was a Tractarian, influenced by Pusey and Newman, who eventually converted to Roman Catholicism and joined the Jesuit order. Although he was willing to renounce poetry, and, in fact, burned much of his early work, his superiors in the Jesuit order encouraged his writing, though little of it was published in his lifetime. His poetics takes the Tractarian tradition of analogy between material and spiritual things further by actually locating religion *within* natural objects instead of "behind" them,[23] an idea that Hopkins expressed through his concept of "inscape," which is the unique, distinctive, and inherent quality of a thing, its dynamic essence. This poetic theory explained and helped produce some of the most original religious verse ever written, and when it was finally published in the twentieth century, it had a profound effect on modernist poetry.

While the Bible enjoyed the largest circulation of any book in Victorian Britain, there were many other religious best sellers that significantly influenced Victorian culture, from Keble's *Christian Year* and Ward's *Robert Elsmere*, to hymnals, tracts, sermons, and religious magazines. Much of this religious literature still remains to be explored. But the more of it we are able to explore, the better we will understand the mainstream literature of the nineteenth century, which engages with many of the same issues and draws on the same store of religious images and narratives. All of this literature testifies to the centrality of religion in Victorian culture and to its amazing—sometimes bewildering—diversity.

7

Women and Religious Life

In the drama of women's emancipation, patriarchal religion has often been cast as villain—and not without reason. Certainly, through the twentieth century, patriarchal Western religions, including Judaism, Christianity, and Islam, have tended to promulgate conservative views about women's social roles. Moreover, they have usually lagged behind the secular world in accepting women's leadership: Women who could be doctors, military officers, and elected officials were still banned from leadership roles in their synagogues, churches, or mosques—and some still are.

At other times and under other social conditions, however, religion could play a liberatory role in women's lives—and those conditions prevailed in nineteenth-century Britain. Far from lagging behind the secular realm, religion was for Victorian women one of the few areas of life in which they could claim equality—even superiority—and religious activity was one of the few socially approved outlets for their talent, energy, and creativity. As a result, women contributed significantly to Victorian religious life and thought.

The idea that men and women had different natures particularly suited to fulfilling their different duties—often called "separate spheres ideology"—assigned women a crucial role in religion. An earlier view had held that women were merely inferior men—weaker, less intelligent, less capable of moral restraint, but essentially similar. Separate spheres ideology saw women as having an essentially different nature, more sensitive and more compassionate. Although men still enjoyed stronger bodies and minds, women came to be regarded as morally and spiritually superior—sexually purer, more self-sacrificing, and more spiritually acute. In 1797 William Wilberforce, the great Evangelical reformer, claimed "that [female] sex seems, by the very constitution of nature, to be more favorably disposed than ours to the feelings and offices of

Religion,"[1] an observation later lent support by statistics on church attendance and other forms of religious involvement. Sometimes this superiority was attributed to Nature, as in Wilberforce, at other times to circumstances: their insulation from the competitive, amoral economic sphere, or their suffering, as in this 1842 article from the *Christian Lady's Magazine*:

> "In Christ Jesus there is neither male nor female": both are accountable creatures . . . and both, if they enter heaven at all, must enter "through much tribulation." But if it be so, that natural sorrow, when sanctified by divine grace, becomes instrumental in perfecting the heirs of glory; then we may reasonably look for the most frequent exemplification of Christian character in that sex which has to bear the largest burden of natural grief . . . the sorrows of the woman are "greatly multiplied" . . . so are the minor trials and vexations which assail the woman, sharper, and more difficult to meet and overcome, than the "thorns and thistles" with which man has to contend: and by so much the more . . . do they tend to produce that true spirit of self-denial: that daily martyrdom for duty's sake; whose conflicts are all unseen, unheard of; and whose praise is not of men but of God.[2]

Here, women are claimed to be more like Christ himself in their humility, suffering, and self-denial.

Although the identification of women with Christ sounds radical, in some ways this spiritual superiority was consistent with women's relegation to the private sphere. After all, religion in Victorian England was part of the private sphere—a matter of individual faith and domestic devotion. But, as we have seen, Victorian religion was also public, and it was widely agreed that Christianity provided both the foundation and the blueprint for a healthy society. In this way, women's acknowledged spiritual superiority could be used to argue for a voice on social issues and a larger role in Victorian society.

Some writers, however, used religious justifications to argue *against* women's participation in the public realm. Most of these writers made their arguments by using a form of natural theology. Natural theology attempts to discern the nature of God and of God's will through observations of the world, His creation. Conservative Christians could argue that existing social arrangements, including women's social roles, were providentially ordained and should not be changed. As Sarah Lewis argued in *Woman's Mission* (1839), a woman should be "content with the sphere of usefulness assigned her by nature and nature's God."[3] Other Christians, however, rejected the idea that the status quo represented God's will; this was a fallen world, and its institutions were as likely to be of diabolical as of divine origin. It was only through "special revelation"—in the Bible or in private experience—that people could hope to find truth about God's will. Thus Christian women could use evidence from the Bible or claims of divine vocation to override traditional restrictions on women's public roles.

This was one of the motivations behind the many books and articles discussing women of the Bible. In fact, relatively few women play major roles in biblical narrative, and these articles often had to recruit figures such as "Manoah's wife" and "Jephthah's daughter" in order to make up their numbers. But these female characters, especially from the Old Testament narratives, could be interpreted in ways that expanded women's opportunities.

The most powerful female character in traditional Christianity is the Virgin Mary, but she proved an equivocal model for Victorian women. Her vocation is merely to (virginal) motherhood, and, as Marina Warner points out in *Alone of All Her Sex*, Mary's "characteristics . . . establish her as the ideal woman—with her submission and her purity and her gentleness. She acts positively only through the principal man in her life, who is, in this case of a virgin birth, her son."[4] During certain historical periods, of course, Christians have accorded her a veneration bordering on worship, with full recognition of her power as well as her virtue. But the image of a powerful Mary was unavailable to most nineteenth-century English women. The Protestant Mary was, in the words of popular hymns, "the pure and lowly maid," or "Mary, Mother meek and mild."[5] When religious women writers do invoke Mary, in fact, it is not her motherhood that is praised but her poetry, the song she sings at the moment of Annunciation, as in Felicia Hemans's "The Song of the Virgin." Here she is a poet, a woman with a unique, divinely revealed vocation of sacred song.

The story of Mary and Martha, the sisters of Lazarus, could be used to sanctify women's traditional domestic roles (by focusing on Martha), to justify the abandonment of those roles in favor of religious life (by focusing on Mary), or to urge a combination of the two: In 1870 an article in the *Christian World Magazine* entitled "Far Above Rubies" interpreted the story of Mary and Martha as a new vision of womanhood, which integrates the domestic and spiritual: "Practical yet intellectual, strong yet tender, broad yet devout, many-sided in apprehension of gifts and graces."[6]

Miriam, the Hebrew priestess and the sister of Moses, served as a model for women's religious leadership. The *Christian World Magazine* published a series of articles about biblical women by American novelist Harriet Beecher Stowe, with the unlikely title, "Portraits of the Patriarchs," and she derives the following lessons from the story of Miriam: "The prophetic gift was without respect of sex, and raised woman at once to the rank of a public teacher; and we shall find in subsequent Jewish history how this gift, in certain instances, exalted a woman to be for a time the head and leader of the State."[7]

An even more radical departure from women's traditional roles came in the person of Deborah, whose story is recorded in the Bible in Judges 4–5. As this writer for the *Christian Lady's Magazine* noted, she could be used to justify

Edward Burne-Jones represents the Virgin Mary not as
a Madonna with Child, but at the moment of Annunciation, in his "Study for the Head of the Virgin" in
"The Annunciation" from Cosmo Monkhouse's *British
Contemporary Artists* (New York: Scribner's, 1899).

women's participation even in military and political life, as well as in inspired
poetry:

> ... [T]hough, as a general rule, the sphere of woman leads her far from
> the strife and shew of life, and bids her rather to retire and submit, than to
> come forward and act: yet the voice of nature and revelation alike sanction
> those occasional instances in which she has emerged from obscurity, to
> enact the part of a ruler or a patriot; or to bow the hearts of all by strains
> of eloquence and passion.[8]

Crucial to all these stories is the idea of vocation, of God's calling one individual to undertake a particular task or fulfill a particular role. Conveniently
beyond human refutation, vocation was a psychologically and rhetorically powerful justification for women undertaking nontraditional public work. This justification was theoretically available to any Christian woman, but it was easier
for Evangelical women to deploy than for their sisters in the High Church,

Gustave Doré's engraving of the prophetess "Deborah," from Cassell's *Doré Gallery*, shows her as a woman of power and inspiration (New York: Cassell, 1885), p. 62.

since Evangelicals placed more emphasis on individual conscience and less on traditional practice. Some High Church women, however, began to focus on the lives of female saints, finding in them models of vocation. Especially notable is the work of Elizabeth Rundle Charles, who recovered the lives of women saints in *Sketches of the Women of Christendom* (1880), *Martyrs and Saints of the*

First Twelve Centuries (1887), as well as a book on Joan of Arc, a woman whose divine vocation took her well beyond traditional female roles.

Women could use the widespread belief in their moral and spiritual superiority to claim a larger role in religious life, and they could use the doctrine of vocation to widen the possibilities for their religious service. As a result, Victorian women participated enthusiastically in nearly every facet of Victorian religious life, within the church and beyond.

WOMEN'S WORK IN THE CHURCH

In every major Christian denomination in Victorian Britain, women were barred from becoming ministers. The exceptions to this rule were rare and marginal. Quakers, who had no hierarchy and believed that the Spirit could speak through any Christian, allowed women more equality in ministry, and a few of the smaller Methodists sects continued to allow women to preach, though not to lead congregations. In the early days of Methodism, when the sense of the urgency of the mission was strongest, John Wesley had authorized some women to become itinerant preachers. After his death, however, when authority in the Methodist Church was codified and centralized in 1804, women's preaching was suppressed. Nevertheless, the Primitive Methodists continued to sanction women's preaching, and Victorians in more mainstream sects continued to be intrigued by the idea of women as preachers. George Eliot sets her novel *Adam Bede* in 1799 in order to allow Dinah Morris, her heroine, to be a Methodist field preacher, calling people to love and community in God, and Christian periodicals for women often printed stories about female religious leaders, such as the Shakers' Ann Lee, eighteenth-century women preachers, and American women ministers.

Still, although British women's voices were seldom heard in the pulpit, their perspective was not absent from the services of the church: Many of the most popular hymns sung in churches across England and America were written by women. They were also adopted across denominations, so that the lyrics of Baptist hymnist Anne Steele appeared in Methodist and Anglican hymnals as well, and Anglican Harriet Auber's hymn, "My Blest Redeemer, Ere He Breathed," became one of the most anthologized hymns of the century. Women were especially well-represented as writers of children's hymns: perhaps the most important Victorian children's hymnist was Cecil Frances Alexander, author of "There is a Green Hill Far Away" and "All Things Bright and Beautiful." In addition, the most popular wedding hymn, "O Perfect Love" was the work of Dorothy F. Gurney. But women's hymns appeared in every section of the hymnals. Encouraged by the evangelical spirit of the age, they wrote dozens of missions hymns, including Claudia Frances Hernaman's "The Call to Arms is Sounding" and Jane Laurie Borthwick's "Come, Labour on!" Borthwick, her sister Sarah Findlater, Frances E. Cox, and Catherine Winkworth were also important as translators of German hymns: Through their selection of hymns to translate and publish, and through their sometimes quite free translations, these women interpreted the German hymn tradition for English congregations in ways that tended to emphasize feminine elements in Christian experience. Other popular hymns by women include Frances Ridley Havergal's "Take my Life and Let It Be," Sarah Flower Adams's "Nearer, My God, To Thee," and Charlotte Elliott's "Just As I Am." Through their hymns, women's religious ideas and experiences became part of Christian worship.

Women also played important roles in ecclesiastical and paraecclesiastical organizations. Women figured prominently as Sunday school teachers and district visitors in every major denomination. They also often ran church-related women's organizations that supported the work of the church by visiting the poor and sick in the parish, collecting and distributing charitable donations of money or goods for the poor, and helping with the maintenance of the church interior. While men occupied positions of public authority and power, women often contributed more to the day-to-day functioning of the parish.

WOMEN'S WORK BEYOND THE CHURCH

Although women might be important within the local churches, their major contributions to British religious life occurred outside the institutional context. We have already seen in Chapter 6 how important their contributions were in the field of religious literature. Barred from the pulpit, religious writers such as Charlotte M. Yonge, Elizabeth Sewell, Felicia Skene, and Emma Jane Worboise "preached" through their novels. Women poets including Elizabeth Barrett Browning and Christina Rossetti felt themselves called to write religious poetry. Women editors of Christian periodicals sought to deepen the faith and broaden the horizons of their mostly female readers, encouraging them to see themselves as part of a vibrant Christian communion and urging them to participate actively in its work within their own local communities.

Religious literature was by this point a socially acceptable forum for women, but because Christians believed that all aspects of their lives should be influenced by their faith, religious literature gave women the opportunity to write on a wide variety of social and political issues as well as on topics concerning private or domestic devotion. In her first "Editorial Address," Emma Jane Worboise justifies the broad content of her magazine in these terms:

Nothing will be admitted to the pages of this magazine that is not of a Christian tone.... We need not say that science, art, the history of nations, the common daily tasks, our youthful loves, our struggles with the busy world, our temporal successes, and our failures, our joys and sorrows, and our losses, should bear the impress of the higher life, that all should teach or comfort, warn or influence, God's blessing being over all, ... because we know full well that life itself, in all its seemings, all its routine, all its trivialities, should be Religion![9]

If religion is relevant to every aspect of human life, public and private, then as a Christian, a woman is entitled to—indeed, obliged to—concern herself with all these aspects. Accordingly, Worboise asserts her right to address any subject, however political or controversial, in her Christian magazine for women. In addition to religious poetry, serialized fiction, explicitly religious articles, and "light" features on botany, health, and "The Domestic Life of the Poets," Worboise includes articles on social issues and national and international politics, including slavery in Central Africa (1867), elections ("Words and Realities: Recent Election Promises" in 1869), and foreign affairs ("The Prussian Campaign in Bohemia" in 1866). Thus, because everything is religious, a religious magazine can offer women a venue for participating in public discourse on topics usually forbidden them.

As we saw in Chapter 5, religion also justified many women in undertaking charitable work of more or less public kinds. Women were involved in religiously inspired charity work at every level, from individual almsgiving and home visits to serving on the board of charitable organizations. They were particularly prominent in charities dedicated to the moral and physical welfare of women and children. They also proved effective fundraisers for charities, many of which organized local women's auxiliaries.

But women went beyond working for various charities and causes to founding charities and spearheading campaigns. Women such as Octavia Hill and Josephine Butler felt their religious calling and religious faith pushing them beyond traditional female roles. If existing conditions are contrary to the will of God, they argued, then Christians have a responsibility to speak out and work to change them. Butler calls for a comprehensive sociopolitical reform, even as she claims a part for women in that reform:

> Looking at any of the great questions before us now—the relations of nation to nation, and of the Anglo-Saxon race to the heathen populations of conquered countries; questions of gold-seeking, of industry, of capital and labour, of the influence of wealth, now so great a power in our country and its dependencies; questions of legal enactments, of the action of Governments, and innumerable social and economic problems—we may ask, "How much of the light of heaven is permitted to fall on those questions?" How many or how few are there among us who ask, and seek, and knock and wait, to know *God's* thoughts on these matters.[10]

Any of those among *us*—woman or man—who knows God's thoughts has every right to promulgate them and to act on them.

Obviously, religious vocation could offer women a transcendent justification for their work outside the home. A few women such as Butler and Florence Nightingale had such a strong sense of vocation that they felt comfortable departing from their traditional female roles to undertake important public work. Most Christian women, however, struggled to balance their traditional domestic or familial duties with a calling to religious work. Where the proper balance lay was a matter of dispute. Nightingale found inspiration from Jesus's rejection of family in favor of religious community and work in Matthew 12: 47–50: when he was told that his mothers and brothers were waiting to speak with him, he replied,

> Who is my mother? And who are my brethren?
> And he stretched forth his hand toward his disciples, and said, behold my mother and my brethren!
> For whosoever shall do the will of my Father which is in heaven, the same is my brother, and sister, and mother.

Here, religious vocation can always trump family responsibilities. On the other extreme, Sarah Lewis wrote in *Woman's Mission* that the only women who should pursue any charitable work beyond the home are "those . . . who can say with truth that for the comfort, the elegance, the happiness of the home of which they are the tutelary divinities, nothing remains to be done."[11] For most women, the balance lay somewhere in between, and while religion provided an opportunity for them to participate meaningfully in the wider community, most continued to perform traditional female roles of daughter, wife, and mother in the patriarchal family.

A few women, however, sought to devote themselves wholly to a religious life, and Victorian Christianity offered them an alternative to these familial roles: life within a religious community.

RELIGIOUS COMMUNITIES

Before the Reformation, Roman Catholic monasteries and convents had thrived in England, but they were disbanded by Henry VIII and their property confiscated. From that time until the nineteenth century, religious orders faced legal barriers and considerable social prejudice, and only a few Catholic convents survived: Cardinal Wiseman estimated that in 1830, there were sixteen convents in England, and no monasteries. But after Catholic Emancipation in 1829 and the restoration of the hierarchy in 1850, dozens of new convents and monasteries sprang up. By the end of the century, there were around 10,000 Roman Catholic nuns in England in nearly 600 convents, as well as more than fifty new monasteries.

But while Roman Catholic women had long had the choice of becoming nuns and devoting themselves to religious service, Anglican women in the early nineteenth century had no such options, and some felt that lack acutely. In *Margaret Percival*, Elizabeth Missing Sewell portrays her heroine's dissatisfaction as a Catholic priest tells her about women's religious orders in his church:

"I have seen women working zealously, humbly, with the greatest success," observed the confessor; "not, indeed, undertaking the duties of men, but watching over the sick and the destitute; standing like ministering angels by the bedside of the dying; and winning souls to Christ by the saint-like purity of their lives. They were members of another communion: you would call them Romanists."

"The sisters of charity," replied Margaret. "Yes, I have read of them, and fancied that if one might dare to choose one's lot in life, theirs would be the safest and the holiest; but they do not act individually."

"No; they are members of a body, bound together by laws, kept under discipline. They act as parts of the Church, and the authority of the Church goes with their efforts . . . But the Catholic Church has peculiar ideas on this subject, she does not contemplate doing good by individuals."

Margaret felt uncomfortable, almost unhappy; yet the very uneasiness she experienced seemed to urge her to continue the conversation.

"We have no institutions of the kind in the English Church," she said.[12]

Eager to restore pre-Reformation institutions and concerned about losing devout women to the Roman Catholic Church, the Tractarians introduced religious orders into the Church of England. The first Anglican convent was founded in 1845 in Park Village West, London, under the spiritual guidance of Edward Pusey; the first Anglican nun, Marian Hughes, had taken her vows in 1841, but had to care for her ailing parents and could not join the community until their deaths in 1849. An even more successful convent was founded in 1848 at Devonport, the Sisterhood of Mercy, with the energetic and talented Lydia Sellon as Mother Superior, and many more followed, notably including the Community of St. Mary the Virgin at Wantage. By the end of the century there were between 2,000 and 3,000 Anglican nuns and sixty Anglican religious orders, many maintaining multiple convents in different towns. Since women could be involved with the convents as "associates" and "tertiaries," not taking vows but participating in the work and worship of the community, these numbers understate how many Anglican women were affected by the revival of religious communities.

Religious orders are divided into the contemplative and the active: contemplative orders withdraw from the world for prayer and worship, while active orders participate in some form of social ministry, such as nursing or teaching. In keeping with the reformism of Victorian culture, almost all the new orders founded in the nineteenth century were active, and many of them were located in areas of particular need, especially large industrial centers. Anglican and Roman Catholic nuns performed many social services: teaching, nursing, caring for the homeless and elderly, visiting prisoners, running orphanages, and "rescuing" prostitutes, an activity considered especially appropriate for communities of celibate women.

Many Victorians greeted the new convents with hostility and suspicion. Some objected to the foundation of Anglican convents as further evidence of the Romanizing tendencies of the Tractarians. Others saw possibilities for sexual transgression in the relationship between nuns and their male confessors, and prurient novels about licentious escapades within convents found a ready audience. Some also regarded the choice of a celibate life as a rejection of the traditional family, and opposed the taking of vows of poverty, chastity, and obedience on the grounds that the fulfillment of the vows might interfere with women's performance of their familial duties. The convents also provoked differing anxieties about women's independence: on one hand, people worried about the individual autonomy that nuns surrendered upon taking a vow of obedience; on the other hand, they worried that these communities of women, although they answered to the church hierarchy, operated apart from traditional forms of patriarchal control.

In the 1860s Anglicans outside the High Church provided a religious order for women that was designed to avoid some of these criticisms. Led by the Broad Church Bishop of London, A. C. Tait, they revived the Anglican order of Deaconesses, which had official endorsement but had long ago been allowed to lapse. Their model was not the Roman Catholic sisterhoods, but the Lutheran Deaconesses at Kaiserwerth, near Dusseldorf, which had been founded in 1836 by Theodor Fliedner to train young women as nurses for the poor. Anglican Deaconesses did many of the same kinds of work as the nuns, but they were directly overseen by the local clergymen, they did not take vows, and they seldom lived communally. These alternative Protestant orders, however, while they performed some valuable work, did not enjoy the success of the new Anglican convents and their religious communities.

Anglican religious orders for men were also founded, notably the Society of St. John the Evangelist at Cowley in 1865, but they never enjoyed the success of the convents, perhaps because Anglican men already had significant opportunities for religious service and meaningful public work outside a monastery. For Victorian women, however, the Anglican and Roman Catholic orders offered something previously unavailable: An official place and recognition within the church; opportunities to participate in meaningful public work; professional training with a chance to assume leadership roles; and an alternative to domestic life in a patriarchal family.

8

The Victorian Religious Unsettlement

The Victorian era experienced a profound unsettlement of faith. Challenges to Christianity seemed to spring simultaneously from many different sources. One source of unsettlement was the increasing sense of individual choice in religious life. As laws that discriminated against them were repealed, non-Anglicans gradually gained acceptance as full British citizens. These repeals created a kind of free market in religion in which each individual could choose his or her favorite "brand," but which undermined the sense that any one brand could make exclusive claims to truth. Moreover, as the empire expanded, information about different religious systems filtered back to Britain. Ironically, much of this information was supplied by Christian missionaries, who had ventured forth to spread Christianity to the heathens, but ended up bringing non-Christian religion back to the British. The knowledge of other cultures and religions caused many Christians to begin to see their own beliefs in a worldwide context, leading some to question their own exclusive possession of truth. Some Victorians even began to question the morality of central Christian doctrines, including eternal damnation and substitutionary atonement, God's demand for innocent blood in exchange for forgiveness for the guilty. Finally, in the intellectual realm, new scientific discoveries and theories undermined claims of biblical accuracy and challenged fundamental Christian understandings of the world, while new ways of interpreting the Bible as a historical document further destabilized a central source of authority for Christians. Together, these different sources of unsettlement had a permanent impact on the prevalence and nature of Christian belief in Britain.

THE FREE MARKET IN RELIGION

It seems paradoxical that the expansion and multiplication of non-Anglican Christian sects, their success in bringing people to Christian worship, should be counted among the sources of religious unsettlement, but the free market in religion did disturb the faith of many Victorian Christians. Dissenters were becoming an important part of English society in the late eighteenth and early nineteenth centuries, and the reduction of their legal and social disabilities only added to their prominence, even as it made conversion to a dissenting denomination more attractive. Similarly, the catholicizing influence of the Oxford Movement, together with legislation that gave increased civil rights to Roman Catholics, increased the frequency of conversions to Roman Catholicism.

Victorian Christians could no longer remain automatically and thoughtlessly faithful to the sect into which they were born. Instead, the brands competing in the religious marketplace were all calling upon each individual to *choose*—to choose for himself or herself. Even the various parties competing for dominance within the Anglican Church encouraged this kind of consumer-consciousness. While most Anglicans chose to remain faithful to the Established Church and their parish clergyman, it was now a *choice* that they had to make, not a fact of life they could take for granted. The call to choose among different brands of Christian belief led many to rethink the foundations of their faith, and some to feel those foundations shaking beneath them.

Autobiographies and fictionalized autobiographical accounts of conversions or near-conversions greatly increased the public perception of the likelihood of conversion (or "perversion," which was the word often used by the opposing faction). Conversions to Roman Catholicism were particularly fraught, signaling not only a rejection of Protestantism but also, it was perceived, a rejection of Englishness itself in favor of Continental superstition. Many novels dramatized such conversions, sometimes intending to justify them, and at other times to discourage them. John Henry Newman published his famous autobiographical novel, *Loss and Gain: The Story of a Convert*, chronicling his 1845 conversion from English Tractarian to Roman Catholic in 1848, but it was itself a reply to another, less positive, story of conversion, a novel by Elizabeth Harris, *From Oxford to Rome: and How It Fared with Some Who Lately Made the Journey* (1847). Elizabeth Missing Sewell, whose High Church Anglican faith was unsettled by news of Newman's conversion, wrote a fictional account of an Anglican girl, Margaret Percival, tempted by the beauty and symbols of feminine power in the Roman church, but in the end almost reluctantly faithful to the church of her birth. Other novels provided lurid accounts of the effects of "perversion" on the family and community. In Emma Jane Worboise's Evangelical novel, *Overdale, or The Story of a Pervert* (1869), for instance, the Anglican vicar's conversion to Catholicism leads to disaster: his wife's disaffection and eventual death, his daughter's joyless confinement in a convent, his son's loss of all faith, and dissension in a previously harmonious community. While most of these literary works were written with didactic intent, to present the arguments in favor of their preferred set of Christian doctrines, their cumulative effect was rather to publicize the grounds of doubt and the possibility of change.

An almost unshakeable British conviction about the superiority of Christianity ensured that non-Christian religions were not competitive in the religious marketplace until very late in the nineteenth century, and even then conversions remained relatively rare, unbelief being the preference of those who rejected the truth of Christianity. But the mere knowledge of other religious systems, often brought back by missionaries and growing rapidly with the expansion of the empire, had an unsettling effect as Britons confronted the reality of whole nations—presumably damned for eternity—who believed in their own religions with the same fervor and earnestness with which British Christians clung to Christianity.

THE MORALITY OF CHRISTIAN TEACHING

Some Victorians also began to have moral qualms about Christian scriptures and doctrine. The narratives of the Old Testament proved particularly disturbing in a society that prided itself on the moral advance of its civilization. Divine commands to wipe out whole cities—"spare them not; slay both man and woman, infant and suckling, ox and sheep, camel and ass" (1 Samuel 15:3)—struck nineteenth-century Britons as barbaric and immoral, as did God's command to Abraham to sacrifice his son, even if it was countermanded at the last minute. Many Christians felt a strong sense of discontinuity between the images of God developed in the Old and New Testaments, and some, including both Dickens and Thackeray, were willing to jettison the Old Testament to save God's reputation as a moral and compassionate Being.

However, doctrines even more central to Christian teaching were not immune from this moral criticism. Were all those heathens in foreign lands really doomed to suffer for eternity because they were unlucky enough not to be European Christians? What of the millions who lived before the birth of Christ? Is such unending punishment just? In this period, many Christians began to question and to reject traditional teachings about Hell, either extending the range of God's mercy beyond previous narrow limits or rejecting the idea of an eternity of physical pain in favor of a spiritualized Hell in which the deprivation of God's presence is the only punishment. Still, even if doctrines of Hell could be adjusted to suit tender Victorian consciences, the central doctrine of Christianity, the death of Christ as an atonement for the sins of others, or substitutionary atonement, also seemed to some both illogical and immoral. What kind of Deity would demand the death of an innocent person to compensate for the failings of others? In a religious culture based upon blood sacrifice and, originally, tribal responsibility, substitutionary atonement made a kind of sense. In Victorian Britain, which insisted on individual responsibility, it seemed barbaric. While few who remained Christians went so far as to abandon this fundamental doctrine, the nineteenth century saw a gradual shift in the emphasis of Christian teaching, placing less emphasis on the atonement and more on the incarnation as the central event of Christian history.

But even as moral considerations led some people to question Christian texts and doctrines, new discoveries and theories in textual criticism and in the sciences further undermined the foundations of Christian faith.

GENESIS AND GEOLOGY

When most modern readers think about the conflict between science and religion, what looms largest in their minds is the controversy surrounding Charles Darwin's *Origin of Species* (1859). Certainly, that is the controversy with the greatest staying power, at least in the United States, where it is still agitating school boards and courts at the start of the twenty-first century. But before Darwin published his revolutionary ideas, Victorians were disturbed by the challenge offered by a different science: geology.

The account of creation given in the book of Genesis formed the basis for Christian ideas of the origins of the earth, a theory that came to be known as "Mosaic Cosmogony." Using biblical sources, particularly the lengthy genealogies—"And Arphaxad begat Salah; and Salah begat Eber; and unto Eber were born two sons" (Genesis 10:24–25)—a seventeenth-century arch-bishop, James Usher, had calculated the date of creation, assigning it to the year 4004 BCE, which would make the earth around 6,000 years old. Even Christian writers who doubted that the date could be so accurately determined accepted the idea of a young earth created over six days, as specified in Genesis. But in the eighteenth century geologists began to unearth evidence that the earth was considerably older—millions, not thousands, of years old. Moreover, the fossil record seemed to indicate that different species appeared gradually over the course of these millions of years, rather than being created on a few successive days. Even more disturbingly, the fossil record suggested that many species had become extinct. For a Christian, this meant that God created certain species only later to destroy them, an act not in keeping with traditional ideas of a benevolent Providence: his eye may be on the sparrow, as the hymn has it, but not, apparently, on the Tyrannosaurus Rex. Finally, the geological record did not clearly include anything that could be equivalent to the universal flood that occasioned Noah's need for an ark.

By the 1830s many Christians were well aware of this challenge to the Bible's accuracy. The discovery of dinosaur fossils had captured the popular imagination, and fossil hunting was a popular hobby. Because geology was such a young science, amateurs, both men and women, could make a real contribution to its development. (In fact, geological study was one of the few sciences that offered women a chance for meaningful participation.) This fascination with dinosaurs and fossils led ordinary people to take an interest in the accounts of modern geology published in the early part of the century—the most important of which was Charles Lyell's *The Principles of Geology* (1830–1833)—and to be disturbed by their implications.

Debate over the interpretation of the new geological discoveries raged both within and beyond scientific circles. Within geology, "uniformitarians," such as Lyell, who believed that rock layers were formed by the uniform working of natural law over long periods of time, clashed with "catastrophists," who favored a theory of geological history that posited a series of cataclysmic events to explain the appearance of the rock layers. Beyond geology, clergymen and others anxious for the authority of Scripture held a wide range of views. A few held determinedly to biblical literalism—a creation in six days and a universal flood. Others, including the professors of Geology at Oxford and Cambridge, both clergymen, initially seized on catastrophist theories, reinterpreting the Genesis narrative's "days" as geological eras and Noah's flood as one of these catastrophic events; this solution, however, was fatally undermined by the triumph of uniformitarian views within geology. Still others began quietly to abandon the claims of the Bible's scientific accuracy. Many ordinary Christians were alarmed by the apparent threat, and Christian periodicals in the 1830s followed the geological debate closely. Even the Evangelical *Christian Lady's Magazine* carried articles and letters on geology and its implications throughout the decade.

Geology also lent new support to an idea that would prove an even larger threat to the Christian worldview: the evolutionary hypothesis. Darwin's *Origin of Species*, with its account of the mechanism of evolutionary change through natural selection, would not be published until 1859, but the fossil record clearly suggested the idea of the gradual development of new species. Jean-Baptist Lamarck (1744–1829), a French scientist, had even posited an explanation of evolution that claimed (among other things) that an animal passed on to its offspring characteristics acquired during its lifetime. In England, the most explicit pre-Darwinian working out of the idea of development appeared in Robert Chambers's *Vestiges of the Natural History of Creation* in 1844. The material was so explosive that Chambers published the book anonymously and never acknowledged authorship during his lifetime. Although it was ridiculed by many scientists for its simplistic Larmarckianism, it created a public outcry, and the scandal produced high sales figures, leading to four editions in the first six months. The Reverend Adam Sedgwick, Professor of Geology at Cambridge, reacted to Chambers's book in a private letter:

> If the book be true, the labours of sober induction are in vain; religion is a lie; human law is a mass of folly, and a base injustice; morality is moonshine; our labours for the black people of Africa mere works of madmen; and man and woman are only better beasts![1]

The most famous account of a layman's reaction to a geological unsettlement of faith comes in Tennyson's *In Memoriam*. The devastating loss of his friend and religious mentor, Arthur Henry Hallam, plunged Tennyson into a morass of grief and doubt, intensified by the new vision of the world promoted by geological science and Lamarckian theories of evolution. First, the poet worries about the apparent lack of concern for the individual organism in the process of evolutionary development:

Are God and Nature then at strife,
    That Nature lends such evil dreams?
    So careful of the type she seems,
So careless of the single life (*In Memoriam* 55: 5–8).

But then he considers the additional problem of extinction, which appeared so clearly in the fossil record:

"So careful of the type?" But no,
    From scarped cliff and quarried stone,
    She [Nature] cries, "A thousand types are gone:
I care for nothing, all shall go" (56: 1–4).

Tennyson then turns to what for him is the central issue—the place of man in this new scientific vision:

. . . And he, shall he,

Man, her last work, who seem'd so fair,
    Such splendid purpose in his eyes,
    Who roll'd the psalm to wintry skies,
Who built him fanes of fruitless prayer.

Who trusted God was love indeed
    And love Creation's final law—
    Tho' Nature, red in tooth and claw
With ravine, shriek'd against his creed—

Who loved, who suffer'd countless ills,
    Who battled for the True, the Just,
    Be blown about the desert dust,
Or seal'd within the iron hills?

No more? A monster then, a dream,
    A discord. Dragons of the prime,
    That tare each other in their slime,
Were mellow music match'd with him (56: 8–24).

If the new geological theories are correct, Tennyson claims, then human life and human aspiration lose all their meaning. Humanity, like the dinosaurs—the "dragons of the prime"—can one day go extinct, becoming no more than a part of the fossil record, "seal'd within the iron hills."

In the course of the poem's 133 lyrics, Tennyson eventually comes to terms with his grief and doubt, basing a new faith on a progressive interpretation of development. This kind of progressivism formed a theme of Chambers' *Vestiges of Creation*, although it would be explicitly rejected by Darwinian theory. At the end of *In Memoriam*, Tennyson imagines progress culminating in a species higher and better than man,

> ... the crowning race
> Of those that, eye to eye, shall look
>   On knowledge; under whose command
>   Is Earth and Earth's, and in their hand
> Is Nature like an open book;
>
> No longer half-akin to brute,
>   For all we thought and loved and did,
>   And hoped, and suffer'd is but seed
> Of what in them is flower and fruit (Epilogue, 128–136).

Despite its optimistic conclusion, the poem still seems, as T.S. Eliot wrote, "not religious because of the quality of its faith, but because of the quality of its doubt." Tennyson represents for us here the effect of a new geological worldview on a generation of Victorian Christians—and prefigures some of the concerns that will be intensified with the publication of Darwin's *Origin of Species*.

GERMAN HIGHER CRITICISM

While geological discoveries did undermine claims of biblical inerrancy, an ultimately more serious threat derived from a variety of historical criticism developed in Germany and known as the German Higher Criticism or "Neology." Classical scholars such as Johann Gottfried Eichhorn, F. A. Wolf, and Barthold Georg Niebuhr, had pioneered a new way of reading classical texts, treating them as historical documents to be studied in the context of the historical period in which they were written. It was Wolf who, using these historical methods, first suggested that Homer was not an individual poet, the author of the *Iliad* and the *Odyssey*; instead, he argued, these poems derived from a long oral tradition and were the work of many different voices. While this claim seemed heretical only to a small group of classical scholars, when the German critics turned their attention to the ancient texts of the Israelites and the New Testament gospel narratives, many more people believed that they were, indeed, spreading heresies. The readings of the German critical theologians denied that the Bible was literally true and inspired throughout, instead

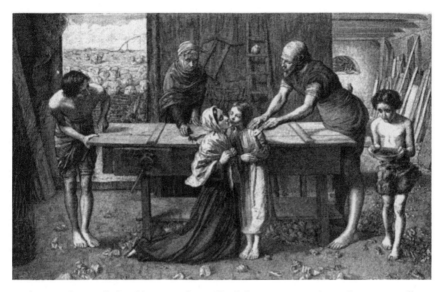

By showing Christ in the humble surroundings of his father's carpenter's shop, John Everett Millais's painting, "Christ in the House of His Parents," provides a visual version of the demythologized lives of Jesus. This picture appears in W. Shaw Sparrow, ed., *The Gospels in Art* (New York: Stokes, 1904), p. 110.

seeing some parts as inspired, others as historical accounts based on fact but written by human beings, others as entirely erroneous. They also cast doubt on the traditional ascriptions of the authorship of many Old Testament texts.

While their attacks on the accuracy, historicity, and inspiration of the Old Testament were troubling, when these critics turned their attention to the New Testament, they were undermining the very foundations of Christianity. They challenged the stories of miracles and, in particular, of the resurrection, as mythological additions to the life story of Jesus. Some of these critics tried to demythologize the narratives, recovering the "historical Jesus" by stripping away the mythological accretions. The most famous of these attempts was D.F. Strauss's *Leben Jesu* (1835), translated into English as *Life of Jesus*.

Nevertheless, for ordinary Christians in the first half of the nineteenth century, geology seemed a much more present threat than the work of German theologians and critics, largely because they knew much less about German Higher Criticism. This was partly because blasphemy laws in England proscribed both blasphemy against God and the questioning of the truth of the Bible. Anyone who published translations of the German critics could be prosecuted under these blasphemy laws, and few people were willing to take the risk. So the dangerous doctrines remained safely hidden away from most English men and women, available only to the intellectuals with easy access to foreign texts and a mastery of the German language. But in 1842, in the case of

Shore v. Wilson, Judge Erskine set a new standard for blasphemy, which required "scoffing" at God or the Bible: a publication that questioned the truth of traditional Christian doctrine "soberly and reverently" was no longer regarded as blasphemous. After this decision, partial translations of Strauss rapidly became available to the public, with the first full English version published in 1846, translated by the young George Eliot (then Marian Evans). A few years later, in 1854, she would also translate an even more thoroughly demythologizing text, Feuerbach's *The Essence of Christianity*, which preached a kind of religion of humanity, based upon the teachings of Christ but denying his divinity and atonement.

Throughout the early part of the century, scientific discoveries and the new historical criticism had been gradually undermining the belief of educated people in the inerrancy and plenary inspiration of Biblical texts. It wasn't until 1859 and 1860, however, that ordinary people recognized how serious the threat to traditional beliefs had become. Those years saw the publication of two of the most controversial books of the century: *Origin of Species* and *Essays and Reviews*.

ORIGIN OF SPECIES: EVOLUTION AND CHRISTIAN FAITH

The Origin of Species was published on November 24, 1859. Darwin's book had been much anticipated in intellectual circles, and all 1,250 copies sold out on the first day. Its publisher quickly ordered another printing of 3,000 copies, and in the end Darwin put out six editions in his lifetime (and it remains a steady seller even today). The book was reviewed in periodicals ranging from the *Times* and the *Athenaeum* to the *Gardener's Chronicle*.

While reactions to Darwin's *Origin of Species* varied considerably, everyone recognized its importance. George Eliot, who had been able to get a copy on the first day, was writing in a letter at the beginning of December that the book "makes an epoch." Novelist and Broad Church clergyman Charles Kingsley also greeted the book enthusiastically and wrote to Darwin, who had sent him an advance copy: "All I have seen of it *awes* me; both from the heap of facts and the prestige of your name, and also with the clear intuition, that if you be right, I must give up much that I have believed and written." Nevertheless, he saw no conflict between the fundamentals of his faith and the theory Darwin proposed:

> I have gradually learnt to see that it is just as noble a conception of Deity, to believe that he created primal forms capable of self development into all forms needful . . . as to believe that He required a fresh act of intervention to supply the lacunas which he himself had made.[2]

But not all clergymen were so happy to accept the new theory. The Reverend Adam Sedgwick, Professor of Geology at Cambridge, wrote that he read

Darwin's work "with more pain than pleasure,"[3] and many other Anglican clergymen had even more violent reactions against the new presentation of evolutionary theory.

Many of the ideas that caused such violent responses, both positive and negative, were not new. The developmental hypothesis, the claim that new species developed gradually over a long period of time from other life forms, was not new; the idea had been discussed by several eighteenth-century thinkers, and the geological record provided strong evidence in favor of this view. It is sometimes claimed that Darwin offered the first account of the mechanism of by which evolution proceeds, natural selection. In fact, others had previously published works putting forth the idea of natural selection, but many readers would first have encountered the idea in the *Origin of Species*. Darwin's major achievement lay in the amount and quality of the evidence he marshaled in support of the theory of evolution by natural selection.

What did many Victorian religious writers find so threatening about Darwin's book? It was clearly a further challenge to biblical literalism, since Genesis 1 chronicled the individual creation of different kinds of plants and animals:

And God said, Let the earth bring forth the living creature after his kind, cattle, and creeping thing, and beast of the earth after his kind: and it was so. And God made the beast of the earth after his kind, and cattle after their kind, and every thing that creepeth upon the earth after his kind: and God saw that it was good (Genesis 1: 24–25).

But geological challenges had already led many Christians to abandon biblical inerrancy about science, and Darwin's theory could make little difference to them.

The theory posed a more serious threat, however, to that foundation of natural theology, the argument from design. According to this argument, the organization and harmony in nature constitute strong evidence of the existence, wisdom, and benevolence of God. But Darwin's theory could account for the appearance of design in nature without resorting to supernatural explanations: the adaptation of animals to their environment was not the result of a wise and benevolent act of creation, but of millennia of random mutations acted upon by a relentless process of natural selection. Darwin also drew attention to elements of the natural world that were anything but harmonious: natural selection worked in part through the deaths by starvation and violence of countless less well-adapted individuals. A vision of constant competition for resources and mates replaced one of peaceful coexistence within a providential plan. That Darwin presented a great deal of detailed evidence that favored this explanation made his book all the more dangerous.

Many of the critics immediately seized on one obvious implication of Darwin's theory. Although Darwin prudently refrained from spelling out the conclusion in *Origin of Species*, saving his discussion of the issue for his 1871 book *Descent of Man*, readers were quick to see that, according to Darwin's theory, human beings were descended from other "lower" forms of life. In addition to the blow to human ego, this claim seemed to challenge the spiritual nature of human beings, their formation "in the image of God," and also, crucially, their moral nature. If people were descended from beasts, if they were essentially no better than beasts themselves, what would prevent their living like beasts?

These issues were discussed in journals, pulpits, and debating halls across the country, but the most famous debate took place on June 30, 1860, when the British Association for the Advancement of Science met in Oxford to discuss Darwin's account of evolution. The event has become the stuff of legend, and, as with many legends, there are several different versions of the clash between Samuel Wilberforce, Bishop of Oxford (and son of the prominent Evangelical politician William Wilberforce), and T.H. Huxley, who became known as "Darwin's bulldog" for his vigorous defense of Darwinian theory. After several speakers had already addressed the issue, Wilberforce presented his arguments against Darwinian theory. The content of the body of his address is not recorded, but since he had recently completed a review of *Origin of Species* for the *Quarterly Review*, we can assume that his speech probably focused on the same material: detailed scientific objections to Darwin's arguments. At the end of his address, however, he turned to the issue of the descent of man. Some accounts claim that he challenged T.H. Huxley directly, asking whether it was through his grandfather or his grandmother that he traced his descent from an ape. Others claim that he appealed to a sexist Victorian chivalry by asking, "If anyone were to be willing to trace his descent through an ape as his *grandfather*, would he be willing to trace his descent similarly on the side of his *grandmother*." According to some versions, upon hearing Wilberforce's rhetorical flourish, Huxley muttered, "The Lord hath delivered him into my hands." Huxley's reply to Wilberforce is variously recorded, but his own account, written later that year, gives the flavor of it:

> If then, said I, the question is put to me would I rather have a miserable ape for a grandfather or a man highly endowed by nature and possessed of great means of influence and yet who employs those faculties and that influence for the mere purpose of introducing ridicule into a grave scientific discussion—I unhesitatingly affirm my preference for the ape.[4]

The Oxford debate is often taken to represent the victory of scientific enlightenment over religious obscurantism, but, in fact, Wilberforce was hardly obscurantist, and Huxley would have been unable at that point to reply convincingly to Wilberforce's substantial objections—though, of course, they would pose no challenge to later, more fully developed versions of evolutionary theory. The debate settled nothing, and religious faith continued to be unsettled by the advance of evolutionary theory over the course of the next century.

PUNCH, OR THE LONDON CHARIVARI—MAY 25, 1861.

THE LION OF THE SEASON.

ALARMED FLUNKEY. "MR. G-G-G-O-O-O-RILLA!"

This cartoon entitled, "The Lion of the Season" from *Punch*, alludes at once to Paul du Chaillu, an explorer of Africa, who wrote about gorillas, and to anxieties caused by the Darwinian theory's suggestion that humans and apes are closely related (*Punch*, 40:213, 1861). Courtesy of the Division of Special Collections, Archives, and Rare Books, University of Missouri at Columbia.

ESSAYS AND REVIEWS: THE EVOLUTION OF CHRISTIAN FAITH

Only a few months after the publication of *Origin of Species*, in February of 1860, Christian orthodoxy received another body blow. This time, though, the attack came from within. Seven Broad Church essayists, six clergymen and one layman, had contributed to a volume with the innocuous title, *Essays and Reviews*; their detractors dubbed them collectively the "Seven against Christ," an allusion to the ancient Greek drama by Aeschylus, *Seven against Thebes*. According to their own views, however, they were writing *for* Christ, not *against* him. All were professed Christians, but they believed that Christianity was endangered by those who attempted to ignore modern scholarship, textual and scientific, and cling instead to untenable intellectual positions; as Benjamin Jowett wrote in the volume, "The Christian religion is in a false position when all the tendencies of knowledge are opposed to it."[5] The Essayists were also frustrated by the limitations on intellectual inquiry that more orthodox Christians attempted to impose. They wanted to address directly the sources of doubt that were causing intellectuals, especially young students, to turn away from Christianity altogether.

Some of the essays were only mildly controversial. Frederick Temple, who, despite the controversy surrounding the volume, later became Archbishop of Canterbury, revised a sermon he had preached, turning it into his essay, "The Education of the World." Only in the context of the other essays could its idea of progressive revelation and its insistence on the careful and unprejudiced study of the Bible be deemed dangerous. Mark Pattison's historical essay on eighteenth-century theology perhaps subtly undermined current theological thought by demonstrating how the circumstances and consuming interests of a historical period can influence its religious ideas, but he was generally condemned only for the company he chose to keep.

The rest of the Essayists, however, addressed directly the most significant challenges to Christian orthodoxy. C.W. Goodwin, the only layman among the Essayists, was also the only one to address the challenges of geology. In his essay, he examined and dismissed various attempts to harmonize biblical narratives with geological discoveries, and ended by urging that such attempts be abandoned: the Bible was not intended as a source of scientific knowledge, but as a source of moral and religious truth, and errors concerning scientific topics did not impugn its authority on spiritual ones. Baden Powell, Professor of Geometry at Oxford and father of the founder of the Boy Scouts, wrote an essay that questioned whether human testimony could establish the reality of a miracle, and further, whether such miracles could constitute any evidence to support Christian teaching.

The most controversial essays, however, were those that focused on the interpretation of the Bible and of Christian doctrine. In the essay that closed the volume, Benjamin Jowett argued that to be understood the Bible must be read "like any other book," without preconceptions and assumptions based upon past interpretations or current doctrinal commitments. Rowland Williams, however, showed just what happened when German critics took that kind of advice to heart. In reviewing the work of a German biblical scholar, Baron Bunsen, Williams brought to the English public the German critical challenge to the historicity of the Bible, to the inspiration of biblical texts, and to the traditionally accepted authorship of some of the books of the Bible. Williams argued that the narratives in the Bible are not meant to be interpreted as literally historical, but rather as communicating spiritual truths. He also responded to the moral sources of unsettlement by reinterpreting problematic Christian doctrines in spiritual rather than physical terms. The atonement, for example, was not a matter of satisfying a justly angry God through the bodily suffering of the innocent, but of "Salvation from evil through sharing the Saviour's spirit."

For the denial of the atonement and the plenary inspiration of the Bible, Williams was tried and condemned in an ecclesiastical court, the Court of Arches; his codefendant was Henry Bristow Wilson, whose essay on "The National Church" provoked just as much controversy. In his essay, Wilson argued that a national church must be a Broad Church, in which there is free inquiry and free speech. In particular, he objected to the requirement that Anglican clergymen sign the Thirty-Nine Articles before ordination in order to prove their orthodoxy. Like Williams, he urged considerable latitude in the interpretation of Scripture, one which recognized that as in a parable or a fable, narrative could contain spiritual truth without being literally true. As he wrote in his essay, "The Word of God is contained in Scripture, whence it does not follow that it is co-extensive with it." The Bible is not as a whole the Word of God, but it still contains God's revelation. He excited even further controversy with his denial of eternal punishment in Hell, a second offense for which he was condemned by the Court of Arches.

Both Williams and Wilson were suspended from their clerical positions for a year, and both appealed their convictions to the civil courts, where they were overturned. But the controversy could not be as easily dismissed as charges of heresy. As in the case of *Origin of Species,* there was nothing radically new in these essays; instead, they seemed to constitute a summary of a half-century's unsettlement of traditional Christian beliefs. Still, while the geological challenges were common knowledge, many ordinary Christians had not given serious consideration to the German Higher Criticism until *Essays and Reviews* made it inescapable. The fact that these views could be held—and even taken for granted—by Anglican clergymen added to the controversy. Over 140 replies to *Essays and Reviews* were published, many of them criticizing the authors for continuing to hold positions in the church while denying some of its central doctrines. Each time one of the replies came out, each time one of the Essayists was recommended for promotion, the controversy was reignited. And, of course, it turned the academic book from a special-interest publication to something approaching a scholarly best seller, with 15,000 copies sold in just the first three months.

Under the circumstances, more orthodox Anglican clergymen felt that they needed to issue a public statement in support of traditional Christian teaching, and in 1864, a majority of the Anglican clergy signed a statement reaffirming the contested doctrines:

> We, the undersigned Presbyters and Deacons in Holy Orders of the Church of England and Ireland, hold it to be our bounden duty to the Church and to the souls of men, to declare our firm belief that the Church of England and Ireland ... maintains without reserve or qualification the plenary Inspiration and Authority of the whole Canonical Scriptures as the Word of God, and further teaches, in the words of our Blessed Lord, that the "punishment" of the "cursed," as the "life" of the "righteous" lasts forever.

But the words of the Essayists could not be unsaid. Their challenge to the authority and inspiration of the Bible and to the doctrine of eternal punishment remained to be answered.

THE EFFECTS OF UNSETTLEMENT

What did the unsettlement of faith mean for ordinary Victorians? Once again, no generalization will suffice, because different people had different reactions to unsettlement. For most Victorian Christians, it was probably a source of periodic unease or confusion, perhaps raising concerns about the future of the nation. Mothers and sisters feared for the faith of their sons and brothers away at university. The prospect of "Papal Aggression" with its attendant conversions disturbed many Victorian Protestants, while the specter of unbelief undermining morality and humanity, perhaps leading to working-class revolutionary violence, worried even more, whether or not they themselves were troubled by doubt about the truth of Christianity. Some Victorians drifted painlessly with the secularizing trend, gradually reducing public and private religious activities without ever officially recanting the faith of their fathers.

For others, however, the unsettlement of faith was much more traumatic. For people of strong religious convictions the loss of faith could topple their worlds, destroying any sense of meaning in their lives, challenging their most fundamental convictions, separating them from family and community. Victorian doubters recorded their experiences in memoirs and novels, and they described emotional upheaval that ranged from unhappiness to near madness.

John Ruskin was raised an Evangelical Anglican, but found his faith challenged by some of the intellectual movements discussed in this chapter. In

1851, he wrote to Henry Acland, who was also experiencing doubts, about his struggles:

> You speak of the Flimsiness of your own faith. Mine, which was never strong, is being beaten into mere gold leaf, and flutters in weak rags from the letter of its old forms; but the only letters it can hold by at all are the old Evangelical formulae. If only the Geologists would let me alone, I could do very well, but those dreadful Hammers! I hear the clink of them at the end of every cadence of the Bible verses.[6]

But Ruskin's reaction seems mild when set against doubters such as J.A. Froude and Elizabeth Missing Sewell.

Froude's novel, *Nemesis of Faith*, described the pain of his own loss of faith; he once "called it 'a cry of pain,' and he told [Charles] Kingsley that he had 'cut a hole in his heart' and written with the blood."[7] His protagonist, Markham Sutherland, pleads with the reader for sympathy for the distraught doubter:

> Ah! You who look with cold eye on such a one, and lift them up to Heaven, and thank God you are not such as he, . . . and call him hard names, and think of him as one who is forsaking a cross, and pursuing unlawful indulgence, and deserving all good men's reproach! Ah! Could you see down below his heart's surface, could you count the tears streaming down his cheeks, as out through some church-door into the street come pealing the old familiar notes, and the old psalms which he cannot sing, the chanted creed which is no longer his creed, and yet to part with which was worse agony than to lose his dearest friend; Ah! You would deal him lighter measure."[8]

Here the doubter suffers from a sense of social ostracism, alienation from his community, represented by the church, as well as from his own younger self, and a painful nostalgia for his old beliefs. Doubters also faced the loss of any hope of immortality and the dramatic change in the way they viewed the meaningfulness of their own lives.

Many accounts of Victorian unsettlement focus on the fascinating stories of men like John Ruskin, J.H. Newman, and J.A. Froude, educated at Oxford or (less often) Cambridge, and unsettled by abstruse intellectual considerations. But many other men and women also faced the unsettlement of religious faith, many without the intellectual armory that allowed some of these men to come to terms with their doubt. Their stories are harder to find, but they are still there, in letters, memoirs, and autobiographical novels. The experience of Elizabeth Missing Sewell can be taken as one example of these often-neglected stories. Sewell was a High Church Anglican and an admirer of Newman; when

Newman converted to Roman Catholicism, Sewell's faith was disturbed, and she describes this disturbance and her own responses in her journal:

> Mr. Meyrick told Edwards there was not a doubt that Newman is going over to Rome . . . It is a horrid, startling notion, but a sermon of Newman's I was reading to-night would be a great safeguard against being led into mischief by it. "Obedience, the remedy for religious perplexity." It is an immense comfort to have one's days so occupied as to leave little time for abstract thought.[9]

But though she sought to avoid "abstract thought," the temptation to follow Newman into the Catholic Church clearly haunted her, and she wrote a novel, *Margaret Percival*, which dramatizes a young girl's struggle as she tries to decide whether or not to convert from Anglicanism to Roman Catholicism. She, like many female doubters, is frustrated with the limited opportunities for participation that her religious tradition allows her, and, as we saw in Chapter 7, she is tempted by the possibility of wider opportunities in Catholicism. Nevertheless, she desires stronger reasons for conversion, but she feels herself unable to decide the question on intellectual grounds, so she has to choose instead between two morally unimpeachable male authority figures, her clergyman-uncle, and a sympathetic Catholic priest:

> My uncle tells me I have been in grievous error. He says that I am ignorant and wilful. He is good, and wise, and self-denying—Father Andrea himself cannot surpass him—and his faith in the English Church is built on a foundation which it seems that nothing can shake; nothing, at least, that I can say, for I know nothing. I must trust either to him or to Father Andrea. There is a horrible conflict in my mind; it has even verged upon madness.[10]

Margaret—and Sewell herself—chooses the Anglican Church, but the decision seems arbitrary. What remains is the story of the struggle and the pain of religious unsettlement.

It is hard to estimate how many people had such strong emotional reaction to the unsettlement of their faith or that of their loved ones, but the popularity of novels on the subject, including those by Froude and Sewell, indicates a widespread concern. As we noted in Chapter 6, Mary Arnold Ward's *Robert Elsmere*, a novel about a young clergyman's loss of faith, became a best seller even though it was very long and fairly intellectual. Thousands of ordinary people were clearly anxious to read a serious consideration of the human problems posed by religious unsettlement.

There were a few Victorians, however, who experienced the loss of faith as a liberation. Marian Evans, who would become the novelist George Eliot, became convinced that her youthful Evangelical faith was intellectually untenable and left it with relatively little regret, even though it caused a serious rift between her and her religious father.

Harriet Martineau's experience was even more dramatic. She was raised in a Unitarian family and began her writing career producing articles for Unitarian periodicals, including the *Monthly Repository*. But she recorded her gradual conversion to atheism in entirely positive terms, almost as a kind of rebirth:

> It took many years . . . But at length I recognized the monstrous super-
> stition in its true character of a great fact in the history of the race, and
> found myself, with the last link of my chain snapped,—a free rover on
> the broad, bright, breezy common of the universe.[11]

Martineau experienced this sense of liberation relatively early in the century, when atheism was still regarded as rare, radical, and dangerous. By the last decades of the nineteenth century, however, atheism and agnosticism had gone public and had acquired a certain degree of public toleration. The story of the gradual acceptance of unbelievers in Victorian society forms an important chapter in the history of Victorian religion.

ATHEISTS, AGNOSTICS, AND FREETHINKERS

While many Victorian Christians experienced an unsettlement of faith, and many more quietly drifted away from religious belief and church attendance, relatively few went so far as to publicly declare their rejection of Christianity. Those who did adopted a variety of names, sometimes signifying slightly different sets of commitments or different social class affiliations: freethinkers, rational religionists, atheists, agnostics, and secularists.

Victorian secularism originated in working-class radicalism, which often included commitments to a belief in reason and scientific progress promoted by eighteenth-century Enlightenment thinkers. Part of the secularists' hostility to religion was rooted in anticlericalism and opposition to the church's role in politics, its defense of the socioeconomic status quo. Early secularists defended a vision of social reform based on scientific knowledge, education, and self-help. They supported a broad view of freedom of speech and freedom of thought, which often led to their identification as "freethinkers." The movement was centered in London, which could offer a critical mass of people alienated from traditional religious beliefs, but there were many smaller provincial groups gathering at Workingmen's Institutes or Halls of Science for mutual support and to further the goals of the movement.

During the early part of the period, reaction to the secularists' activities was strongly negative and sometimes physically violent. Atheism had become bound up in the minds of many Britons with the horrors of the French Revolution, the Terror, and the Napoleonic Wars, which had ended only in 1815. Many believed that religion was the foundation of all social order and all morality—particularly among the working classes—and any threat to religion, especially when combined with political radicalism, seemed to endanger the nation itself. As a result, secularists suffered considerable persecution through much of the nineteenth century; persecution, however, helped create martyrs and sustain the movement, as many usually inactive unbelievers rallied to the cause of freedom.

The first organized atheist group, the Central Secular Society, was founded in 1851 by George Jacob Holyoake with the goals of furthering "the instruction of the members in matters appertaining to this life, the promotion of secular education, of rational amusements, and general culture."[12] Like many others, he had come to secularism from the Owenite movement; founded by Robert Owen, this group sought to remake society on a rational, utilitarian basis, stressing peaceful social change and cooperation rather than competition. Holyoake had served as an Owenite "social missionary," traveling from town to town aiding existing groups and lecturing on social reform. He had come to prominence in 1842 when, as the result of a remark he made in one of his speeches, he was convicted of blasphemy and imprisoned for six months under harsh conditions, during which time his young daughter died of hunger. Radicals rallied to his cause, and Holyoake became the unofficial leader of the movement, founding the Secular Society and, in 1852, taking over as editor of the journal of secularism, the *Reasoner*.

Secularism experienced a period of growth under Holyoake's leadership; between 1851 and 1861, sixty secularist groups were formed in cities across Britain. While he never abandoned his atheist beliefs, Holyoake increasingly sought respectability for the movement, and he was willing to cooperate with believers on socially worthwhile projects. Although secularism remained a fringe movement, under his leadership it moved toward greater social acceptance.

Agnosticism was a later development, one associated less with political radicalism and more with the "honest doubt" of the middle classes. T.H. Huxley, the defender of Darwin's evolutionary theory, coined the term "agnostic" in 1867 to describe a form of unbelief that was less confident—and that to many seemed less dangerous—than atheism or secularism. Huxley defined the central agnostic doctrine thus: "In matters of intellect, do not pretend that conclusions are certain which are not demonstrated or demonstrable." Conclusions about the existence of God, according to Huxley, fell into the category of the undemonstrated and, perhaps, undemonstrable, so that agnostics were obliged to suspend judgment about whether God existed or not.

Even as agnosticism moved closer to the mainstream, atheism became more militant. From 1866, leadership of the secularist movement was taken over by the combative Charles Bradlaugh. In that year he founded the National Secular Society and became its first president. In its constitution, the organization expressed support for "universal education, employment, civil, religious and intellectual liberty," and claimed that religion—"childish and absurd superstition"—stood in the way of human improvement and happiness.[13]

But even as it enjoyed increased membership and reduced persecution under Bradlaugh's leadership, secularism faced internal challenges. Despite its program of rational social reform, secularism remained largely a negative movement, defined by its opposition to religion, which limited its appeal and its ability to retain active members. Moreover, its membership was almost entirely male; the movement was not attractive to women or to families, which meant that children of secularists were seldom raised in the "unfaith." If such a pattern continued, secularism would have to depend entirely on conversion for its continued existence, with every new generation having to begin the process anew. In response, secularists turned some of their attention away from recruitment and toward retention; they attempted to create a positive secularist community, one that would attract women and families into the fold. To do this, many secular societies adopted the trappings of religion, setting themselves up almost as alternative churches—without the supernatural beliefs. They devised rituals for the naming of children, marriage, and burial; they held weekly meetings on Sundays; they compiled hymnals, hoping to enlist the emotions as well as the reason in the secularist cause; and they even offered Secular Sunday school for the young. Their efforts, however, met with limited success; few women joined the movement, and membership continued to fluctuate, growing significantly whenever a new instance of persecution filled the newspapers, and then gradually diminishing—until the next crisis.

One of the more notorious of these crises came with the prosecution of Charles Bradlaugh and Annie Besant on charges of obscenity. Because many Victorians believed that morality was wholly dependent on religious belief, atheists were frequently attacked as immoral and consequently dangerous. This problem was compounded by the fact that many secularists—including Bradlaugh and Besant—were committed to neo-Malthusianism, or the practice of artificial birth control, on the grounds that large families contributed to the cycle of poverty and ignorance in the working class, as well as to the unequal social standing of women. Even those secularists who feared that advocacy of birth control would hurt the movement, however, strongly supported the right of advocates to freedom of speech and publication. So when in 1877 Bradlaugh and Besant deliberately courted prosecution for obscenity by republishing a book describing methods of birth control, many latent secularists rallied to support them. Membership soared. They were duly charged, and both Bradlaugh and Besant conducted their own defenses—which was rare for anyone, but almost unheard of for a woman. Both were eventually convicted and sentenced to six months in jail, though Bradlaugh managed to have the convictions reversed on a technicality. The trial brought both defendants a degree of public recognition, which, however useful it may have been to the secularist movement, had serious personal consequences. Besant lost custody of her young daughter to her estranged husband, and Bradlaugh's reputation inflamed the opposition when in 1880 he was elected to Parliament.

Bradlaugh ran for Parliament as the Liberal Party candidate for Northampton and was elected because of his radical politics and despite some concern over his irreligion. But when he tried to take his seat in Parliament, he faced a problem: members of Parliament had to swear a religious oath on the Bible in order to assume their offices. At first, he hoped to make an affirmation of the kind that nonbelievers had been able to make in court since 1870. When he was forbidden to affirm, he agreed to take the oath as specified, but he was not permitted to do so. Over the next five years, Bradlaugh faced unremitting controversies and a series of hindrances, including lawsuits and even physical ejection from the Houses of Parliament. Finally, in January of 1886, Bradlaugh was permitted to swear the oath and take his place as a Member of Parliament, the first avowed atheist to do so. This victory represented a milestone in the public acceptance of free thought in matters of religion.

Committed secularists were never very numerous—at the height of the movement, they numbered only about 4,000—though they did contribute to several important legal reforms, particularly on issues of freedom of speech and publication. In the final years of the nineteenth century, the secularist movement lost steam. This was partly because political radicals were leaving the secular ranks and turning instead to socialism. But it was also a result of the large changes that Christianity in England had undergone over the course of the century and the gradual waning of religious influence. The religious issues that formed the center of secularist doctrine now mattered less to ordinary people. Their arguments about the inconsistencies in Scripture and the immorality of doctrines of eternal punishment, which had won them converts in the early days of the movement, were now fully endorsed by liberal Christians and accepted by many within the Anglican church. Secularists found themselves arguing not against the establishment, which they had associated with political oppression, but against marginalized groups of fundamentalist dissenters. The political meaning of their religious opposition had changed.

By 1900 religion had lost much of its political and social power, and a movement dedicated to its denial seemed less and less relevant to the concerns of a new century.

CONCLUSIONS

By 1900, religion in Britain was increasingly seen as a private rather than a public matter. Despite late Victorian revivalism, church attendance had declined significantly, and the society, like most European societies, was becoming increasingly secularized. It was clear that religion would not be central to the story of the twentieth century in Britain as it had been to the nineteenth.

The story of Victorian religion was one of controversies, conflicts, and constant change. It was the story of how the unity represented by the Established Church of England gave way to religious pluralism and diversity and of how Britain adapted to this pluralistic society through the growth of religious tolerance and a more religiously neutral polity. It was the story of Tractarians trying to reform their church and its priests, renewing their sense of high mission; of Evangelical activists trying to remake the world according to God's will; of Broad Church academics searching for an intellectually tenable faith. It was the story of challenges to faith from science, from textual studies, and from individual conscience and experience.

It was the story of bishops and cardinals, prime ministers and popes, Oxford dons and scientific mavericks. And it was the story of millions of ordinary people, each with his or her own story to tell of religious consolation, of communion and community, of vocation and service, of assurance or the loss of certainty, of conversion or the loss of faith, be it painful or joyous.

The next centuries would have their own religious stories. There would be new challenges as people of faith tried to cope with the horrendous cruelties that marked the era with its world wars and its genocidal regimes. Many of our stories, however, seem like sequels that take up the themes of the Victorian era.

The twentieth- and twenty-first centuries still struggle with conflicts over the role of women in religious life. The Roman Catholic Church in the early twenty-first century maintains an all-male priesthood, but many other Christian denominations allow women a larger role. The Church of Scotland ordained a woman in 1969; the first woman to become a priest in the Church of England was ordained in 1994. The worldwide Anglican communion, which includes the U.S. Episcopal Church, is still split over the issue: while most (though not all) of the churches ordain women as priests, there is no agreement over whether women should be ordained as bishops. Most of the Protestant dissenting denominations in Britain also ordain women. Jewish women, too, have assumed roles of religious leadership: in Reform, Reconstuctionist, and Conservative Judaism, women can become rabbis, though Orthodox and Hasidic Jews still refuse women "semicha" (rabbinical ordination). The role of women in Islam is, of course, a matter of increasing controversy. The struggle to define women's religious roles that began in the Victorian era continues in modern societies.

The conflict between science and religion also continues into the twenty-first century. While in most of Europe, including Britain, evolutionary theory seems to have been incorporated into religious belief, in America debates over the teaching of evolution in public schools rage on, in terms that Thomas Huxley and Samuel Wilberforce would have found familiar. But scientific discoveries also present new challenges to the religious worldview, as neuroscience investigates the neurological basis of religious experience and explores the physical foundations of human action, which complicate religious issues of sin and punishment. The sense of divergence between a scientific and religious worldview, which the Victorians clearly experienced, still causes anxiety for Western societies.

Issues concerning faith and practice in religiously pluralistic societies also trouble modern nations as they troubled the Victorians. To what extent can religious precepts guide legislation for a pluralistic society? How can the rights of religious minorities best be guaranteed? What are the limits of religious toleration? What is the proper role of religion in public life? Just as Victorian Evangelicals made a concerted attempt to legislate morality—from imposing their own views of slavery on a reluctant plantation culture in Jamaica to forcing everyone to observe their version of the Sabbath, so evangelical Christians in modern societies, particularly in the United States, bring their religious convictions to twenty-first-century politics, whether they are working to ban abortion or improve environmental standards.

Finally, our story has one more theme in common with the Victorian story: the persistent search for meaning both within and beyond religious traditions. The Victorians found themselves in a world where the old religious certainties were called into question: centuries of religious forms and religious beliefs seemed inadequate to meet the challenges of modern knowledge and modern life. Many sought to renew or remake the old faiths that had once served so well. Some tried to find alternative sources of meaning in art, in human love, and in political activism. That search for meaning and for a worldview adequate to our world continue for us today.

APPENDIX 1: THE THIRTY-NINE ARTICLES

ARTICLE 1—OF FAITH IN THE HOLY TRINITY

There is but one living and true God, everlasting, without body, parts, or passions; of infinite power, wisdom, and goodness; the maker and preserver of all things both visible and invisible. And in unity of this Godhead there be three Persons, of one substance, power, and eternity; the Father, the Son, and the Holy Ghost.

ARTICLE 2—OF THE WORD, OR SON OF GOD, WHICH WAS MADE VERY MAN

The Son, which is the Word of the Father, begotten from everlasting of the Father, the very and eternal God, and of one substance with the Father, took man's nature in the womb of the blessed Virgin, of her substance: so that two whole and perfect natures, that is to say, the Godhead and manhood, were joined together in one person, never to be divided, whereof is one Christ, very God and very man, who truly suffered, was crucified, dead, and buried, to reconcile His Father to us, and to be a sacrifice, not only for original guilt, but also for all actual sins of men.

ARTICLE 3—OF THE GOING DOWN OF CHRIST INTO HELL

As Christ died for us, and was buried, so also is it to be believed that He went down into Hell.

ARTICLE 4—OF THE RESURRECTION OF CHRIST

Christ did truly rise again from death, and took again His body, with flesh, bones, and all things appertaining to the perfection of man's nature, wherewith He ascended into Heaven, and there sitteth until He return to judge all men at the last day.

ARTICLE 5—OF THE HOLY GHOST

The Holy Ghost, proceeding from the Father and the Son, is of one substance, majesty, and glory with the Father and the Son, very and eternal God.

ARTICLE 6—OF THE SUFFICIENCY OF THE HOLY SCRIPTURE FOR SALVATION

Holy Scripture containeth all things necessary to salvation: so that whatsoever is not read therein, nor may be proved thereby, is not to be required of any man, that it should be believed as an article of the faith, or be thought requisite or necessary to salvation.

In the name of Holy Scripture, we do understand those Canonical books of the Old and New Testament, of whose authority was never any doubt in the Church.

The names and number of the Canonical Books:

Genesis	The First Book of Kings
Exodus	The Second Book of Kings
Leviticus	The First Book of Chronicles
Numbers	The Second Book of Chronicles
Deuteronomy	The First Book of Esdras
Joshua	The Second Book of Esdras
Judges	The Book of Esther
Ruth	The Book of Job
The First Book of Samuel	The Psalms
The Second Book of Samuel	The Proverbs
Ecclesiastes, or the Preacher	Four Prophets the Greater
Cantica, or Songs of Solomon	Twelve Prophets the Less

All the books of the New Testament, as they are commonly received, we do receive, and account them canonical.

And the other books (as Hierome saith) the Church doth read for example of life and instruction of manners; but yet it does not apply them to establish any doctrine. Such are these following:

The Third Book of Esdras	Baruch the Prophet
The Fourth Book of Esdras	The Song of the Three Children
The Book of Tobias	The Story of Susanna
The Book of Judith	Of Bel and the Dragon
The rest of the Book of Esther	The Prayer of Manasses
The Book of Wisdom	The First Book of Maccabees
Jesus the Son of Sirach	The Second Book of Maccabees

ARTICLE 7—OF THE OLD TESTAMENT

The Old Testament is not contrary to the New; for both in the Old and New Testament everlasting life is offered to mankind by Christ, who is the only Mediator between God and man, being both God and man. Wherefore there are not to be heard which feign that the old fathers did look only for transitory promises. Although the law given from God by Moses, as touching ceremonies and rites, do not bind Christian men, nor the civil precepts thereof ought of necessity to be received in any commonwealth; yet, notwithstanding, no Christian man whatsoever is free from the obedience of the commandments which are called moral.

ARTICLE 8—OF THE THREE CREEDS

The three Creeds, Nicene Creed, Athanasius' Creed, and that which is commonly called the Apostles' Creed, ought thoroughly to be received and believed; for they may be proved by most certain warrants of Holy Scripture.

ARTICLE 9—OF ORIGINAL OR BIRTH SIN

Original sin standeth not in the following of Adam (as the Pelagians do vainly talk), but it is the fault and corruption of the nature of every man that naturally is engendered of the offspring of Adam, whereby man is very far gone from original righteousness, and is of his own nature inclined to evil, so that the flesh lusteth always contrary to the spirit; and therefore in every person born into this world, it deserveth God's wrath and damnation. And this infection of nature doth remain, yea, in them that are regenerated, whereby the lust of the flesh, called in Greek *phronema sarkos* (which some do expound the wisdom, some sensuality, some the affection, some the desire of the flesh), is not subject to the law of God. And although there is no condemnation for them that believe and are baptized, yet the Apostle doth confess that concupiscence and lust hath itself the nature of sin.

ARTICLE 10—OF FREE WILL

The condition of man after the fall of Adam is such, that he cannot turn and prepare himself, by his own natural strength and good works, to faith and calling upon God. Wherefore we have no power to do good works pleasant and acceptable to God, without the grace of God by Christ preventing us that we may have a good will, and working with us when we have that good will.

ARTICLE 11—OF THE JUSTIFICATION OF MAN

We are accounted righteous before God, only for the merit of our Lord and Saviour Jesus Christ by faith, and not for our own works or deserving. Wherefore that we are justified by faith only is a most wholesome doctrine, and very full of comfort; as more largely is expressed in the Homily of Justification.

ARTICLE 12—OF GOOD WORKS

Albeit that good works, which are the fruits of faith and follow after justification, cannot put away our sins and endure the severity of God's judgement, yet are they pleasing and acceptable to God in Christ, and do spring out necessarily of a true and lively faith, insomuch that by them a lively faith may be as evidently known as a tree discerned by the fruit.

ARTICLE 13—OF WORKS BEFORE JUSTIFICATION

Works done before the grace of Christ and the inspiration of His Spirit, are not pleasant to God, forasmuch as they spring not of faith in Jesus Christ, neither do they make men meet to receive grace, or (as the School authors say) deserve grace of congruity: yea, rather for that they are not done as God hath willed and commanded them to be done, we doubt not but they have the nature of sin.

ARTICLE 14—OF WORKS OF SUPEREROGATION

Voluntary works besides, over and above, God's commandments which they call Works of Supererogation, cannot be taught without arrogancy and impiety. For by them men do declare that they do not only render unto God as much as they are bound to do, but that they do more for His sake than of bounden duty is required: Whereas Christ saith plainly, When ye have done all that are commanded to you, say, We be unprofitable servants.

ARTICLE 15—OF CHRIST ALONE WITHOUT SIN

Christ in the truth of our nature was made like unto us in all things, sin only except, from which He was clearly void, both in His flesh and in His spirit.

He came to be the lamb without spot, Who by sacrifice of Himself once made, should take away the sins of the world: and sin, as Saint John saith, was not in Him. But all we the rest, although baptized and born again in Christ, yet offend in many things: and if we say we have no sin, we deceive ourselves, and the truth is not in us.

ARTICLE 16—OF SIN AFTER BAPTISM

Not every deadly sin willingly committed after Baptism is sin against the Holy Ghost, and unpardonable. Wherefore the grant of repentance is not to be denied to such as fall into sin after Baptism. After we have received the Holy Ghost, we may depart from grace given and fall into sin, and by the grace of God we may arise again and amend our lives. And therefore they are to be condemned, which say, they can no more sin as long as they live here, or deny the place of forgiveness to such as truly repent.

ARTICLE 17—OF PREDESTINATION AND ELECTION

Predestination to life is the everlasting purpose of God, whereby, before the foundations of the world were laid, He hath constantly decreed by His counsel secret to us, to deliver from curse and damnation those whom He hath chosen in Christ out of mankind, and to bring them by Christ to everlasting salvation as vessels made to honour. Wherefore they which be endued with so excellent a benefit of God be called according to God's purpose by His Spirit working in due season; they through grace obey the calling; they be justified freely; they be made sons of God by adoption; they be made like the image of His only-begotten Son Jesus Christ; they walk religiously in good works; and at length by God's mercy they attain to everlasting felicity.

As the godly consideration of Predestination and our Election in Christ is full of sweet, pleasant, and unspeakable comfort to godly persons and such as feel in themselves the working of the Spirit of Christ, mortifying the works of the flesh and their earthly members and drawing up their mind to high and heavenly things, as well because it doth greatly establish and confirm their faith of eternal salvation to be enjoyed through Christ, as because it doth fervently kindle their love towards God: so for curious and carnal persons, lacking the Spirit of Christ, to have continually before their eyes the sentence of God's Predestination is a most dangerous downfall, whereby the devil doth thrust them either into desperation or into wretchlessness of most unclean living no less perilous than desperation.

Furthermore, we must receive God's promises in such wise as they be generally set forth in Holy Scripture; and in our doings that will of God is to be followed which we have had expressly declared unto us in the word of God.

ARTICLE 18—OF OBTAINING ETERNAL SALVATION ONLY BY THE NAME OF CHRIST

They also are to be had accursed that presume to say that every man shall be saved by the law or sect which he professeth, so that he be diligent to frame his life according to that law and the light of nature. For Holy Scripture doth set out to us only the name of Jesus Christ, whereby men must be saved.

ARTICLE 19—OF THE CHURCH

The visible Church of Christ is a congregation of faithful men, in which the pure word of God is preached and the sacraments be duly ministered according to Christ's ordinance in all those things that of necessity are requisite to the same. As the Church of Jerusalem, Alexandria, and Antioch have erred: so also the Church of Rome hath erred, not only in their living and manner of ceremonies, but also in matters of faith.

ARTICLE 20—OF THE AUTHORITY OF THE CHURCH

The Church hath power to decree rites or ceremonies and authority in controversies of faith; and yet it is not lawful for the Church to ordain anything contrary to God's word written, neither may it so expound one place of Scripture, that it be repugnant to another. Wherefore, although the Church be a witness and a keeper of Holy Writ: yet, as it ought not to decree anything against the same, so besides the same ought it not to enforce anything to be believed for necessity of salvation.

ARTICLE 21—OF THE AUTHORITY OF GENERAL COUNCILS

General Councils may not be gathered together without the commandment and will of princes. And when they be gathered together, forasmuch as they be an assembly of men, whereof all be not governed with the Spirit and word of God, they may err and sometime have erred, even in things pertaining to God. Wherefore things ordained by them as necessary to salvation have neither strength nor authority, unless it may be declared that they be taken out of Holy Scripture.

ARTICLE 22—OF PURGATORY

The Romish doctrine concerning Purgatory, Pardons, worshipping and adoration as well of Images as of Relics, and also Invocation of Saints, is a fond thing vainly invented, and grounded upon no warranty of Scripture; but rather repugnant to the word of God.

ARTICLE 23—OF MINISTERING IN THE CONGREGATION

It is not lawful for any man to take upon him the office of public preaching or ministering the sacraments in the congregation, before he be lawfully called and sent to execute the same. And those we ought to judge lawfully called and sent, which be chosen and called to this work by men who have public authority given unto them in the congregation to call and send ministers into the Lord's vineyard.

ARTICLE 24—OF SPEAKING IN THE CONGREGATION IN SUCH A TONGUE AS THE PEOPLE UNDERSTANDETH

It is a thing plainly repugnant to the word of God and the custom of the primitive Church, to have public prayer in the Church, or to minister the sacraments in a tongue not understanded of the people.

ARTICLE 25—OF THE SACRAMENTS

Sacraments ordained of Christ be not only badges or tokens of Christian men's profession, but rather they be certain sure witnesses and effectual signs of grace and God's good will towards us, by the which He doth work invisibly in us, and doth not only quicken, but also strengthen and confirm, our faith in Him.

There are two Sacraments ordained of Christ our Lord in the Gospel, that is to say, Baptism and the Supper of the Lord.

Those five, commonly called Sacraments, that is to say, Confirmation, Penance, Orders, Matrimony, and Extreme Unction, are not to be counted for Sacraments of the Gospel, being such as have grown partly of the corrupt following of the Apostles, partly are states of life allowed in the Scriptures; but yet have not the like nature of Sacraments with Baptism and the Lord's Supper, for that they have not any visible sign or ceremony ordained of God.

The Sacraments were not ordained of Christ to be gazed upon or to be carried about, but that we should duly use them. And in such only as worthily receive the same, have they a wholesome effect or operation: but they that receive them unworthily, purchase to themselves damnation, as Saint Paul saith.

ARTICLE 26—OF THE UNWORTHINESS OF THE MINISTERS, WHICH HINDERS NOT THE EFFECT OF THE SACRAMENTS

Although in the visible Church the evil be ever mingled with the good, and sometime the evil have chief authority in the ministration of the word and sacraments; yet forasmuch as they do not the same in their own name, but in Christ's, and do minister by His commission and authority, we may use their ministry both in hearing the word of God and in the receiving of the sacraments. Neither is the effect of Christ's ordinance taken away by their wickedness, nor the grace of God's gifts diminished from such as by faith and rightly do receive the sacraments ministered unto them, which be effectual because of Christ's institution and promise, although they be ministered by evil men. Nevertheless it apperaineth to the discipline of the Church that inquiry be made of evil ministers, and that they be accused by those that have knowledge of their offences; and finally, being found guilty by just judgement, be deposed.

ARTICLE 27—OF BAPTISM

Baptism is not only a sign of profession and mark of difference whereby Christian men are discerned from other that be not christened, but is also a sign of regeneration or new birth, whereby, as by an instrument, they that receive baptism rightly are grafted into the Church; the promises of the forgiveness of sin, and of our adoption to be the sons of God, by the Holy Ghost are visibly signed and sealed; faith is confirmed, and grace increased by virtue of prayer unto God. The baptism of young children is in any wise to be retained in the Church as most agreeable with the institution of Christ.

ARTICLE 28—OF THE LORD'S SUPPER

The Supper of the Lord is not only a sign of the love that Christians ought to have among themselves, one to another, but rather it is a sacrament of our redemption by Christ's death: insomuch that to such as rightly, worthily, and with faith receive the same, the bread which we break is a partaking of the body of Christ, and likewise the cup of blessing is a partaking of the blood of Christ.

Transubstantiation (or the change of the substance of bread and wine) in the Supper of the Lord, cannot be proved by Holy Writ, but is repugnant to the plain words of Scripture, overthroweth the nature of a Sacrament, and hath given occasion to many superstitions.

The body of Christ is given, taken, and eaten in the Supper, only after an heavenly and spiritual manner. And the mean whereby the body of Christ is received and eaten in the Supper is faith.

The Sacrament of the Lord's Supper was not by Christ's ordinance reserved, carried about, lifted up, or worshipped.

ARTICLE 29—OF THE WICKED WHICH DO NOT EAT THE BODY OF CHRIST, IN THE USE OF THE LORD'S SUPPER

The wicked and such as be void of a lively faith, although they do carnally and visibly press with their teeth (as S. Augustine saith) the sacrament of the body and blood of Christ, yet in no wise are they partakers of Christ, but rather to their condemnation do eat and drink the sign or sacrament of so great a thing.

ARTICLE 30—OF BOTH KINDS

The Cup of the Lord is not to be denied to the lay people; for both parts of the Lord's sacrament, by Christ's ordinance and commandment, ought to be ministered to all Christian men alike.

ARTICLE 31—OF THE ONE OBLATION OF CHRIST FINISHED UPON THE CROSS

The offering of Christ once made is the perfect redemption, propitiation, and satisfaction for all the sins of the whole world, both original and actual, and there is none other satisfaction for sin but that alone. Wherefore the sacrifices of Masses, in which it was commonly said that the priests did offer Christ for the quick and the dead to have remission of pain or guilt, were blasphemous fables and dangerous deceits.

ARTICLE 32—OF THE MARRIAGE OF PRIESTS

Bishops, Priests, and Deacons are not commanded by God's laws either to vow the estate of single life or to abstain from marriage. Therefore it is lawful also for them, as for all other Christian men, to marry at their own discretion, as they shall judge the same to serve better to godliness.

ARTICLE 33—OF EXCOMMUNICATED PERSONS, HOW THEY ARE TO BE AVOIDED

That person which by open denunciation of the Church is rightly cut off from the unity of the Church and excommunicated, ought to be taken by the whole multitude of the faithful as an heathen and publican, until he be openly reconciled by penance and received into the Church by a judge that hath authority thereto.

ARTICLE 34—OF THE TRADITIONS OF THE CHURCH

It is not necessary that traditions and ceremonies be in all places one or utterly alike; for at all times they have been diverse, and may be changed according to the diversity of countries, times, and men's manners, so that nothing be ordained against God's word.

Whosoever through his private judgement willingly and purposely doth openly break the traditions and ceremonies of the Church which be not repugnant to the word of God, and be ordained and approved by common authority, ought to be rebuked openly that others may fear to do the like, as he that offendeth against common order of the Church, and hurteth the authority of the magistrate, and woundeth the conscience of the weak brethren.

Every particular or national Church hath authority to ordain, change, and abolish ceremonies or rites of the Church ordained only by man's authority, so that all things be done to edifying.

ARTICLE 35—OF HOMILIES

The second Book of Homilies, the several titles whereof we have joined under this Article, doth contain a godly and wholesome doctrine and necessary for these times, as doth the former Book of Homilies which were set forth in the time of Edward the Sixth: and therefore we judge them to be read in Churches by the ministers diligently and distinctly, that they may be understanded of the people.

Of the Names of the Homilies:

1. Of the right Use of the Church
2. Against peril of Idolatry
3. Of the repairing and keeping clean of Churches
4. Of good Works: first of Fasting
5. Against Gluttony and Drunkenness
6. Against Excess of Apparel
7. Of Prayer
8. Of the Place and Time of Prayer
9. That Common Prayers and Sacraments ought to be ministered in a known tongue
10. Of the reverend estimation of God's Word
11. Of Alms-doing
12. Of the Nativity of Christ
13. Of the Passion of Christ
14. Of the Resurrection of Christ
15. Of the worthy receiving of the Sacrament of the Body and Blood of Christ
16. Of the Gifts of the Holy Ghost
17. For the Rogation-days
18. Of the state of Matrimony
19. Of Repentance
20. Against Idleness
21. Against Rebellion

ARTICLE 36—OF CONSECRATION OF BISHOPS AND MINISTERS

The Book of Consecration of Archbishops and Bishops and ordering of Priests and Deacons, lately set forth in the time of Edward the Sixth and confirmed at the same time by authority of Parliament, doth contain all things necessary to such consecration and ordering; neither hath it anything that of itself is superstitious or ungodly.

And therefore whosoever are consecrated or ordered according to the rites of that book, since the second year of King Edward unto this time, or hereafter shall be consecrated or ordered according to the same rites, we decree all such to be rightly, orderly, and lawfully consecrated or ordered.

ARTICLE 37—OF THE CIVIL MAGISTRATES

The Queen's Majesty hath the chief power in this realm of England and other her dominions, unto whom the chief government of all estates of this realm, whether they be ecclesiastical or civil, in all causes doth appertain, and is not nor ought to be subject to any foreign jurisdiction.

Where we attribute to the Queen's Majesty the chief government, by which titles we understand the minds of some slanderous folks to be offended, we give not to our princes the ministering either of God's word or of sacraments, the which thing the Injunctions also lately set forth by Elizabeth our Queen doth most plainly testify: but only that prerogative which we see to have been given always to all godly princes in Holy Scriptures by God himself, that is, that they should rule all estates and degrees committed to their charge by God, whether they be temporal, and restrain with the civil sword the stubborn and evil-doers.

The Bishop of Rome hath no jurisdiction in this realm of England.

The laws of the realm may punish Christian men with death for heinous and grievous offences.

It is lawful for Christian men at the commandment of the Magistrate to wear weapons and serve in the wars.

ARTICLE 38—OF CHRISTIAN MEN'S GOODS WHICH ARE NOT COMMON

The riches and goods of Christians are not common, as touching the right, title, and possession of the same, as certain Anabaptists do falsely boast; notwithstanding every man ought of such things as he possesseth liberally to give alms to the poor, according to his ability.

ARTICLE 39—OF A CHRISTIAN MAN'S OATH

As we confess that vain and rash swearing is forbidden Christian men by our Lord Jesus Christ, so we judge that Christian religion doth not prohibit but that a man may swear when the magistrate requireth in a cause of faith and charity, so it be done according to the Prophet's teaching in justice, judgement, and truth.

APPENDIX 2: THE CREEDS

THE APOSTLES' CREED

I believe in God the Father Almighty,
Maker of heaven and earth:

And in Jesus Christ His only Son our Lord;
Who was conceived by the Holy Ghost,
born of the Virgin Mary,
suffered under Pontius Pilate,
was crucified, dead, and buried.
He descended into hell;
The third day He rose again from the dead;
He ascended into heaven,
and sitteth on the right hand of God the Father Almighty;
from thence He shall come to judge the quick and the dead.

I believe in the Holy Ghost;
the Holy Catholic Church;
the communion of saints;
the forgiveness of sins;
the resurrection of the body;
and the life everlasting.
Amen.

THE NICENE CREED

I believe in one God the Father Almighty,
Maker of heaven and earth,
and of all things visible and invisible:

And in one Lord Jesus Christ,
the only begotten Son of God,
begotten of His Father before all worlds,
God of God, Light of Light,
very God of very God,
begotten, not made,
being of one substance with the Father,
by Whom all things were made;
Who for us men and for our salvation
came down from heaven,
and was incarnate by the Holy Ghost of the Virgin Mary,
and was made man,
and was crucified also for us under Pontius Pilate.
He suffered and was buried,
and the third day He rose again
according to the Scriptures,
and ascended into heaven,
and sitteth on the right hand of the Father.
And He shall come again with glory,
to judge both the quick and the dead;
Whose kingdom shall have no end.

And I believe in the Holy Ghost,
the Lord, the giver of life,
Who proceedeth from the Father and the Son,
Who with the Father and the Son together
is worshipped and glorified,
Who spake by the prophets.
And I believe one holy Catholic and Apostolic Church.
I acknowledge one baptism for the remission of sins.
And I look for the resurrection of the dead,
and the life of the world to come.
Amen.

THE ATHANASIAN CREED

Whosoever will be saved, before all things it is necessary that he hold the Catholic Faith. Which Faith except everyone do keep whole and undefiled, without doubt he shall perish everlastingly.

And the Catholic Faith is this: That we worship one God in Trinity, and Trinity in Unity, neither confounding the persons, nor dividing the substance;

For there is one Person of the Father, another of the Son, and another of the Holy Ghost. But the Godhead of the Father, of the Son, and of the Holy Ghost, is all one, the Glory equal, the Majesty co-eternal.

Such as the Father is, such is the Son, and such is the Holy Ghost.

The Father uncreate, the Son uncreate, and the Holy Ghost uncreate.

The Father incomprehensible, the Son incomprehensible, and the Holy Ghost incomprehensible.

The Father eternal, the Son eternal, and the Holy Ghost eternal.

And yet they are not three eternals, but one eternal.

As also there are not three incomprehensibles, nor three uncreated, but one uncreated, and one incomprehensible.

So likewise the Father is Almighty, the Son Almighty, and the Holy Ghost Almighty.

And yet not three Almighties, but one Almighty.

So the Father is God, the Son is God, and the Holy Spirit is God. And yet they are not three gods, but one God.

So likewise the Father is Lord, the Son Lord, and the Holy Spirit Lord. And yet not three lords, but one Lord.

For like as we are compelled by the Christian verity to acknowledge each Person by Himself to be God and Lord,

So we are also forbidden by the Catholic Religion to say there be three Gods, or three Lords.

The Father is made of none, neither created, nor begotten.

The Son is of the Father alone, not made, nor created, but begotten.

The Holy Ghost is of the Father, and of the Son, neither made, nor created, nor begotten, but proceeding.

So there is one Father, not three Fathers; one Son, not three Sons; one Holy Ghost, not three Holy Ghosts.

And in this Trinity none is afore or after other; none is greater or less than another,

But the whole three Persons are co-eternal together and co-equal.

So that in all things, as is aforesaid, the Unity in Trinity and the Trinity in Unity is to be worshipped.

He therefore that will be saved must think thus of the Trinity.

Furthermore, it is necessary to everlasting salvation that he also believe rightly the Incarnation of our Lord Jesus Christ.

For the right Faith is, that we believe and confess, that our Lord Jesus Christ, the Son of God, is God and Man;

God, of the Substance of the Father, begotten before the worlds; and Man of the substance of His Mother, born in the world;

Perfect God, and perfect man, of a reasonable soul and human flesh subsisting.

Equal to the Father, as touching His Godhead; and inferior to the Father, as touching His Manhood;

Who, although He be God and Man, yet He is not two, but one Christ;

One, not by conversion of the Godhead into flesh, but by taking of the Manhood into God;

One altogether, not by confusion of Substance, but by unity of Person.

For as the reasonable soul and flesh is one man, so God and Man is one Christ;

Who suffered for our salvation, descended into hell, rose again the third day from the dead.

He ascended into heaven, He sitteth at the right hand of the Father, God Almighty, from whence He shall come to judge the quick and the dead.

At Whose coming all men shall rise again with their bodies and shall give account for their own works.

And they that have done good shall go into life everlasting; and they that have done evil into everlasting fire.

This is the Catholic Faith, which except a man believe faithfully, he cannot be saved.

NOTES

INTRODUCTION

1. Jane Austen, *Mansfield Park* (Oxford: Oxford University Press, 1980), 82.
2. Ibid., 98.
3. Irene Collins, *Jane Austen and the Clergy* (London: Hambledon Press, 1994), 27.
4. Jane Austen, *Sense and Sensibility* (Oxford: Oxford University Press, 1980), 246–247.
5. Jane Austen, *Pride and Prejudice* (Oxford: Oxford University Press, 1980), 340.
6. Collins, *Jane Austen and the Clergy*, 27.
7. Ibid., 27–28.
8. Ibid., 30.
9. Austen, *Sense and Sensibility*, 241.
10. Collins, *Jane Austen and the Clergy*, 43.
11. Ibid., 43.
12. Ibid., 145.

1: CHURCH AND STATE: POLITICS AND THE VICTORIAN CHURCH OF ENGLAND

1. M.V. Hughes, *A London Child of the 1870s* (Oxford: Oxford University Press, 1977), 72.
2. Charles Dickens, *Sunday Under Three Heads*, Project Gutenberg, http://infomotions.com/etexts/gutenberg/dirs/etext97/suths10.htm, 1997.
3. Owen Chadwick, *The Victorian Church* (Oxford: Oxford University Press, 1966–1970), I:456.
4. Dickens, *Sunday Under Three Heads*.
5. Charles Dickens, *Hard Times* (Harmondsworth, Middlesex, UK: Penguin, 1995), 79.
6. Chadwick, *The Victorian Church*, I:483.

7. Kathleen Heasman, *Evangelicals in Action* (London: G. Bles, 1962), 14.

8. George Eliot, *Middlemarch* (Harmondsworth, Middlesex, UK: Penguin, 1985), 662.

9. D.W. Bebbington, *Evangelicalism in Modern Britain: A History from the 1730s to the 1980s* (London: Unwin Hyman, 1989), 130.

10. Eliot, *Middlemarch*, 191.

11. Chadwick, *The Victorian Church*, I:168.

12. A similar account occurs in Luke 22:19–20.

13. John Henry Newman, *Apologia Pro Vita Sua* (New York: W.W. Norton, 1968), 78–79.

14. Arthur Penrhyn Stanley, *Essays Chiefly on Questions of Church and State* (London: Murray, 1884), 7, 16.

15. Chadwick, *The Victorian Church*, I:353.

16. *Hymns, Ancient and Modern: Historical Edition* (London: William Clowes, 1909), nos. 25, 421, 470, 483.

2: VARIETY IN VICTORIAN RELIGIOUS EXPERIENCE

1. Owen Chadwick, *The Victorian Church* (Oxford: Oxford University Press, 1966–1970), I:402.

2. Harriet Martineau, *Autobiography* (Boston, MA: J.R. Osgood, 1877), 30.

3: A CLERGYMAN'S LIFE

1. Francis Knight, *The Nineteenth-Century Church and English Society* (Cambridge: Cambridge University Press, 1995), 134.

2. Alan Haig, *The Victorian Clergy* (London: Croom Helm, 1984), 8.

3. Ibid., 146.

4. Ibid., 142.

5. Knight, *The Nineteenth-Century Church and English Society*, 129.

6. Haig, *The Victorian Clergy*, 222.

7. Knight, *The Nineteenth-Century Church and English Society*, 132.

8. Ibid., 131.

9. Anthony Trollope, *The Last Chronicle of Barset*, Project Gutenberg, http://www.gutenberg.org/catalog/world/readfile?fk_files=284934&pageno=23, 2002, 23.

10. John Gott, *The Parish Priest of the Town* (London: Society for Promoting Christian Knowledge, 1906), 7.

11. Owen Chadwick, *The Victorian Church* (Oxford: Oxford University Press, 1966–1970), II:347.

12. Anthony Trollope, *Barchester Towers* (New York: New American Library Signet Classics, 1983), 18.

4: RELIGION AND DAILY LIFE

1. Francis Knight, *The Nineteenth-Century Church and English Society* (Cambridge: Cambridge University Press, 1995), 83–84.

2. M.V. Hughes, *A London Child of the 1870s* (Oxford: Oxford University Press, 1977), 100–101.

3. Knight, *The Nineteenth-Century Church and English Society*, 84.

4. Charles Dickens, *Hard Times* (Harmondsworth, Middlesex, UK: Penguin, 1995), 29.

5. Hughes, *A London Child of the 1870s*, 100.

6. Knight, *The Nineteenth-Century Church and English Society*, 39.

5: RELIGION AND REFORM

1. Leslie Howsam, *Cheap Bibles: Nineteenth-Century Publishing and the British and Foreign Bible Society* (Cambridge: Cambridge University Press, 1991), 207.

2. Philip B. Cliff, *The Rise and Development of the Sunday School Movement in England, 1780–1980* (Nutfield, Redhill, Surrey: National Christian Education Council, 1986), 27.

3. Ibid., 101.

4. Ibid., 124.

5. Ibid., 95–96.

6. Marianne Farningham, *A Working Woman's Life* (London: James Clarke, 1907), 111–130.

7. Nancy Boyd, *Three Victorian Women Who Changed Their World: Josephine Butler, Octavia Hill, Florence Nightingale* (Oxford: Oxford University Press, 1982), 133.

8. Ibid., 91.

9. Andrew Porter, *Religion versus Empire? British Protestant Missionaries and Overseas Expansion, 1700–1914* (Manchester: Manchester University Press, 2004), 41.

10. Ibid., 8–9.

6: THE BIBLE AND OTHER BEST SELLERS

1. Francis Knight, *The Nineteenth-Century Church and English Society* (Cambridge: Cambridge University Press, 1995), 175.

2. Leslie Howsam, *Cheap Bibles: Nineteenth-Century Publishing and the British and Foreign Bible Society* (Cambridge: Cambridge University Press, 1991), 178.

3. *Hymns, Ancient and Modern* (1861), nos. 2, 11, and 71, respectively.

4. Owen Chadwick, *The Victorian Church* (Oxford: Oxford University Press, 1966–1970), I:443–444.

5. Josef L. Altholz, *The Religious Press in Britain, 1760–1900* (Westport, CT.: Greenwood Press, 1989), 72.

6. Ibid., 79.

7. Charlotte Yonge, "Autobiography" in *Charlotte Mary Yonge: Her Life and Letters* by Christabel Coleridge (London: Macmillan, 1903), 65.

8. Elaine Showalter, *A Literature of Their Own: British Women Novelists from Bronte to Lessing* (London: Virago, 1982), 145.

9. Margaret M. Maison, *Search Your Soul, Eustace: A Survey of the Religious Novel in the Victorian Age* (London: Sneed Stagbooks, 1961), 139–140.

10. Emma Jane Worboise, "'Inkshed' and 'Authorship': To Intending Contributors," *Christian World Magazine* 18 (1882):34.

11. Mary Summers, "Anne Brontë's Religion," *Transactions of the Bronte Society* 25 (2000):20.

12. Charlotte Brontë, *Jane Eyre* (Harmondsworth, Middlesex, UK: Penguin, Signet Classics, 1997), 65.

13. Ibid., 63.

14. Ibid., 111.

15. Ibid., 461.

16. Elizabeth Rigby, "Vanity Fair—and Jane Eyre," *Quarterly Review* 84 (December 1848).

17. Charlotte Yonge, *The Daisy Chain, or Aspirations* (Project Gutenberg, http://www.gutenberg.org/etext/3610, 2003), Chapter 22.

18. George Eliot, *Middlemarch* (Harmondsworth, Middlesex, UK: Penguin, 1985), 619.

19. Thomas Hardy, *Tess of the D'Urbervilles* (Harmondsworth, Middlesex, UK: Penguin, 1985), 128.

20. Ibid., 378.

21. Mark Knight and Emma Mason, *Nineteenth-Century Religion and Literature: An Introduction* (Oxford: Oxford University Press, 2006), 100.

22. Ibid., 101.

23. Ibid., 109.

7: WOMEN AND RELIGIOUS LIFE

1. William Wilberforce, *A Practical View of the Prevailing Religious System of Professed Christians in the Higher and Middle Classes in the Country, Contrasted with Real Christianity* (London: 1797), 434.

2. Lydia (pseud.), "Female Biography of Scripture: Manoah's Wife," *Christian Lady's Magazine* 17 (1842):503ff.

3. Elizabeth K. Helsinger, Robin Lauterbach Sheets, and William Veeder. *The Woman Question: Defining Voices*, 1837–1883, vol. 1 (New York: Garland, 1983), 10.

4. Marina Warner, *Alone of All Her Sex: The Myth and the Cult of the Virgin Mary* (New York: Random House, 1976), 288.

5. *Hymns, Ancient and Modern*, nos. 330, 322.

6. "Far Above Rubies," *Christian World Magazine* 6 (1870):305.

7. Harriet Beecher Stowe, "Portraits of the Patriarchs: Miriam and Moses," *Christian World Magazine* 9 (1873):373.

8. Lydia (pseud.), "Female Biography of Scripture: Deborah," *Christian Lady's Magazine* 16 (1841):337–349.

9. Emma Jane Worboise, "Editorial Address," *Christian World Magazine* 1 (1866):2.

10. Nancy Boyd, *Three Victorian Women Who Changed Their World: Josephine Butler, Octavia Hill, Florence Nightingale* (Oxford: Oxford University Press, 1982), 63.

11. Helsinger, Sheets, and Veeder, *The Woman Question: Defining Voices*, 10.

12. Elizabeth Missing Sewell, *Margaret Percival* (London: Longmans, 1846), I:353.

8: THE VICTORIAN RELIGIOUS UNSETTLEMENT

1. Robin Gilmour, *The Victorian Period: The Intellectual and Cultural Context of English Literature, 1830–1890* (New York: Longman, 1993), 122.

2. Charles Kingsley, Letter to Charles Darwin, November 18, 1859, Darwin Correspondence Project, Letter 2534, http://www.darwinproject.ac.uk/darwinletters/calendar/entry-2534.html.

3. Adam Sedgwick, Letter to Charles Darwin, November 24, 1859. Darwin Correspondence Project, Letter 2548, http://www.darwinproject.ac.uk/darwinletters/calendar/entry-2548.html.

4. J.R. Lucas, "Wilberforce and Huxley: A Legendary Encounter," *Historical Journal* 22(2) (1979), http://users.ox.ac.uk/~jrlucas/legend.html.

5. Benjamin Jowett, "On the Interpretation of Scripture," in *Essays and Reviews* (London: John W. Parker, 1860), 374.

6. George P. Landow, *The Aesthetic and Critical Theories of John Ruskin* (Princeton: Princeton University Press, 1971), 266.

7. Basil Willey, *More Nineteenth Century Studies: A Group of Honest Doubters* (New York: Columbia University Press, 1956), 121.

8. J.A. Froude, *Nemesis of Faith* (London: Chapman, 1849), 116–117.

9. Elizabeth Missing Sewell, *Autobiography*, ed., Eleanor L. Sewell (London: Longmans, Green, 1907), 119.

10. Elizabeth Missing Sewell, *Margaret Percival* (London: Longmans, 1846), I:353, II:281.

11. Harriet Martineau, *Autobiography* (Boston, MA: J.R. Osgood, 1877), 89.

12. Susan Budd, *Varieties of Unbelief: Atheists and Agnostics in English Society, 1850–1960* (London: Heinemann, 1977), 28.

13. Budd, *Varieties of Unbelief: Atheists and Agnostics in English Society*, 42.

GLOSSARY

Advent: A holy season of Christian churches; a period of preparation for the celebration of the birth of Christ on Christmas. Advent begins on Advent Sunday, the fourth Sunday before Christmas day.

Agnostic: A person who suspends judgment on the question of the existence or nonexistence of God on the grounds of insufficient evidence.

Aisles: In church architecture, passageways on either side of the nave, usually separated from it by colonnades.

Alb: A long white linen tunic, often belted with a long rope-like cord, worn by clergymen when administering the Eucharist. The alb, like other more elaborate liturgical vestments, was associated in the Victorian period with the ritualist movement in the Church of England.

Altar: In Christian churches, the table or other structure upon which the bread and the wine for the celebration of the Eucharist are placed. The altar, located in the sanctuary at the east end of the church, is generally considered the holiest part of the church.

Anglican: Pertaining to the Church of England, the established church in England and Wales. The Anglican Communion, led by the Archbishop of Canterbury, now encompasses churches throughout the world, including the Church of Ireland, the Church of Wales, and the American Episcopal Church.

Anglo-Catholic: A member of the High Church party of the Church of England who emphasizes the church's continuity with its Roman Catholic traditions. Victorian Anglo-Catholics reintroduced into the Anglican Church many Roman Catholic traditions including auricular confession and adoration of the Virgin Mary, and they stressed clerical authority and the sacramental nature of the Eucharist. *See also* Tractarian and Ritualist.

Apocrypha: Jewish and Christian religious texts that were accepted by some religious groups as canonical, representing revelation from God, and were included as part of their Bible, but were rejected by other groups. Listed as noncanonical in the Thirty-Nine

Articles of the Anglican Church, the Apocrypha includes 3 Esdras, 4 Esdras, the Book of Tobit, the Book of Judith, the rest of the Book of Esther, the Book of Wisdom, Eccesiasticus (Sirach), Baruch, Song of the Three Children, the Story of Susanna, Of Bel and the Dragon, the Prayer of Manasses, 1 Maccabees, and 2 Maccabees.

Apostolic Succession: A doctrine, held by Roman Catholics and by British Tractarians, according to which Jesus Christ originally ordained his Apostles to lead the church, and their authority was subsequently passed down through ordination to a new generation of bishops, who in turn ordained their successors, and so on, in unbroken succession to the present day. Priestly authority thus derives, through this unbroken line of ordination, from Christ himself, and no one outside this line of succession can claim such authority.

Apse: A semicircular or polygonal section of the sanctuary of a church, located at the east end, beyond the altar.

Archbishop: A clergyman, ranking above the bishops in the church hierarchy, who has jurisdiction over an archdiocese, or group of dioceses. The Church of England has two archbishops, the Archbishop of York and the Archbishop of Canterbury; the Archbishop of Canterbury serves as leader of both the Church of England and the Anglican Communion. The Church of Ireland also has two archbishops, the Archbishop of Armagh and the Archbishop of Dublin.

Archdeacon: A clergyman chosen by the bishop to assist him with the oversight of the parishes in his diocese. The archdeacon oversees an archdeaconry, which is part of the diocese, visiting parish clergy and inspecting church property. He ranks above vicars and rectors and is just below the bishop in the church hierarchy.

Archdiocese: The geographical area, encompassing a group of dioceses, under the jurisdiction of an archbishop.

Arminian: Adhering to a Christian theological doctrine that opposes Calvinistic predestination, claiming instead that Christian salvation is open to anyone who has faith in Jesus Christ and that human beings can, by their free will, accept or reject the offer of salvation.

Assembly Movement: *See* Plymouth Brethren.

Atheist: Someone who believes that God does not exist.

Atonement, Doctrine of: A central Christian belief that claims that the sacrificial death of Jesus Christ served as a kind of payment for the sins of believers and allowed reconciliation between human beings and God.

Banns: An announcement of a bride and groom's intention to wed. The banns had to be read out in the bride's and groom's parish churches for three consecutive Sundays before the wedding could take place, unless a license or special license was obtained. The announcement would be made as follows: *I publish the Banns of Marriage between Mary Jones of Grimsby and Christopher Johnson of Stickford. If any of you know cause, or just impediment, why these two persons should not be joined together in Holy Matrimony, ye are to declare it. This is the first [or second or third] time of asking.*

Baptism: A ritual in the Christian church in which water is sprinkled or poured on the head, or, less frequently, a person is entirely immersed in water, to enact or symbolize purification from sin and to initiate membership in a Christian church. Baptism is a sacrament for almost every Christian denomination, but denominations differ in their practice and doctrine of baptism. Most denominations, including Anglicans, Presbyterians, and Methodists, baptize infants, as well as adult converts, by sprinkling water. Baptists reject the baptism of infants and baptize by total immersion only those who have made a confession of Christian faith, a practice known as "believer's baptism."

Baptismal Regeneration: The doctrine that being baptized removes the guilt of original sin and confers salvation. The Book of Common Prayer endorses this doctrine, and it is accepted by most Anglicans, but some Victorian Evangelicals objected that repentance and faith, rather than external ritual, are necessary for the forgiveness of sin.

Baptist: Dissenter belonging to one of several Protestant denominations, including General Baptists, Particular Baptists, and Strict and Particular Baptists. Although Baptists were part of Old Dissent and some Baptists retained Calvinist doctrines of salvation, Victorian Baptists were otherwise evangelical in belief and practice. Their distinctive beliefs included a rejection of infant baptism, an insistence that only those who professed Christian faith could be baptized, baptism by total immersion, and the independent governance of each local congregation.

Basilican: In church architecture, a term used to describe a longitudinal layout of a church, in which a long nave on the west end of the church, sometimes flanked by aisles, leads to a sanctuary, with or without an intervening choir, on the east end. Many British churches use this basilican design, to be contrasted with the other common layout, the cruciform church.

Benefice: A position in the church that has attached to it a source of income, such as rights to rents or tithes. The word can also refer to the income itself.

Bible Christians: Members of a Dissenting denomination derived from Wesleyan Methodism. Founded in 1815 by William O'Bryan, the Bible Christians gained a significant following in Devon and Cornwall. Their doctrine was fundamentally the same as Wesleyan Methodism, with additional emphasis on the centrality of biblical authority, but, unlike the Wesleyans, they continued to allow women to preach and they strongly supported the temperance movement.

Bishop: In the Anglican Church, a clergyman, ranking above vicars and rectors in the church hierarchy, who has jurisdiction over a large group of parishes, known as a diocese, and over the clergymen working within those parishes. (*But see also* "Suffragan Bishop.") The diocesan bishop's church is a cathedral, where he has his episcopal throne or "cathedra"; he is addressed as "the Right Reverend." The Methodists also have bishops who exercise administrative jurisdiction over groups of clergy working in a particular geographical region.

Book of Common Prayer: In the Anglican Church, the book setting out the words and structure of worship services. The 1662 version was the one in use throughout the nineteenth century.

Broad Church: A party within the Anglican Church, liberal and theologically progressive, which believed that the Church of England should be tolerant of a broad range of opinion in theology and practice and should remain open to new ideas.

Calvinist: Adhering to the theological tenets of John Calvin (1509–1564), particularly the doctrines that human beings are totally depraved, unable to choose to follow God on their own, and that some people (the "elect") are chosen ("predestined") by God to be saved, while others are predestined to damnation for their sins. Victorian Anglicans were generally moderate Calvinists, but virtually all Calvinists—including Presbyterians, Congregationalists, and many Baptists—moderated their views over the course of the nineteenth century.

Canon: In the Anglican Church, a clergyman appointed by the bishop to assist the dean in the operation of the cathedral. Some canons had specific responsibilities within the cathedral or diocese. After 1840, each cathedral had between four and six canons.

Canon, Minor: In the Anglican Church, a clergyman appointed to sing services at a cathedral. Minor canons did not participate in the governance of the cathedral.

Canon, Nonstipendiary: An honorary position carrying neither salary nor responsibilities within a cathedral.

Canticle: A hymn, other than the psalms, taken from the Bible. Canticles appear frequently in Anglican worship as specified in the *Book of Common Prayer*.

Cassock: An ankle length black robe worn by clergymen, often for ordinary occasions as well as services. A bishop's cassock is traditionally purple rather than black.

Catechism: A summary of doctrine, usually presented in a question-and-answer format. Generally, a catechism is memorized by a young person and recited publicly before his or her confirmation. The Anglican catechism includes the Ten Commandments, the Apostles' Creed, and the Lord's Prayer, as well as questions about the sacraments.

Cathedral: A church, often large and ornate, which contains the throne of the bishop, the "cathedra." In Britain, only if a population center has a cathedral can it officially be designated a city. The cathedral city gives its name to the diocese of which it is the center.

Chancel: The space around the altar at the east end of a church, encompassing the sanctuary and the choir.

Chapel: A place of religious worship. In the Victorian period, it was primarily used to refer to dissenting houses of worship, as opposed to Anglican "churches." But it can also refer to a particular area of a large church or cathedral; a place for religious worship within a school, hospital, or prison; a private space for worship established for a noble family, either within the manor house or in a separate building on the estate; and a smaller building for worship, a "Chapel of Ease," constructed for the convenience of worshippers whose parish church was too distant.

Chapter: The governing body of a cathedral, consisting of the dean and the resident canons. The chapter is responsible for all operations of the cathedral, including maintenance, finances, and worship services. The chapter also must confirm certain decisions and appointments made by the bishop and may also serve as an advisory body for him.

Chasuble: The outermost garment worn by a clergyman celebrating the Eucharist. The chasuble is a kind of poncho, often elaborately embroidered, worn over the alb and stole. The color of the chasuble worn—whether white, gold, purple, red, or green— depends upon the season of the Christian year. In the Victorian period, the chasuble was associated with the ritualist movement.

Choir (or Quire): Group of singers, amateur or professional, who regularly participate in worship services; in church architecture, the area between the nave and the sanctuary where such a choir would sit. In some churches the choir and sanctuary would be separated from the nave by an ornate lattice known as a choir screen (also chancel screen, rood screen).

Christening: Another term for infant baptism: the ceremony in which an infant is baptized and named.

Christian Socialism: A largely Anglican movement, initially inspired by the Chartist revolts of 1848, which emphasized messages of equality and social justice in Christian teachings. The leaders of the movement, including F.D. Maurice and Charles Kingsley, criticized the system of industrial capitalism and promoted the interests of the working classes through educational initiatives, workers' cooperative societies, and support for trade unions.

Christmas: The Christian holy day celebrating the birth of Jesus Christ, generally observed on December 25.

Churching of Women: In the Anglican Church, a service in which a woman who had recently given birth was blessed and thanks were given for her safe delivery of the child.

Church of England: The established Church of England and, in the Victorian period, of Wales. Members of the church, known as Anglicans, are Christian Protestants. The nominal head of the church is the reigning monarch of Great Britain, but the Archbishop of Canterbury provides religious and administrative leadership; governance is conducted by the church hierarchy, including its bishops and its archbishops. The doctrine and liturgy of the church are set out in the Thirty-Nine Articles and the *Book of Common Prayer.*

Church of Ireland: The Irish branch of the Anglican Church, which was the official state church in Ireland until it was disestablished in 1871.

Church of Scotland: In the Victorian period, the established church in Scotland. Also known as the Kirk, it is Presbyterian in doctrine and church governance. *See* Presbyterian.

Church Rate: A tax on all property owners in a parish to pay for the upkeep and the operational expenses of the Anglican Church in the parish. Dissenters objected to being forced to give money to the Anglican Church, and in 1868 the compulsory church rate was abolished.

Churchwarden: In the Anglican Church, a lay official of the parish church, elected by the vestry or parish council and usually working part-time, who is responsible for the upkeep of the church property in the parish, including the buildings, the churchyard, and any moveable goods, and for the maintenance of peace and order on church grounds.

Collect: A short prayer forming part of a liturgical worship service. The word is pronounced with an accent on the first syllable.

Colonnade: A long row of columns; in churches, these generally separate the nave from the aisles.

Communion: *See* Eucharist.

Confession, Auricular: A form of confession of sins in which the penitent meets with the priest privately to recount and repent of his or her sins and receive absolution, or forgiveness of those sins, which the priest pronounces as the representative of God and the church. The penitent may be required to carry out some form of penance, a form of punishment or of partial atonement for the sin, which might take the form of prescribed prayers. Auricular confession in the Victorian Church of England was controversial and generally practiced only by those with extreme High Church views.

Confirmation: A ceremony in the Anglican church in which a young person, having come to years of discretion, affirms in the presence of the bishop of his or her diocese the promises made on his or her behalf at baptism. Most Victorian Anglicans were confirmed between the ages of fourteen and nineteen, and it served as a rite of passage into adulthood. Prior to being confirmed, the candidate had to memorize the catechism and, often, attend catechism classes with his or her local minister.

Congregationalist: Member of a denomination of Old Dissent that stressed the independence of each local congregation: each chapel was self-governing, choosing its own minister, administering its own affairs, and recognizing no required creed. Also known as Independents, Victorian Congregationalists were evangelicals and moderate Calvinists.

Cope: A very long cloak or mantle worn by some Anglican clergymen over the cassock and surplice for processions and special services. Its use in the Victorian period is associated primarily with the ritualists of the High Church.

Cottage Meeting: A meeting held in a private home, usually on a weeknight, for the purposes of Bible study, prayer, and Christian fellowship. Cottage meetings were pioneered by Methodists in the eighteenth century, when many Methodist congregations had no chapel in which to gather, and they continued in Methodism and in other evangelical denominations through the nineteenth century and were adopted by some Anglican Churches.

Creed: A statement or confession of fundamental beliefs, often recited as part of a worship service. Important creeds for Victorian Anglicans included the Nicene Creed, the Apostles' Creed, and the Athanasian Creed. *See* Appendix 2.

Cruciform: Cross-shaped; used to describe churches built in the shape of a cross, with the nave, choir, and sanctuary extending west to east, and transepts, forming the arms of the cross, extending out to the north and south of the choir.

Curate: In the Anglican Church, a clergyman hired by an incumbent clergyman to assist him with the work of the parish. Curates could serve as substitutes for nonresident incumbents, performing all or most of the work of the parish in exchange for part of the incumbent's remuneration, or they could serve as assistants alongside the incumbent, particularly in large urban parishes. Curates tended to have meager salaries and little job security.

Darbyites: *See* Plymouth Brethren.

Deacon: In the Anglican Church, the lowest level of ordained clergyman, who could perform some, but not all, ministerial functions. A deacon could conduct worship services, baptize, and sometimes perform marriages, but could not administer Eucharist, absolve sins, or bless someone in the name of the church. He was addressed as "the Reverend." For most Victorian clergymen, becoming a deacon was a stage on the way to ordination to the priesthood, and they remained deacons only for one probationary year.

Deaconess: In the nineteenth century, a woman who was a member of a Protestant order of deaconesses. The Anglican Church revived the order of deaconesses in the 1860s as an alternative to conventual life; deaconesses performed various kinds of charitable work, including nursing, teaching, and prison visiting, but they did not take religious vows and seldom lived communally.

Dean: In the Anglican Church, the clergyman primarily in charge of the operation of a cathedral. Appointed by the Queen, he serves as president of the chapter and performs specified parts of the cathedral services. He occupies a high position in the Anglican hierarchy, and is addressed as "the Very Reverend."

Diocese: The geographical area under the jurisdiction of a particular bishop; a diocese will include a large number of parishes.

Disestablishment: The act of divesting a state church of its privileged status and government support.

Dissenter: In England and Wales, any non-Anglican Protestant. Old Dissent refers to denominations in existence at the time of the Act of Uniformity of 1662, which demanded conformity to Anglican doctrines and practices and forced many people with different beliefs to withdraw from the Anglican Church: these include Baptists, Congregationalists, Presbyterians, and Quakers. New Dissent refers to protestant denominations that came into existence after 1662, including Unitarianism and the many forms of Methodism.

Don: A person holding an academic appointment at Oxford or Cambridge University.

Doxology: A short hymn of praise to God. This word usually refers to the Trinitarian doxology: *Glory be to the Father, and to the Son: and to the Holy Ghost; as it was in the beginning, is now, and ever shall be: world without end. Amen.*

Easter: The Christian holy day celebrating the resurrection of Jesus Christ after his crucifixion and burial. Easter is a "moveable feast," meaning that its date varies from year to year, because it is determined according to the lunar calendar. Although the rules for determining the date of Easter are complex, Easter is generally observed on the Sunday after the first full moon on or after March 21.

Epiphany: Christian holiday celebrating the revelation of Jesus as God in human form and connected with the adoration of the Christ child by the three wise men or Magi. Epiphany is celebrated on January 6, the twelfth day after Christmas, and marks the end of the Christmas season; it is also known as Twelfth Day or, more commonly, as Twelfth Night.

Established Church: A church officially established and supported by the government of a particular country. In the Victorian period the Church of England (the Anglican or Episcopal church) was the established church in England; the Church of Scotland (Presbyterian) was the established church in Scotland; and the Church of Ireland (Anglican/Episcopalian) was the established church in Ireland until 1871, when Parliament disestablished it.

Eucharist: A rite celebrated in some form by nearly every Christian denomination in fulfillment of the injunction of Jesus recorded in Luke 22: 19–20 and 1 Corinthians 11: 25–26. During the ceremony, regarded by most denominations as a sacrament, bread and wine (the Host), representing the body and blood of Jesus Christ, are blessed and then distributed to each member of the congregation in remembrance of the self-sacrifice of Jesus. This ceremony is also called communion, the Lord's Supper, and among High Churchmen, Mass. (*See also* "Transubstantiation.")

Evangelical Movement: A large interdenominational Christian movement originating in the eighteenth century which, despite considerable diversity, shared doctrinal emphases including the need for conversion, the authority of the Bible, the immediacy of an individual's relationship to God, the assurance of salvation, and the necessity of social involvement and activism. While some evangelicals belonged to dissenting denominations, the Evangelical party within the Anglican Church was active and influential, particularly early in the nineteenth century.

Font: A piece of church furniture designed to hold the water for baptism by aspersion (sprinkling). It usually takes the form of a basin with a pedestal and is placed in the western end of the nave.

Free Church: In Scotland, a Presbyterian denomination that broke away from the established Church of Scotland in 1843 over the issue of state encroachment on the church's spiritual independence.

Freethinker: A person who rejects tradition, authority, or religious dogma as the foundation of his or her beliefs; in Victorian usage, it usually refers to someone who rejects all orthodox religious beliefs in favor of atheism or agnosticism.

German Higher Criticism: A school of biblical scholarship, pioneered by German scholars including Friedrich Schleiermacher, which focused attention on the sources of biblical texts, calling into question the authorship and reliability of parts of the Bible and the historicity of biblical narratives. Other thinkers associated with higher criticism include David Friedrich Strauss and Ludwig Feuerbach.

Glebe: An area of land belonging to a particular benefice in the Church of England, which could be used by the incumbent clergyman to supplement his income, either by renting it out or by farming it himself.

Godparent: In the Anglican church, a person chosen by the parents of an infant to participate in the child's baptism by making a declaration of faith and obedience on the child's behalf. Each child has one or two godparents of its own sex and one of the opposite sex. Godparents nominally had responsibility for the child's religious education, but this function was widely neglected.

Good Friday: The Christian holy day celebrating the crucifixion of Jesus Christ, whose sacrificial death, according to Christian theology, brought the possibility of salvation for humanity.

Guy Fawkes Day: In Britain, an annual celebration held on November 5 to commemorate the 1605 failure of the Gunpowder Plot, in which Catholic conspirators, including Guy Fawkes, planned to blow up the Houses of Parliament while the King was present there. Effigies of the conspirators (and, occasionally, of the Pope), called "guys," are traditionally burnt publicly. The celebration is also known as Bonfire Night.

High Church: In the Anglican Church the party that emphasizes the spiritual authority of the church and clergy and defends their central position in society. While unemotional and uninspiring eighteenth-century clergy were sometimes referred to as "High and Dry," the High Church through most of the nineteenth century consisted of the Tractarians and Ritualists, those who emphasized the Roman Catholic traditions within Anglican doctrine and liturgy.

Holy Orders: The traditional levels of the Christian ministry, including bishop, priest, and deacon. "To take holy orders" means to be ordained to the ministry as deacon or priest; "to be in holy orders" means to have been ordained as a minister.

Holy Week: The week immediately preceding Easter Sunday. It begins on Palm Sunday and includes Maundy Thursday, Good Friday, and Holy Saturday. Pious Victorian Christians often attended services daily during Holy Week.

Host: The consecrated bread and wine used in the celebration of the Eucharist.

Incarnation, Doctrine of: The belief that God, in particular the Second Person of the Trinity, took on material form or "became flesh" in the womb of Mary and was born as a human being, Jesus of Nazareth, who was both wholly divine and wholly human.

Incumbent: In the Church of England, the parish clergyman who holds the benefice for that parish and receives its income, whether or not he performs most of the clerical duties of the parish. The incumbent may be a rector, a vicar, or a perpetual curate, depending on the nature of the benefice.

Independent: *See* Congregationalist.

Jesuit: A member of the Society of Jesus, a male religious order of the Roman Catholic Church founded by Ignatius Loyola in the 1530s and renowned for academic prowess and breadth of learning. Jesuits were active in efforts to convert non-Christians and Protestants to Roman Catholicism, and Victorian Protestants entertained an exaggerated fear of Jesuits, whom they portrayed as secret agents of the Pope.

Kilhamites: A breakaway Methodist sect founded by Alexander Kilham in 1797, which stressed greater participation of the laity in church governance.

Kirk: *See* Church of Scotland.

Laity: All persons connected to a church who are not members of the clergy.

Layman: A person who is not a member of the clergy.

Lectionary: A book containing a list of passages from the Bible to be read on particular days of the year, generally as part of a worship service.

Lent: The forty-day period preceding Easter Sunday, a time of preparation for the celebration of the resurrection of Jesus Christ on Easter. It begins on Ash Wednesday and ends on Holy Saturday, the day before Easter. The day before Lent begins is known as Shrove Tuesday; in Britain this has traditionally been celebrated as Pancake Day. The tradition of serving pancakes on Shrove Tuesday originated as a way of using up rich ingredients and enjoying a final indulgence before the Lenten season of fasting.

License, Special License (Marriage): Special arrangements for marriage in the Church of England that do not require the reading of banns and the delay entailed by this requirement. A license issued by a local clergyman, costing a few pounds, would allow a couple to marry in any parish in which one of them had been in residence for fifteen days; a special license, issued by the Archbishop of Canterbury and costing around £28, allowed the marriage to take place in any Anglican parish.

Litany: A responsive prayer used in public worship consisting of a series of petitions recited by a leader, followed by fixed responses by the congregation.

Lord's Prayer: A Christian prayer that appears in the Gospels (Matthew 6: 9–13 and Luke 11: 2–4) as a model prayer provided by Jesus to his disciples. This prayer is frequently recited in worship services in many denominations, including the Anglican Church. The 1662 Prayer Book version is as follows: *Our Father, Which art in Heaven, hallowed be Thy Name. Thy Kingdom come. Thy will be done, in earth as it is in Heaven. Give us this day our daily bread. And forgive us our trespasses, as we forgive them that trespass against us. And lead us not into temptation; but deliver us from evil. For Thine is the Kingdom, the Power, and the Glory, for ever and ever. Amen.*

Lord's Supper: *See* Eucharist.

Lutheranism: A Protestant denomination founded on the teachings of Martin Luther (1483–1546), a German reformer. Lutherans affirm the ultimate authority of the Bible, and they believe that a person is saved not by works but by God's grace and individual faith through the atoning work of Jesus Christ. Lutheranism became the most important Protestant denomination in Germany and throughout northern Europe, and it influenced the English reformation and contributed significantly to English hymnody, but it was not a major denomination in nineteenth-century Britain and was confined mainly to German-speaking congregations.

Mass: The celebration of the Eucharist in a worship service. In the Church of England, the use of the term was confined to Anglo-Catholics.

Methodist, New Connexion: *See* Kilhamites.

Methodist, Primitive: A breakaway sect of Methodism that split from Wesleyan Methodists in 1810 as a result of the increasing conservatism of the Wesleyans and their move away from early Methodist practices such as open-air preaching. Also called "Ranters," they practiced noisy public evangelism and, like the early Wesleyans, allowed women to preach.

Methodist, Wesleyan: A denomination of New Dissent founded in the eighteenth century by John Wesley. The largest and most important dissenting denomination in Victorian Britain, Wesleyan Methodists were evangelicals with Arminian views of salvation. They popularized hymn singing in Britain.

Michaelmas: A day in the Christian calendar dedicated to the Archangel Michael, observed on September 29. Marking the beginning of autumn, it was a traditional day for the celebration of a quarterly communion service, for the settling of accounts, for the start of new terms of employment, and for the beginning of the academic term.

Millenarianism: Interest in the imminent end of the world.

Minister: General term used to refer to a clergyman below the level of archdeacon or bishop, including Anglican deacons and priests, whatever their clerical appointments, and also dissenting clergy.

Mormonism: Religious sect founded in America by Joseph Smith in 1830; in that year he published the *Book of Mormon,* which Mormons regard as a sacred and divinely inspired text. Also known as the Church of Jesus Christ of the Latter-Day Saints, it enjoyed a brief period of growth in Victorian England from 1837 to 1852, when the revelation of the Mormon Church's endorsement of polygamy caused a rapid decline.

Muscular Christianity: A movement among Victorian Anglicans that promoted a vision of Christian manhood combining physical strength and health with Christian ethical ideals. Having its greatest effect in British public schools, it was popularized in the works of Charles Kingsley and Thomas Hughes.

Narthex: A vestibule or lobby area located at the west end of a church.

Natural Theology: A set of beliefs about the nature of God supposedly derivable without any special revelation (the Bible, the teachings of Jesus) from evidence found in God's creation, including both the natural world and human nature.

Nave: The area in a church, generally the largest area, where the congregation gathers, facing the sanctuary.

Neology: Rationalist theology originating in Germany in the eighteenth century and regarded as a threat to orthodox Christianity and to biblical authority. *See* German Higher Criticism.

Nonconformist: Used as a synonym for a Dissenter or a non-Anglican Protestant.

Ordination: In the Anglican and other churches, the rite of consecration, generally performed by a bishop, by which a person becomes a Christian minister.

Oxford Movement: *See* Tractarian.

Parish: In the Church of England, the territorial area for which a particular Anglican incumbent—the rector, vicar, or perpetual curate—had responsibility. The parish also became the unit of local government in Britain.

Parish Clerk: In the Anglican Church, a lay official who assists the presiding minister in the conduct of worship services by reading the biblical lessons and epistles, announcing the hymns, leading the congregational responses, and assisting at the altar during communion services.

Parson: In the Anglican Church, a rector or vicar of a parish. The term was also used more loosely to describe any clergyman with responsibility for a parish, including perpetual curates and sometimes even assistant curates.

Parsonage: A house, owned by the Church of England, provided for the use of the incumbent clergyman of a parish.

Pentecost: Christian celebration held on the fiftieth day after Easter commemorating the coming of the Holy Spirit upon the followers of Jesus as related in the Bible in Acts 2. In England, it is also called Whitsun or Whitsunday.

Perpetual Curate: An incumbent clergyman in an Anglican parish who is paid a salary by the diocese, rather than deriving his income from tithes and church lands like vicars and rectors.

Pervert: A convert to a religious sect regarded by the writer or speaker as holding mistaken and injurious doctrines.

Pew, Box: In a church, bench seating with high back and sides, entered through a door. Usually located nearest the altar, box pews were reserved for church members of higher social standing, who paid regular pew rent for the privilege.

Pluralism: Practice of simultaneously holding two or more clerical benefices. Pluralism declined over the course of the nineteenth century as the result of legal reforms and changing attitudes.

Plymouth Brethren: A conservative evangelical Christian sect founded in Ireland in the 1820s and brought to Plymouth, England, by John Nelson Darby in 1830. Also called the Assembly Movement and the Darbyites, the Plymouth Brethren were individualistic and egalitarian: they had no central governing organization, no creed, and no ordained ministers. They were a millenarian sect, expecting the imminent end of the world.

Prayer Book: *See Book of Common Prayer.*

Prayer, Responsive: A form of public prayer used as part of a worship service in which a worship leader, often the presiding minister, recites a prayer and the congregation recites corporate responses.

Preaching Robe: Also called a Geneva gown or pulpit gown, this long black gown with bell sleeves, very much like modern-day doctoral gowns, was the traditional dress of Anglican clergy conducting services in which a sermon was preached, and some clergy continued to wear it throughout the nineteenth century, even as more elaborate vestments gained popularity. It gradually became associated with the Evangelical movement within the Anglican Church. It was also worn by Congregational and Presbyterian ministers.

Prebend, Prebendary: In the Anglican Church, the stipend that a canon receives from the income of the cathedral; also used to refer to the canon receiving such a stipend.

Precentor: A canon of a cathedral with primary responsibility for the worship services, particularly the musical portions.

Predestination, Doctrine of: Calvinist doctrine holding that God in his sovereignty has foreordained all things, especially that God has elected certain people to receive eternal salvation.

Presbyterian: In Scotland, a member of the established Church of Scotland (the Kirk) or of one of several dissenting denominations that broke with the established church, including the Free Church and the United Presbyterians. In England, a member of a dissenting denomination of Old Dissent. Presbyterians held Calvinist doctrines of predestination; church governance was carried out by representative bodies known as Presbyteries, made up of representatives from local congregations.

Priest: In the Anglican Church, a clergyman who has undergone the second level of ordination, or been "priested," and is entitled to perform most ecclesiastical functions, including celebration of the Eucharist and absolution of sins. (Only bishops, however, could perform ordinations and confirmations.) The use of the term "priest" was often associated with the Anglican High Church.

Protestant: Member of any non-Catholic Christian sect founded after the start of the Protestant Reformation in 1517.

Psalmody: Tradition of congregational singing, dominant in English churches into the eighteenth century, which holds that the only songs appropriate for use in worship services are the inspired songs recorded in Scripture, especially the Psalms. English metrical versions of the Psalms were published in two influential Psalters: the Old Version (1562) by Sternhold and Hopkins and the New Version (1696) by Tate and Brady.

Pulpit: An elevated platform to the left of the altar of a church from which the Gospel lesson is read and the sermon delivered.

Puseyite: *See* Tractarian.

Quakers: Members of an egalitarian and pacifist dissenting Christian sect of Old Dissent. Quakers believed in the Inner Light, a direct revelation of God's will available to every believer, according to which all activities of life should be conducted. They rejected all formal religious ceremony and hierarchy of every kind. At religious services, held in simple Meeting Rooms, Quakers sat in silence until a member of the group was moved by the Spirit to speak. Quakers were conspicuous in society for their plain dress and their use of the informal second person—"thee" and "thou"—indicating their refusal to recognize social distinctions.

Real Presence: Doctrine of the Eucharist, held by Roman Catholics, High Church Anglicans, and some Broad Church Anglicans, which claims that the body and blood of Jesus

Christ are really present in the consecrated bread and wine used in the sacrament, either physically through transubstantiation, or in some spiritual sense.

Rector: Incumbent clergyman of an Anglican parish whose income includes the "great tithes" on cereal crops and the "small tithes" on all other farm produce, as well as income from church land (the glebe).

Rectory: A house, owned by the Church of England, provided for the use of the current rector of the parish.

Reserve, Doctrine of: A belief held by the Tractarians and other High Church Anglicans that some spiritual truths should not be communicated to the uninitiated. The doctrine tended to discourage the discussion of religious matters in secular contexts. It caused some other Christian sects to suspect the Tractarians of duplicity or insincerity.

Reverend: Honorary prefix used when addressing a clergyman, often abbreviated as Rev. Clergymen below the level of archdeacon or bishop, including deacons, are addressed as "the Reverend John Smith" or "the Reverend Mr. Smith" or, if they have a higher academic degree, "the Reverend Dr. Smith." Bishops are addressed as "the Right Reverend," deans as "the Very Reverend," and archbishops as "the Most Reverend." The proper prefix for archdeacons is "the Venerable."

Ritualist: A member of the Anglican High Church who attempted to introduce some of the rituals of Roman Catholic worship into Anglican services.

Rural Dean: A parochial clergyman appointed by the bishop to help oversee the work of the other local clergyman in his district, or "deanery."

Sabbatarian: A Christian who believes in the strict observance of Sunday as the Sabbath day, a day of rest and worship.

Sacrament: A rite of the church, instituted by Christ, which is generally defined as an outward sign that itself conveys an inward, spiritual grace. The Anglican church officially recognizes only two sacraments, baptism and the Eucharist, but some Anglo-Catholics follow the Roman Catholic church in counting five further rites as sacraments: confirmation, matrimony, ordination, confession, and last rites.

Salvation Army: Evangelical Christian organization founded in London's East End by Methodist evangelists William and Catherine Booth to minister to the poorest members of society. Organized along military lines with its officials, both men and women, taking the titles of military officers, it became famous for its street preaching, its brass bands, and its social activism on behalf of the destitute and homeless.

Sanctuary: The holiest part of the church, where the altar is located and where the clergy performs the service; this area at the east end of the church is reserved for the clergy.

Secularist: A member of a Victorian atheistic movement closely connected with working-class radicalism and Enlightenment rationalism.

See: The office held by a bishop or, by extension, the geographical area under his jurisdiction, his diocese.

Sexton: In the Anglican Church, a lay official who serves as church caretaker, with responsibility for the buildings and/or the graveyard of a local parish church; the sexton would often have duties that included ringing bells for service and digging graves.

Stole: A long, wide band of cloth (approximately 3–4" × 7–9'), traditionally of silk and often embroidered, worn by a clergyman while conducting services. The stole is worn around the neck, either hanging down in front or crossed over the body, over a surplice or alb.

Suffragan Bishop: A bishop who serves as an assistant to a bishop in charge of a particular diocese.

Sunday School: Charity school for children of the lower classes intended to provide basic literacy and, sometimes, elementary mathematical skills, as well as religious training. The first schools were founded in the late eighteenth century, and thereafter Sunday schools run by religious groups and sometimes by individuals proliferated. After the Education Act of 1870, Sunday schools increasingly focused on religious knowledge and began to welcome students from all social classes.

Surplice: A wide-sleeved, full, white linen tunic, reaching below the knees, worn by some Anglican clergymen when conducting worship services. The surplice is worn over a cassock. Its use was endorsed by the Elizabethan Act of Uniformity (1559), which forbade the use of albs, chasubles, and stoles, so the surplice was not closely associated with the Victorian ritualist movement.

Temperance Movement: A social movement that aimed to reduce or eliminate the consumption of alcoholic beverages.

Tertiary: An associate of a religious community who, though not taking vows as a monk or nun, participates in the work and worship of the community.

Thirty-Nine Articles: Central defining statement of Anglican doctrine, established in 1563. *See* Appendix 1.

Tithe: A tax on the farm produce of a parish, which was supposed to provide an income for the incumbent clergyman. The "great tithes" were levied on cereal crops such as wheat and oats, while the "small tithes" were levied on all other produce.

Tractarian: A member of the High Church party in the Church of England in the 1830s and 1840s, which stressed the continuity of Anglican doctrine and practice with Roman Catholic traditions. The name "Tractarian" derives from the series of publications, the *Tracts for the Times* (1833–1841), in which leading High churchmen argued for their interpretation of Anglican doctrine; they are sometimes known as Puseyites, after one of their leading members, Edward Bouverie Pusey. The movement in which they were involved is also called the Oxford Movement because so many of its founders, including John Keble and John Henry Newman, were academics at Oxford University.

Transept: In a cruciform ("cross-shaped") church, the part of the building set crosswise to the nave, forming the "arms" of the cross and separating the nave from the sanctuary. The area where the transept and the nave intersect (the crossing) is often topped by a spire, a tower, or a dome.

Transubstantiation: Doctrine of the Eucharist held by Roman Catholics and some Anglo-Catholics claiming that the bread and wine when consecrated by the priest actually become the body and blood of Jesus Christ, even while retaining the appearance of bread and wine.

Trinity, Doctrine of: Belief that God is one Being which contains three distinct Persons: God the Father, God the Son (incarnated as Jesus Christ), and God the Holy Spirit.

Twelfth Night: *See* Epiphany.

Unitarian: A member of a nonevangelical dissenting denomination remarkable for its denial of the doctrine of the Trinity and thus of the divinity of Jesus Christ. Unitarianism preached a rational, ethical religion, closely related to eighteenth-century deism, and encouraged social activism rather than evangelism.

Venerable: Honorary prefix used when addressing an archdeacon. For example, such a man may be properly called Archdeacon Grantly, the Venerable Theophilus Grantly, or the Venerable Mr. Grantly.

Vestment: Clerical clothing worn by the clergyman only while conducting religious services.

Vestry: (1) A storage room attached to a church where vestments and other goods used in worship services are kept, often used as a changing room for those participating in the service; (2) An elected council responsible for the administration of the local parish church, including, until 1837, local administration of the Poor Law. Their name reflects their usual meeting place, in the local church vestry.

Vicar: Incumbent clergyman of an Anglican parish who does not receive the "great tithes" on cereal crops, but derives his income from church land (the glebe) and from the "small tithes," or tithes on all other farm produce.

Vicarage: A house, owned by the Church of England, provided for the use of the current vicar of the parish.

Whitsun, Whitsunday: *See* Pentecost.

BIBLIOGRAPHY

Altholz, Josef L. *The Religious Press in Britain, 1760–1900*. Westport, CT: Greenwood Press, 1989.

Austen, Jane. *Mansfield Park*. Oxford: Oxford University Press, 1980 [1814].

———. *Pride and Prejudice*. Oxford: Oxford University Press, 1980 [1813].

———. *Sense and Sensibility*. Oxford: Oxford University Press, 1980 [1811].

Bebbington, D.W. *Evangelicalism in Modern Britain: A History from the 1730s to the 1980s*. London: Unwin Hyman, 1989.

Boyd, Nancy. *Three Victorian Women Who Changed Their World: Josephine Butler, Octavia Hill, Florence Nightingale*. Oxford: Oxford University Press, 1982.

Brontë, Charlotte. *Jane Eyre*. Harmondsworth, Middlesex, UK: Penguin, Signet Classics, 1997 [1847].

Budd, Susan. *Varieties of Unbelief: Atheists and Agnostics in English Society, 1850–1960*. London: Heinemann, 1977.

Chadwick, Owen. *The Victorian Church*. 2 vols. Oxford: Oxford University Press, 1966–1970.

Christian Lady's Magazine. Edited by Charlotte Elizabeth (Tonna). London: Seeley, Burnside, and Seeley, 1834–1846.

Christian World Magazine. Edited by Emma Jane Worboise. London: James Clarke, 1866–1886.

Cliff, Philip B. *The Rise and Development of the Sunday School Movement in England, 1780–1980*. Nutfield, Redhill, Surrey: National Christian Education Council, 1986.

Collins, Irene. *Jane Austen and the Clergy*. London: Hambledon Press, 1994.

Dickens, Charles. *Hard Times*. Harmondsworth, Middlesex, UK: Penguin, 1995 [1854].

———. *Sunday Under Three Heads*. Project Gutenberg, http://infomotions.com/etexts/gutenberg/dirs/etext97/suths10.htm, 1997 [1836].

Eliot, George. *Middlemarch*. Harmondsworth, Middlesex, UK: Penguin, 1985 [1871].

Farningham, Marianne. *A Working Woman's Life*. London: James Clarke, 1907.

Froude, J.A. *Nemesis of Faith*. London: Chapman, 1849.

Gilmour, Robin. *The Victorian Period: The Intellectual and Cultural Context of English Literature, 1830–1890*. New York: Longman, 1993.

Gott, John. *The Parish Priest of the Town*. London: Society for Promoting Christian Knowledge, 1906 [1885].

Haig, Alan. *The Victorian Clergy*. London: Croom Helm, 1984.

Hardy, Thomas. *Tess of the D'Urbervilles*. Harmondsworth, Middlesex, UK: Penguin, 1985 [1891].

Heasman, Kathleen. *Evangelicals in Action: An Appraisal of Their Social Work in the Victorian Era*. London: G. Bles, 1962.

Howsam, Leslie. *Cheap Bibles: Nineteenth-Century Publishing and the British and Foreign Bible Society*. Cambridge: Cambridge University Press, 1991.

Hughes, M.V. *A London Child of the 1870s*. Oxford: Oxford University Press, 1977 [1934].

Hymns, Ancient and Modern. Historical edition. London: William Clowes, 1909.

Jowett, Benjamin. "On the Interpretation of Scripture." In *Essays and Reviews*. London: John W. Parker, 1860.

Kingsley, Charles. Letter to Charles Darwin, November 18, 1859. Darwin Correspondence Project: Letter 2534, http://www.darwinproject.ac.uk/darwinletters/calendar/entry-2534.html.

Knight, Frances. *The Nineteenth-Century Church and English Society*. Cambridge: Cambridge University Press, 1995.

Knight, Mark, and Emma Mason, *Nineteenth-Century Religion and Literature: An Introduction*. Oxford: Oxford University Press, 2006, 100.

Landow, George P. *The Aesthetic and Critical Theories of John Ruskin*. Princeton, NJ: Princeton University Press, 1971.

Lucas, J.R. "Wilberforce and Huxley: A Legendary Encounter." *Historical Journal*, 22(2) (1979): 313–330, http://users.ox.ac.uk/~jrlucas/legend.html.

Lydia (pseud.). "Female Biography of Scripture: Manoah's Wife." *Christian Lady's Magazine* 17 (1842): 503ff.

———. "Female Biography of Scripture: Deborah." *Christian Lady's Magazine* 16 (1841): 337–349.

Maison, Margaret M. *Search Your Soul, Eustace: A Survey of the Religious Novel in the Victorian Age*. London: Sneed Stagbooks, 1961.

Martineau, Harriet. *Autobiography*. Boston, MA: J.R. Osgood, 1877.

Newman, John Henry. *Apologia Pro Vita Sua*. New York: W.W. Norton, 1968 [1864].

Porter, Andrew. *Religion versus Empire? British Protestant Missionaries and Overseas Expansion, 1700–1914*. Manchester: Manchester University Press, 2004.

Rigby, Elizabeth. "Vanity Fair—and Jane Eyre." *Quarterly Review* 84 (December 1848): 153–185, http://faculty.plattsburgh.edu/peter.friesen/default.asp?go=252.

Sedgwick, Adam. Letter to Charles Darwin, November 24, 1859. Darwin Correspondence Project: Letter 2548, http://www.darwinproject.ac.uk/darwinletters/calendar/entry-2548.html.

Sewell, Elizabeth Missing. *Autobiography*. Edited by Eleanor L. Sewell. London: Longmans, Green, 1907.

———. *Margaret Percival*. London: Longmans, 1846.

Showalter, Elaine. *A Literature of Their Own: British Women Novelists from Bronte to Lessing*. London: Virago, 1982 [1977].

Snell, K.D.M. and Paul S. Ell, *Rival Jerusalems: The Geography of Victorian Religion*. Cambridge: Cambridge University Press, 2000.

Stanley, Arthur Penrhyn. *Essays Chiefly on Questions of Church and State*. London: Murray, 1884.

Stowe, Harriet Beecher. "Portraits of the Patriarchs: Miriam and Moses." *Christian World Magazine* 9 (1873): 368–373.

Summers, Mary. "Anne Brontë's Religion." *Transactions of the Bronte Society* 25 (2000): 18–30.

Trollope, Anthony. *Barchester Towers*. New York: New American Library Signet Classics, 1983 [1857].

Trollope, Anthony. *The Last Chronicle of Barset*, Project Gutenberg, http://www.gutenberg.org/catalog/world/readfile?fk_files=284934&pageno=23, 2002[1867].

Warner, Marina. *Alone of All Her Sex: The Myth and the Cult of the Virgin Mary*. New York: Random House, 1976.

Wilberforce, William. *A Practical View of the Prevailing Religious System of Professed Christians in the Higher and Middle Classes in the Country, Contrasted with Real Christianity*. London: T. Cadell and W. Davies, 1797.

Willey, Basil. *More Nineteenth Century Studies: A Group of Honest Doubters*. New York: Columbia University Press, 1956.

Worboise, Emma Jane. "Editorial Address." *Christian World Magazine* 1 (1866): 1–3.

———. "'Inkshed' and 'Authorship': To Intending Contributors." *Christian World Magazine* 18 (1882): 34.

Yonge, Charlotte. "Autobiography." In *Charlotte Mary Yonge: Her Life and Letters* by Christabel Coleridge. London: Macmillan, 1903.

———. *The Daisy Chain, or Aspirations*. Project Gutenberg, http://www.gutenberg.org/etext/3610, 2003 [1856].

INDEX